Early Childhood Education and Care in Ireland

Early Childhood Education and Care in Ireland

Charting a Century of Developments (1921–2021)

Nóirín Hayes and Thomas Walsh (eds)

Peter Lang

Oxford • Bern • Berlin • Bruxelles • New York • Wien

Bibliographic information published by Die Deutsche Nationalbibliothek
Die Deutsche Nationalbibliothek lists this publication in the Deutsche Nationalbiblio-
grafie; detailed bibliographic data is available on the Internet at
http://dnb.d-nb.de.

A catalogue record for this book is available from the British Library.
Library of Congress Cataloging-in-Publication Data

Names: Hayes, Nóirín, editor. | Walsh, Thomas, 1976- editor.
Title: Early childhood education and care in Ireland : charting a century
  of developments (1921-2021) / Nóirín Hayes, Thomas Walsh, Editors.
Description: Oxford ; New York : Peter Lang, [2022] | Includes
  bibliographical references and index.
Identifiers: LCCN 2021038386 (print) | LCCN 2021038387 (ebook) | ISBN
  9781789978681 (paperback) | ISBN 9781789978698 (ebook) | ISBN
  9781789978704 (epub)
Subjects: LCSH: Early childhood education--Ireland--History--20th century.
  | Early childhood education--Ireland--History--21st century. | Early
  childhood education--Parent participation--Ireland--History--20th
  century. | Early childhood education--Parent
  participation--Ireland--History--21st century.
Classification: LCC LB1139.3.I73 E27 2022 (print) | LCC LB1139.3.I73
  (ebook) | DDC 372.2109417--dc23
LC record available at https://lccn.loc.gov/2021038386
LC ebook record available at https://lccn.loc.gov/2021038387

Cover design by Brian Melville for Peter Lang.

ISBN   978-1-78997-868-1 (print)
ISBN   978-1-78997-869-8 (ePDF)
ISBN   978-1-78997-870-4 (ePub)

© Peter Lang Group AG 2022

Published by Peter Lang Ltd, International Academic Publishers,
52 St Giles, Oxford, OX1 3LU, United Kingdom
oxford@peterlang.com, www.peterlang.com

Nóirín Hayes and Thomas Walsh have asserted their right under the Copyright, Designs
and Patents Act, 1988, to be identified as Editors of this Work.

This publication has been peer reviewed.

Contents

Figure

Tables

Foreword

A noticeable feature about the development of early childhood education and care across the century has been the vibrancy, innovation and vision of people, mostly women. None of the events described in this book would have taken place without their enthusiastic participation, input and support over the years.

This book takes the reader on a historical tour of the origins and development of the key features and themes of the ECEC sector over the past 100 years. As I read it, I was taken back to the visit of Maria Montessori to Waterford in the 1920s and the vibrant Montessori provisions since that time. Indeed, the various chapters elucidate the complex relationship between the State and the ECEC sector over the decades, particularly the stance of Rev Professor Timothy Corcoran SJ in the early years of the Irish Free State. The book also reminded me of the pivotal decade of the 1960s not only in the development of services and the creation of organisations, but also the changing of attitudes towards women, children and ECEC. The influential Plowden Report in the UK impacted significantly on the Primary School Curriculum of 1971 which gradually impacted on practice in the infant classes of primary schools. The various chapters prompted me to remember that societal changes and the impact of European funding in the 1990s catalysed significant developments, including the OMNA project in the DIT, the Early Childhood Education Forum and the seminal White Paper on Early Childhood Education, *Ready to Learn*. This laid a foundation for subsequent developments, most particularly the increasing and ongoing professionalisation of the sector. A particular contribution of the book is the tracing of parallel developments in Northern Ireland in the same period, noting the similarities and differences in the pathways travelled. All of the above appear in much more detail in this fascinating book. I can assure the reader that the authors of all the chapters, most of whom I know, argue their case with passion and expertise.

In my role in the development of Early Childhood Studies in UCC, I experienced this commitment and the importance of the 'behind the scenes' activity which plays such an important part in all the initiatives in ECEC that have taken place in Ireland. At an institutional level, academic and political, the command structure has to 'buy in' to proposals and new ideas for change to happen. While people change events, luck also plays a part! For example, good luck can be seen in the appointment of Micheál Martin as Minister of Education in the late 1990s which resulted in the very important National Forum on Early Childhood Education taking place and the subsequent White Paper which flowed from it. Bad luck resulted in the decision to close down the CECDE due, in part, to the financial crash of 2008. I personally regard this decision as one of the greatest set-backs to ECEC in recent times.

Concerning the two editors of this book, I became aware of the existence of Tom Walsh whilst talking to the late Professor John Coolahan at a meeting. He was eulogising his good fortune at having acquired this brilliant PhD student! My subsequent dealings with Tom back this up and I am particularly grateful for his Directory of Early Years Research in Ireland which he compiled whilst working for the CECDE. It has been an invaluable aid to research into the domain ever since.

Likewise, with Nóirín Hayes! I was at a meeting in the early 1980s when Séamus McGuiness of TCD informed me that he had an excellent student writing her M.Ed dissertation on the education of young children. As we all know, Nóirín has gone on to become the longest serving, high profile, and most respected academic in ECEC in Ireland. Her contribution to the sector is incalculable.

I would like to take the liberty of also highlighting two other people who represent the best in Ireland with respect to the Early Years. Irene Gunning, formerly CEO of the IPPA, for her devotion to duty, irrepressible enthusiasm, and her constant desire to gain recognition for all those serving young children (and not least for bringing the most important 'influencers' from across the world to our shores!). I would also like to say the same about Professor Mathias Urban of DCU who continues this visionary work today.

This book very much connects the past to the future. It 'sparks off' in Jung's words 'Memories, Dreams, Reflections'. It is an excellent book and I highly recommend it.

Emeritus Professor Francis Douglas
Director of Early Childhood Studies UCC, 1995–2009
1st August 2021

THOMAS WALSH AND NÓIRÍN HAYES

Introduction

Like many good ideas, the genesis of this book can be traced back to a chat over coffee involving both co-editors in late 2018. The absence of a dedicated volume delineating the historical development and evolution of the complex and multidimensional early childhood education and care (ECEC) sector was something that, we felt, affected contemporary understandings of a vibrant and integral aspect of the education system. The motivation for the book was to provide an anthology that would retrace some of the origins and foundations of the sector in order to comprehend its current, complex, structures. In compiling this book our goal was to explore the evolution of the ECEC system since the establishment of the Free State and critique the historical and contemporary provision in Ireland under a number of key themes. As the centenary of the establishment of the Irish Free State (later the Republic of Ireland) approached, we believed the time was opportune to capture the salient milestones and markers on the sector's historical landscape. Focusing on the 100 years from 1921 to 2021, and on the age range of birth to 6 years of age, offered a framework for the book and provided a fitting tribute to the pioneering work of the sector's founders, almost exclusively dynamic women who fought against the odds to provide quality ECEC experiences for children. While the book acknowledges the pivotal role of parents in caring for and educating their children within the home, the key focus is on the provisions outside the home for children from birth to 6 years.

We immediately concluded that an edited book was the best approach considering the diversity and complexity of the sector. Our involvement in the sector in various ways enabled us to identify expert authors who could provide rich personal and professional insights on the sector from a range of perspectives. In selecting contributors and topics, we sought to achieve a careful balance in documenting the past, profiling the present and signposting the future across the various chapters. The aim was to explicitly identify authors, and indeed create co-authoring opportunities, to present a range of diverse experiences, perspectives and trajectories within the sector. We were delighted with the response from chapter authors contacted and with their engagement throughout the eighteen-month process of developing the edited book. The chapter authors brought a nuanced and insightful perspective to their chapters based on their professional expertise, and indeed their contributions and commitments to the sector over extended periods of time. Individually and collectively, the chapters reveal profound insights on the development of many critical aspects of the ECEC sector in the last century and deepen our appreciation of contemporary opportunities and challenges. While each chapter provides a rich account of a particular theme, many transversal themes permeate the book and are brought together in the Conclusion. While the focus is on the past and the present, the book also has an eye to the future in terms of signalling prospective opportunities, challenges, hopes and possibilities. Our sincere thanks to each of the chapter authors for their generosity in sharing their expertise and indeed for their forbearance with us throughout the writing process.

Before turning to outline the various chapter contributions, it is important to provide a brief historical context for the book.

Background and context

The development of the ECEC sector in Ireland, like all jurisdictions, followed a unique trajectory that was influenced by its political, religious, socio-economic, cultural and international context. Following the foundation of the Irish Free State in 1921, the symbiotic relationship between the Catholic Church and the State had a profound effect on the shaping of Irish society. The ideologies and values emerging from the Church-State alliance as they related to children, women and families were enshrined within the Constitution of Ireland (Government of Ireland 1937). These impacted considerably on societal attitudes and the extent of State services in the ECEC realm for many decades. For the first fifty years following the establishment of the Irish Free State, societal configurations and expectations meant that ECEC services were not a necessity for most parents and families. Indeed the only constant in terms of provision is the infant classes of primary schools where children aged from 3 to 4 years and upwards have attended since the 1920s. When wider societal developments necessitated increased provisions for children prior to attending the infant classes of primary schools from the late 1960s onwards, the embedded structures and ideologies resulted in a fragmented, laissez-faire and ad hoc State response to such societal needs. Unfortunately what resulted was an embedding of a 'care' and 'education' divide, both conceptually and practically, the legacy of which still impacts adversely on the sector today.

While each chapter delineates the historical backdrop and foundations for the issues under consideration over the past 100 years, the focus of most chapters is on the rich and complex activity in the last twenty to thirty years. International influences, and more importantly funding from the EU, have been key catalysts in the development of the sector since the 1990s. What becomes immediately apparent is the lack of an overarching child-centred vision or strategy for the ECEC sector at this time of exponential growth and development, leading to fragmentation at both policy and practice levels. A sector traditionally at the margins of public policy has become a core focus of government policy in recent years. This has emerged from a range of motives and been driven by varying perspectives, including labour force activation, equality for women and indeed increased understanding of the critical importance of quality ECEC for young children. The historical foundations and fault lines on which the sector has emerged continue to impact its development in the contemporary context. This book tells the story of the origins, lines of development, key milestones and markers, and the policy and practice drivers that have shaped and continue to shape the ECEC sector, both historically and contemporaneously.

A note on terminology

Spanning such an extensive time period, one of the key strengths of this book is that it captures evolving understandings, developments and ideologies as they relate to ECEC. Underpinning this richness is the changing language and terminology used over the past 100 years to name both the sector itself and its workforce, but also the various organizations and ECEC services available. In line with the approach advocated by John Bennett and his colleagues as part of the *Starting Strong* project (Organisation for Economic Co-operation and Development [OECD] 2001), this book employs early childhood education and care (ECEC) as the key overarching term for the sector throughout. However, as you will read, each author has used the particular term or phrase relating to the sector or aspect of the sector that was used in various epochs, eras and contexts. In this way, many chapters employ a range of terminology for the same construct or issue as they chart the journey of evolution historically. This approach provides an authenticity and sympathy to context throughout the chapters and book, while the overarching term demonstrates a commitment to the inseparability of care and education in the lives of young children.

It is not only in the overarching term for the sector that terminology proved challenging within this book. The various ways in which those working within the sector have been named over the past 100 years, indeed in the contemporary context, lack consistency and agreement. So throughout the book various terms such as practitioner, early childhood educator, teacher and early years professional are used by authors to best represent the way in which those working within various elements of the sector were termed throughout the period. Work currently underway in terms of naming and framing the sector and its professionals may help to bring greater cohesion to its identity.

Last of all, it is unsurprising that many departments, agencies and organizations were created, closed and morphed in various ways over such an extensive time frame. For example, the name of the Department of Education has changed on a number of occasions, coming full cycle to be once again known as the Department of Education in 2020. To provide an overview:

- The Department of Education was established in 1924.
- It was renamed the Department of Education and Science (DES) in 1997.
- It was then renamed the Department of Education and Skills (DES) in 2010.
- In 2020, it was renamed as the Department of Education.

Another example of this is the reconfiguration of the Department of Children and Youth Affairs (DCYA), initially established in 2011, as the Department of Children, Equality, Disability, Integration and Youth (DCEDIY), in 2020. Similarly, many State agencies, non-voluntary organizations and voluntary bodies were established, merged or ceased to exist throughout the last century. The terms used throughout the book align to the formal name of the department, agency or organization at the relevant time of the event under consideration. To assist readers, a timeline of key events has been compiled from the chapters in this book to provide an overview of significant developments in the sector since 1900 (see Appendix).

Chapter outlines

The book begins with Thomas Walsh's profiling of the key actors, agencies, departments and organizations that have played central roles in the development of ECEC policy and the provision of services from the 1920s to 2000 in Chapter 1. While the Department of Education and the Department of Health had national policy responsibility for young children, it was in the non-statutory realm that the greatest dynamism and innovation existed. When traced longitudinally, the evolution and development of the ECEC sector reveals a patchwork of ad hoc provisions for young children and their families, which grew in momentum in the last decades of the twentieth century. The analysis reveals a lethargic

State in the development of ECEC policy or provisions and the sterling efforts of many pioneering women in establishing organizations to promote and provide innovative ECEC experiences for young children, as well as wider family supports. Such provisions, both statutory and non-statutory, remained very fragmented, patchy and variable for most of the twentieth century. The chapter provides a backdrop to many later chapters which unpack in greater detail the policy and practices emerging from these foundational structures.

Nóirín Hayes succeeds in the challenging task of judiciously mapping the key features of the ECEC policy landscape over the past century in Chapter 2. The chapter is structured around three key phases, with a particular emphasis on the last two decades. What emerges from this analysis is the complexity of the ECEC policy terrain, intersecting as it does with so many competing agendas, aspects of social policy, constitutional and legislative provisions, and societal values. The chapter explores the origins of the conceptual and practical structural divides between 'care' and 'education' that are still firmly embedded within policy and practice. Tracing the impact of international influences and funding in the Irish policy for ECEC from the late 1990s is a key contribution of the chapter. The section focusing on policy developments in the past two decades is extremely rich and provides a useful critique of the successes and shortcomings of recent developments. What emerges is a picture of rapid development but with little underpinning transformation. While the historical legacy weighs heavily on the contemporary system, the chapter ends with a note of optimism regarding the achievement of a 'renewed vision for an integrated high-quality, affordable and sustainable model of ECEC'.

In Chapter 3, Maura O'Connor comprehensively delineates the provision of early childhood education in the infant classes of primary schools over the past 100 years. The chapter is central to this book as children's experiences in the infant classes represented the only State and universal provision for early childhood education for much of the period under review. The journey of curriculum development and enactment is systematically charted across five key policy areas, noting the international, political, religious, cultural, and economic and social changes that impacted on the learning experiences and outcomes of young children. Points of convergence and divergence are perceptively noted across the eras, highlighting the many resonances between present and past inherent within infant class policy and practice. The critical and pioneering role of infant class teachers in advancing pedagogical practices across the school system is very well captured. Central to the chapter is the conceptualization and experience of the child and the impact, both positive and negative, of curriculum policy on their childhood experiences and future opportunities. The chapter concludes with a note of optimism for the future as a conceptualization of the agentic, competent, caring and confident child is deeply embedded within the current draft curriculum framework that will inform future infant class pedagogical practices.

Máire Mhic Mháthúna and Mairéad Mac Con Iomaire provide, in Chapter 4, a rich and detailed account of provision for Irish-medium preschools in Ireland from the inception of the first naíonraí (Irish-medium preschool settings) in the 1960s. The chapter begins with a very useful statistical overview of the current situation before tracing the development and evolution of the sector in a systematic and comprehensive manner. The authors capably navigate the very complex landscape of Irish-medium provision, detailing the many and various organizations (and their changing titles and functions) that supported Irish-medium ECEC over the past century. One of the key strengths of this chapter is the skilful weaving in of the voice of many of the pioneers, almost exclusively females, who championed the establishment and development of Irish-medium services from the 1970s. A particular focus is placed on the pedagogical resources produced by organizations and individuals over the decades, and the bibliography is a real boon for those exploring such publications. Parallel provisions in Northern Ireland are also charted. The chapter concludes with a presentation of a range of challenges, recommendations and opportunities for the future development of Irish-medium ECEC in Ireland.

The curriculum for young children is the key focus of Carmel Brennan and Arlene Forster in Chapter 5. Bringing their respective expertise and experience in curriculum development and enactment across the sector, the authors insightfully trace the key milestones and developments in curriculum policy, practice and research over the past half century. Excellent emphasis is placed on international influences and influencers on Irish curriculum provision, particularly in the early decades of curriculum de-velopment. The philosophy, values and commitments underpinning early childhood educators to play-based learning from the 1960s, and the evolving understanding of approaches, are clearly presented. Following the overview of earlier developments, a comprehensive account of the development and enactment of *Aistear, the Early Childhood Curriculum Framework*, is pro-vided. The chapter perceptively captures the many tensions and challenges on the curriculum landscape when various agencies and actors, which had worked in varying philosophical and practice-based traditions, began to work collaboratively on curriculum development in recent decades. The chapter reminds readers that the curriculum journey is ongoing, and the next steps are already being written as both *Aistear* and the Primary School Curriculum engage in review and redevelopment processes.

The journey towards professionalization of the ECEC workforce is traced in detail by Mary Moloney and Geraldine French in Chapter 6. As with many other chapters, the historical evolution of ECEC education and training is firmly embedded in the wider policy landscape and these links are capably charted in the opening sections. The authors argue that a key factor in the non-linear and slow process of professionalization has been the conceptual and practical split of 'care' and 'education' in ECEC policy. Key milestones that prompted policy development and action (and indeed inaction) in relation to professional education and training are highlighted along this journey. Various efforts, particularly from 2002 onwards, to sup-port professionalization of the sector are very comprehensively delineated. Despite the many efforts and multiple policies, the chapter reveals many contradictions, gaps and unintended consequences within the policy land-scape that work against the achievement of the government's stated aim of a graduate-led ECEC workforce. The chapter concludes on a hopeful note that current policy development processes regarding professionalization will enhance the situation, asserting that our youngest children deserve no less quality of provision than any other sector of the education system.

Elizabeth Dunphy and Máire Mhic Mháthúna capably chart the origins, work and ultimate closure of the Centre for Early Childhood Development and Education (CECDE) in Chapter 7. The authors them-selves occupied a range of senior leadership roles throughout the operation of the Centre and offer very perceptive and nuanced insights on its functioning and role. Situating the establishment of the Centre in the wider ECEC landscape, the authors explore the various tensions and dilemmas that policy makers addressed prior to its official launch. The chapter is structured around the key functions of the CECDE, exploring the successes and challenges in their achievement between 2002 and 2008. An excellent focus is placed on the process of developing *Síolta, The National Quality Framework for Early Childhood Education*, as well as on its impact on policy and practice since its publication in 2006. Useful insider insights frame the key factors which led to the unexpected closure of the CECDE in 2008, and the impact this had on ECEC developments at a national level. The chapter is of particular interest and importance representing as it does the most comprehensive account of the role of the CECDE written to date.

The legislative and regulatory landscape for ECEC in Ireland is comprehensively charted by Anne Egan and Sheila Garrity in Chapter 8. Beginning with the 1908 Children Act, the chapter is essential to our understanding of the key direct and indirect legislative provisions that have impacted on the care and education of young children in Ireland. Indeed, much of the legislation affecting young children has been focused on other stakeholders, particularly women and employers. The authors impressively introduce and critique the significance of multiple legislative and regulatory provisions, exploring their interface with one another and their impact on wider policy developments. An evolution from a more punitive and controlling approach to a more progressive and liberalizing discourse underpinning legislative and regulatory provision is evident in the analysis. Excellent emphasis is also placed on direct and indirect international influences on the legislative landscape in Ireland. The increasing complexity of the regulatory and legislative landscape in the past three decades is immediately evident from the chapter, and it is equally apparent that this momentum is likely to continue into the future.

Chapter 9, co-authored by Maresa Duignan and Fiona McDonnell, provides a comprehensive overview of the evolution of inspection systems in the ECEC sector. Framed by the broader developments in the policy and legislative landscape, the chapter traces the various systems, regulations and organizations with responsibility for overseeing the quality of provisions for young children in both preschools and school settings. While the chapter is structured primarily around the provisions of the two key agencies with responsibility for the inspection of ECEC services (Tusla and the Department of Education Inspectorate), useful linkages and tensions are explored relating to the interface of provisions. As the authors occupy senior managerial roles in both the Tusla Early Years Inspectorate and in the Department of Education Inspectorate, the chapter provides valuable insights into how the philosophy, systems, regulations and procedures for inspection have been developed and the factors that have influenced their evolution over time. The chapter concludes with some musings on a common agenda for the inspection of ECEC settings into the future. The comprehensive bibliography will be a significant resource for readers wishing to explore further the historical evolution of ECEC inspection policy in Ireland, particularly over the last three decades.

Chapter 10, the final chapter, provides readers with an overview of the key provisions for ECEC in Northern Ireland over the past 100 years. This insightful chapter by Noel Purdy and Diane McClelland offers readers perceptive understandings into the key developments north of the border following partition in the 1920s. The chapter usefully focuses on four key aspects of provision in order to achieve depth of treatment: key policy and legislative provisions, the evolution of curriculum provision, the development of the ECEC workforce, and an exploration of key contemporary issues and challenges for the sector. The chapter provides a very useful touchstone for readers by charting parallel developments in the same time period. It is interesting to note that despite a common policy and practice landscape prior to the 1920s, both jurisdictions followed largely distinct paths following partition. While some parallels are evident at times in terms of developments North and South, these have only become more pronounced and visible in recent decades. However, despite the different trajectories, both jurisdictions share a number of common challenges and opportunities in the contemporary context. The Conclusion chapter brings together key issues and discourses from the book under a range of themes and provides some signposts for the future development of the ECEC sector.

Note

This book received support from the Maynooth University Publication Fund and the Researching Early Childhood Education and Care Collaborative (RECEC) at the School of Education, Trinity College Dublin.

Bibliography

Government of Ireland (1937). *Constitution of Ireland*. Dublin: The Stationery Office. Available at: <http://www.irishstatutebook.ie/pdf/en.cons.pdf>.
Organisation for Economic Cooperation and Development (2001). *Starting Strong: Early Childhood Education and Care*. Paris: OECD.

THOMAS WALSH

1 Key actors and organizations in the development and evolution of early childhood education and care provision in Ireland in the twentieth century

Introduction

The evolution of the early childhood education and care (ECEC) sector in Ireland over the twentieth century is best described as a patchwork of developments that reacted to need as opposed to proactively providing for the changing needs of children and their families. While the ECEC sector in 2021 is a crowded space in terms of policy, practice and research, this contemporary reality follows a period of State lethargy and inactivity in the twentieth century in terms of out-of-home ECEC provision. In the absence of State facilities and with a pervasive social and constitutional doctrine that 'a woman's place was in the home', a number of organizations and agencies emerged in Irish society to meet the need of parents seeking 'childcare' or ECEC provisions. These organizations ranged in focus from provisions targeted at the most marginalized and disadvantaged in society to those catering for middle- and upper-class children and their families.

This chapter traces the origins and development of the role of a range of government departments, agencies and organizations that emerged and evolved from the early 1900s up to 2000. To situate this development, the chapter begins with a short background and context for the specific developments explored later in the chapter. The next section analyses the role of the government departments and agencies in the provision of ECEC, most particularly the Department of Health and the Department of Education.

It then moves to explore the roles of a wide range of non-statutory organizations in the provision and promotion of ECEC services, including
secular, religious, community, private and voluntary actors. The interface
between the statutory and non-statutory agencies and organizations will
be explored. Finally, the origins of a number of organizations comprising
the current National Voluntary Childcare Collaborative are presented. The
chapter endeavours to capture the innovative and ground-breaking work
of the key pioneers of these organizations, almost exclusively female, in
the development of the sector and the provision of services for children
and families.

Background and context

Before moving to examine the actors and organizations, a brief background and context is useful to situate the developments that emerged
throughout the 1900s, particularly in the latter part of the century.
Historically, the State has had minimal involvement in the provision of
early childhood services in Ireland (Gilligan 1991, Hennessy and Hayes
1997). The origins of this traditional neglect are largely rooted in ideological and doctrinal discourses regarding the position of children, women
and families in society (Glendenning 1999). Constitutional provisions
(Government of Ireland 1937), reinforced by legislation and regulations
such as the 'marriage bar', underpinned the dominant model for much
of the twentieth century of 'breadwinner husband with dependent wife
and children' (Kennedy 1989: 11). It also concretized a subsidiary role for
the State in terms of family and children, ultimately supporting the view
that children were a private family responsibility (Hayes 2002). Arguably,
it was societal attitudes to the role of women throughout the twentieth
century that remained the greatest barrier to ECEC developments, with
a pervasive and largely unchallenged expectation that a 'woman's place
was in the home', certainly that of a married woman. As late as the 1970s,
this societal attitude to married women working outside the home and

availing of ECEC services is captured well by the Commission on the Status of Women, which stated:

> We wish to stress that we are unanimous in the opinion that very young children, at least up to 3 years of age, should, if at all possible, be cared for by the mother at home and that as far as re-entry to employment is concerned, the provision of day-care for such children must be viewed as a solution to the problems of the mother who has particularly strong reasons to resume employment. (Commission on the Status of Women 1973: paragraph 310)

Socio-economic, educational and international factors led to shifting attitudes towards women and children from the 1960s. Increased urbanization of families away from familial networks (Humphreys 1966, Kennedy 1989) and a growing economy requiring female labour force activation catalysed the need for childcare support beyond the home and family. This, in turn, was driven by increased universal provision for post-primary education and increasing emphasis on equal status for men and women in the workforce. The increase in married women in the workforce was particularly pronounced, rising from 5 per cent in 1961 to 37 per cent in 1996 (Kennedy 2001: 63). There was a change in societal values regarding the family with enhanced State intervention in supporting families through an increased range of welfare payments. Research was emerging highlighting the importance of ECEC for cognitive, social and emotional development, especially for children affected by educational disadvantage (Holland 1979). International thinking and ideas regarding early childhood education and pedagogy also increasingly permeated thinking and approaches in Ireland, championed by many of the Irish pioneers who attended conferences and engaged with emerging research. This trend was in line with other international experiences in the latter part of the twentieth century (Singer and Wong 2018, 2021). Vatican II thinking from the 1960s reduced sensitivities to State involvement in the lives of children and families (Whyte 1979). Ireland's enhanced connectivity with a wide range of international organizations and agencies, particularly our accession to the European Economic Community in the 1970s, exposed national thinking to more diverse discourses, expectations and obligations. Ireland became a signatory to many international charters and conventions relating to young children, including, albeit belatedly, the United Nations Convention on the Rights of the Child (UN 1989) in 1992. Collectively, this reduced Ireland's insularity and led to a shift in focus from social expenditure in relation to education and children to one of investment and future employability (Department of Education 1965).

One might expect seismic parallel developments in the provision of ECEC services to respond to this evolving societal situation from the 1970s. This was not the case. Despite increasing demands, support or provision for childcare was slow to translate into significant changes in policy or practice at a national level. The provision that developed was largely ad hoc, responding to local need and initiated by voluntary, community and private providers. The absence of a State, or indeed State-aided, system led to the growth of a myriad of service types that varied in terms of ethos, philosophy, pedagogy, duration and quality. These included childminding (both family relatives and non-familial), domestic help (including au pairs), naíonraí (Irish language medium or bilingual preschools), home and community playgroups, crèches, community playgroups, day nurseries, preschools and, effectively, the infant classes of primary schools.

Statutory agencies

Up to 2000, there was a division in terms of funding and policy responsibility for ECEC between the Department of Health and the Department of Education at a national level. This led to a largely split system, whereby provision for preschool children was largely perceived to be a 'health' issue while provision from the infant classes onwards was the responsibility of the Department of Education (Hayes et al. 1997). The split system between 'care' and 'education' in Ireland has long historical roots and remains deeply embedded at a structural and conceptual level (Walsh 2016). The roles of these two government departments are now explored in turn.

Department of Education

Historically, preschool provision in Ireland for children prior to attending the infant classes of primary schools was limited and varied. While all children were obliged to attend school from the age of 6, the reality was that approximately half of all 4-year-olds and almost all 5-year-olds attended the infant classes of primary schools in the 1900s (Coolahan 2017). For example, in 1988–1989, 1 per cent of 3-year-olds and under, 56 per cent of 4-year-olds and more than 99 per cent of 5-year-olds were receiving full-time education (Department of Education 1989: 3). As Gilligan (1991: 71) states:

> These trends are due presumably to the absence of alternative pre-schools, kindergarten or nursery school facilities, which in other developed countries frequently serve as a formal introduction to the educational system.

However, many of these infant classes up to the 1980s had up to forty children in each class, often in multi-grade classes in smaller schools. Arguably, the early enrolment of pupils in primary schools at this time and the low number of mothers in the workforce resulted in a lack of public concern for preschool education. Even in the 1950s, the Council of Education Report warned against early enrolment in primary schools, asserting the suitability of the child's home for ECEC:

> that in the average home the young child lives in his natural environment, which no school no matter how perfect, can provide and the benefit of which are immeasurable. (Department of Education 1954: 82)

The Department of Education supported some limited provision for preschool and school-age children considered at risk of educational disadvantage or who had special educational needs. A number of special schools were established from the 1920s, with initial provisions focusing on children with sensory needs (McGee 1990). From the 1950s, schools for 'emotionally disturbed' children were established by religious organizations or by pioneers such as Nancy Jordan who founded a school in Assumpta House in Blackrock in 1962 which employed Montessori methods. In 1969, the Department of Education, in conjunction with the

Bernard van Leer Foundation, supported the Rutland Street Project, an early intervention project for disadvantaged preschool children and their families in inner-city Dublin (Holland 1979). Traveller preschools were also funded from the 1980s (Kernan 2000) and these were followed by Early Start settings in designated disadvantaged schools for 3 and 4-year-old children from 1994. By the 1990s, specific Department of Education support for ECEC included the Rutland Street Project, thirty-three Early Start settings and forty Traveller Preschools catering for 400 children (O'Flaherty and Hayes 1997: 49).

Department of Health

The Department of Health assumed responsibility for providing services for young children at risk as determined under the *Children Act 1908*. Later, the *Health Act 1970* (Government of Ireland 1970) created a role for the Department of Health in the support of childcare services in limited circumstances through local Health Boards. This empowered Health Boards to provide grants to voluntary groups or local management committees towards the operating costs of centres catering for children or families in need of special support. The Department of Health became the main department supporting childcare, particularly in the Eastern Health Board region, based on the conviction that supporting day care provision represented a feasible form of preventative action from an operational and economic perspective (Gilligan 1991: 139). However, direct support remained very limited throughout the twentieth century.

In the latter decades of the twentieth century, the Department of Health established a number of committees to examine the role and need for childcare. The *Task Force on Child Care Services* reported in 1980 and while its focus was on residential and alternative care for children, it acknowledged the special position of children in society; asserting that 'there is a connection between the care of children and the good of society' (Department of Health 1980: 37). The committee investigating the *Minimum Legal Requirements and Standards for Day Care Services* (Department of Health 1985) was appointed by the Minister for Health, Barry Desmond, with a view to contributing to a Children's Bill and Child Care Act (Cowman 2007: 50). The report, which was never published, advocated a compulsory registration system of day care facilities and made recommendations regarding staff ratios, training requirements, administration of the system of registration and the importance of parent and community involvement. Concurrently, the *Working Party on Childcare Facilities for Working Parents*, under the Minister for Labour, recommended alternative working arrangements for working parents and the regulation of day care facilities (Government of Ireland 1983). A decade of reports culminated in the *Child Care Act 1991* (Government of Ireland 1991) and the subsequent *Child Care (Preschool Services) Act 1996* (Department of Health and Children 1997) in relation to the inspection of childcare settings.

Non-statutory agencies

This section delineates the origins, evolution and contribution of a range of non-statutory agencies in the provision and promotion of ECEC services, with a key focus on their organization and structure. Given the extensive time period, this is an indicative rather than exhaustive account of the many varied ways in which ECEC was advanced in Ireland in the twentieth century.

The Women's National Health Association and the Civics Institute

The Women's National Health Association was founded in 1907 by Lady Aberdeen, wife of the Viceroy (Carruthers 2001). The Association focused on the role of housewives and mothers as key agents in improving the health of the population. It established a number of Babies' Clubs with a doctor and nurse attached and opened its first school medical centre in 1916 (Kennedy 2001: 104). The Women's National Health Association collaborated with the Civics Institute and Dublin Corporation in the

1930s through a Joint Playgrounds Committee, advocating the need for safe spaces for child recreation.

Lady Aberdeen was central to the establishment of The Civics Institute of Ireland in 1914, a voluntary organization founded to identify social issues and opportunities and to promote ideas and measures to address these issues among the special bodies best placed to do so (Kernan 2005). Its membership comprised professional and businessmen, and some women. While its initial focus was on the entire island of Ireland, its activities primarily related to Dublin. Public health, including the health and welfare of families and children, were central to its work with an emphasis on improving the civic spirit and amenities of cities. ECEC became a focus of the Civics Institute from its inception.

In 1933, the Civics Institute initiated and managed the first City Corporation children's playground at Broadstone in Dublin and it managed ten playgrounds by 1940 where children aged between 4 and 14 could play, with the sites and apparatus provided by Dublin Corporation. The playgrounds operated under the guidance of play leaders, financed by Dublin Corporation, as well as volunteers and elected playground captains (children). Kernan argues that in addition to their role protecting children from street dangers and safeguarding the streets from groups of unsupervised children, playgrounds served an educative social purpose (Kernan 2005). The supervised element of the playgrounds underpinned a pedagogical practice by the Civics Institute to develop a spirit of citizenship and patriotism in young children, developing attitudes and behaviours of good citizenship in line with the nationalist, Gaelic vision. Kernan also asserts that a further element inherent in the provision of playgrounds was a social support for parents, particularly mothers, by providing respite to parents from child-rearing duties (Kernan 2005: 683). Attendance at the playgrounds dropped by the 1970s in light of tenement resettlement and other social factors and the Civics Institute handed over responsibility for the management of the playgrounds to Dublin Corporation in 1971.

The Civics Institute also pioneered the opening of day nurseries. The main aim of these nurseries was to support parents with inadequate financial or social resources, primarily mothers, to work outside the home, as well as to support the early development and education of children. They provided full day care to preschool children for prolonged periods of time and children were often referred to these by doctors, social workers, welfare societies or clergy (Cowman 2007: 15). The Liberty Crèche was founded in 1892 as part of the Sick Poor Institute and was run by the Civics Institute, with the supervision of a voluntary committee (Cremin 1993). It catered for twenty-four children from 8.30 a.m. to 6 p.m. The Civics Institute established St Brigid's Nursery Centre at Mountjoy Square in 1939 for children aged 2 to 5 years (Cowman 2007: 4). It was financed initially by a foreign businessman who worked on Mountjoy Square and voluntary subscriptions, while the site was provided by Dublin Corporation. Hayes and Kernan (2008) argue that its operation was governed by middle class ideals with a strong focus on developing children's social skills. Provision included three meals a day with time for rest and play for deprived children from the surrounding area. From 1950, it was aided by the Department of Health, Dublin Corporation and subsequently Dublin Health Authority. Its management was taken over by the Daughters of Charity in 1986, the year in which the Civics Institute ceased to operate. In 1955, the Civics Institute also opened a purpose-built day care nursery, St Joseph's, in Cork Street, Dublin. Its development was supported by the Minister for Health, Dublin Corporation and the finances of Dublin businesses.

Daughters of Charity

The Daughters of Charity were also pioneers in the provision of social and educational supports to young children and their families in Ireland. The Henrietta Street Crèche, founded in 1923, was a voluntary community service which was financed by the Daughters of Charity, and later partially supported by the Dublin Health Authority. It originally catered for up to forty children of working mothers, aged from 6 months to 8 years. Sr Anthony Hegarty was the Director and it also enjoyed outdoor play facilities in a garden and adjoining parks (Cowman 2007: 8). The Henrietta Street Crèche was closed, refurbished and reopened as St Mary's Day Nursery in 1964, catering only for preschool children. The Health Authority paid 70 per cent of costs and the remainder was met through parent fees and fundraising. Children were selected on the basis of their mother's need to work by the Director of the Nursery, public health nurses and social workers. Sr Monica Cowman (Director 1964–1969) was trained at the Royal Society of Day Nurseries, London in 1933. She maintained many international links throughout her career, particularly through her involvement in the *Organisation Mondiale pour l'Education Prescolaire* (OMEP), that informed and progressed ECEC practice both in St Mary's and more broadly in Ireland (see below).

By 1992, the Daughters of Charity directed or were centrally involved in fourteen nurseries and preschool centres in Dublin, Cork, Belfast and Drogheda (Cowman 2007: 24). The ownership and initiation of some of these premises rested with the Health Boards, Corporations, various community groups and trusts while others were owned, initiated and managed by the Daughters of Charity. The mission of the Daughters of Charity Child and Family Services was to provide professional and therapeutic services to children, in partnership with families, with a view to achieving a more just and equitable society. Afterschool services were added to nurseries such as St Vincent's Day Nursery in Ballyfermot in 1992 and parenting courses were offered in many centres. Some nurseries offered both sessional and full day care service (Cowman 2007: 24–30).

OMEP Ireland (Organisation Mondiale pour l'Education Prescolaire)

OMEP is an international organization affiliated to UNESCO. It was established in 1948 to promote a greater understanding of the needs of young children in the age category birth to 8 years. OMEP Ireland was founded in Ireland in 1966 with a purpose to learn from the experiences of other countries and to provide a forum to bring together existing practice in Ireland (Douglas 1994). From the outset, OMEP Ireland published a newsletter, organized a number of seminars and events, and gathered data on existing and expanding preschool provision in Ireland in the 1960s. More importantly, it provided a forum and context for organizations and individuals concerned with the welfare of young children to network and interact. OMEP Ireland was strategic in inviting successive

Ministers for Health to attend and speak at OMEP conferences, using these opportunities to inform them of the work and of the needs of child-care workers. Sr Monica Cowman attributed the later establishment of the Irish Preschool Playgroups Association (IPPA), the Association for the Welfare of Children in Hospital and the initiation of courses for pre-school personnel to the work of OMEP Ireland (Cowman 2007: 21). Moreover, an open meeting hosted by OMEP in May 1993 to discuss actions following Ireland's ratification of the UNCRC had a direct influence on the establishment of the Children's Rights Alliance in 1995.

One of the key concerns of the Irish National Committee of OMEP was the development and provision of a training course to prepare personnel to look after young children outside their homes. A sub-committee of OMEP Ireland was established 'to investigate and report on the present position of training facilities for those looking after groups of children and to make recommendations' (Cowman 2007: 38). It produced a booklet in 1970 entitled *Training Pre-school Personnel* (McKenna 1970). Following long and protracted efforts, a partnership with the Catering College of the Dublin Institute of Technology, which was already offering a Child Care Diploma Course for people working in residential services, resulted in the development of a certificate course entitled 'Training Pre-school Personnel' under Dr Mona Hearn. The Eastern Health Board took responsibility for the tutor's fee. The course commenced in 1977 with twelve students and with Sr Monica Cowman as the first course tutor. This was expanded to a Diploma course in 1993 and to a degree course in 1999, the BA in Early Childhood Care and Education. By this time, University College Cork was also offering a degree programme and a number of Institutes of Technology were offering diploma courses in ECEC.

Irish Preschool Playgroups Association (IPPA)

The aim of playgroups was to provide preschool children with opportunities for supervised and social play, with most playgroups open for up to three hours per day in women's private homes. Internationally, playgroup movements and associations were founded to support and promote such activities, including in the UK in 1961. Close professional relationships between the UK founders (including Belle Tutaev) and Irish pioneers (including Sr Monica Cowman), catalysed the establishment of the IPPA on 14th May 1969 in Dublin. Support for the IPPA also emanated from the recently established OMEP Ireland organization and the Civics Institute (Hayes and Kernan 2008). Molly Walmsley (a key member of the Civics Institute and OMEP Ireland) became the first member of IPPA and Máirín Hope was its first chairperson. Elizabeth Moloney was the 'face' of the IPPA in its first decade (Douglas 1994: 44).

Central to the aims of the IPPA was the promotion of preschool education, to develop training and networking opportunities for playgroup leaders, to promote the formation of playgroups in Ireland, to develop and maintain a set of standards for playgroups and support for parents and families (Douglas 1994: 28). The key pedagogical vision underpinning the IPPA was placing play at the centre of the child's experience. Not long after its establishment in Dublin, a second branch was opened in Limerick by 1972 and this branch structure continued to develop, leading to thirteen branches by the early 1980s aligned to the then Health Board regions (Douglas 1994: 50). Its first decade witnessed the remarkable growth of the organization, spearheaded by pioneering women of all classes and religions. Its activities were underpinned by its first Constitution, ratified at the 1971 AGM. Membership increased from ninety-nine in 1970 to 1,000 members in 1982, reaching close to 2,000 members by the turn of the twenty-first century. The IPPA undertook a number of organizational reviews, establishing three subcommittees with responsibility for Education, the Newssheet and the AGM in 1981. The IPPA was registered as a limited company from 1987 to ensure that members were not responsible for the liabilities of the Association.

IPPA playgroups ranged from community playgroups (usually established and run by cooperative groups of mothers) to private fee-paying playgroups often run by mothers in their home. These were generally attended by up to twenty children aged 3 to 5 years of age where the emphasis was on play-based learning. From the outset, it placed a strong focus on provision for 'handicapped children' and collated lists of members who would cater for children with special educational needs. The IPPA placed a particular focus on community playgroups from the mid-1970s through its involvement in the 'Ballymun Experiment', captured in a leaflet entitled *Community Pre-school Playgroups in Ireland*. Community playgroups were non-profit making and organized and run by a committee of parents on a rota basis. By the late 1980s, approximately 15 per cent of IPPA members were community playgroups run under the auspices of a local committee or voluntary body and geared towards serving the needs of an area (IPPA 1990).

Developing standards and introducing a voluntary code of standards were discussed regularly by the IPPA from the 1970s. Its formal registration system and voluntary Code of Standards became operational in the 1980s and it stipulated criteria around accommodation, access to outdoor play, adult-child ratios, age of entry to playgroups, health and safety and record keeping (O'Flaherty and Hayes 1997). This resulted in visits to preschools by the IPPA and the issuing of a Certificate of Registration to those playgroups which were deemed to have met the standards. Support for members was provided by the first National Playgroup Adviser from 1978, Moira Jones, who was joined in the 1980s by Regional Play Advisers. This work was an important preparatory precursor to the Department of Health regulations introduced in 1996 (Department of Health 1996), although these fell short of registration campaigned for by the IPPA and instead introduced a system of notification. The Department of Health, and individual Health Boards, provided grant aid to the IPPA from the early 1980s to support its work in terms of recruiting playgroup advisors and other related activities. Support funding increased exponentially from 2000 onwards through the Equal Opportunities Childcare Programme (EOCP) and the National Childcare Investment Plan (NCIP) funding schemes, directing the work of the IPPA to training, quality improvement and information sharing (IPPA 2004).

In terms of training and education, the IPPA forged strong links with the Sion Hill Training College and with the St Nicholas Montessori Society for Ireland which was founded in 1970. It also directly provided training courses and lecture series that became more formally accredited by organizations such as Vocational Educational Committees (VECs) and the National Council for Vocational Awards (NCVA). Courses offered included introductory, foundation and tutor courses. In the early decades, attendees were not formally assessed on the completion of courses but this practice changed by the early 1990s when the Diploma in Playgroup Practice was introduced in 1993. By 2003, eighty tutors worked alongside IPPA core staff to deliver a wide range of accredited courses (IPPA 2004: 6).

The National Children's Nurseries Association (NCNA)

By the 1980s, there was a growing number of private, full day care services for children and families. The National Children's Nurseries Association (NCNA) was formed in 1988, prior to the introduction of regulations, to coordinate and bring together childcare providers offering such full day care for young children as well as afterschool services. This involved supporting those working in and running nurseries, encouraging the maintenance and raising of quality standards, the creation of public awareness of the role of day care and to act as an advocacy group within the childcare sector. The NCNA was a membership-based voluntary organization and became a limited company with charitable status in 2002. By the end of the twentieth century, the NCNA had 500 members representing 2,147 staff catering for 10,834 children (NCNA 2002).

The structure of the NCNA was that there were three divisions under the National Committee Director of Services: the National Advisor and Regional Support Workers, the Training Co-ordinator and the Administration Team (NCNA 2002). Advisory Services of NCNA included visits to nurseries, assessment of standards in NCNA applicant nurseries, advice to members on establishing and managing a childcare service, as well as advice and support for parents. The provision of training courses for members was a core focus of the work of the NCNA. This included the NCNA Diploma in Nursery Management accredited by University College Dublin as well as a broad range of both non-accredited and accredited courses. Provision expanded significantly from 2000 with increased funding under the EOCP and NCIP. From 2000, the NCNA issued an annual report which reflected the increased professionalization of the organization and the increasing responsibilities of the organization within the childcare sector.

In December 2010, the boards of the IPPA and the NCNA agreed an amalgamation of both organizations into a new organization called Early Childhood Ireland (ECI). This merger is symbolic of the maturation of the sector and would have been considered unfeasible years earlier given the differing philosophical underpinnings of both organizations.

Other organizations

The National Voluntary Childcare Organizations (NCVOs)

A range of organizations was established from the 1970s to support and provide a network for fledgling aspects of the emerging ECEC infrastructure. The establishment and origins of key organizations are briefly profiled below,[1] while their contemporary work is explored across other chapters in this book. From 2000, many of these non-governmental organizations came together under the umbrella of the National Voluntary Childcare Organizations (NCVOs), subsequently known as the National Voluntary Childcare Collaborative, and were supported financially by the EOCP/NCIP and other funding streams to undertake their advisory and support work. There were eight NVCOs, two of which (the IPPA and the NCNA) have already been profiled:

- *Barnardos* was set up by the Irish-born doctor, Thomas Barnardo, in London in the 1870s to support poor and destitute children through housing and education. Services in Ireland began in the 1960s and Barnardos became an independent organization in 1989. Services included day nurseries, children's play buses for areas lacking childcare provision, a playgroup advisory service, toy libraries, a neighbourhood

---

1   For a comprehensive account of the work of each organization, please see Flood and Hardy (2013).

resource service and a parents' advisory service. Barnardos was instrumental in championing the High/Scope curriculum and approach in Ireland from the 1980s. It places a strong emphasis on family support and advocacy. See: <https://www.barnardos.ie/>.

- *Childminding Ireland* is the national body for childminders established in 1983. It promotes quality childminding in small, home-like settings as a form of non-parental care for children of all ages, from infancy to school-age. See: <https://www.childminding.ie/>.
- *Children in Hospital Ireland*: Following an OMEP Ireland survey of seventeen hospitals in Dublin in 1969, The Association for the Welfare of Children in Hospital Ireland was founded in 1970 by Ms Patricia Hemmens. The Association was responsible for introducing play into the wards of general hospitals and providing play sessions for children in hospital, largely staffed by volunteers and students gaining educational or social work experience. It subsequently changed its name to Children in Hospital Ireland. See: <https://www.childreninhospital.ie/>.
- *Forbairt Naíonraí Teo*: From the late 1960s, a number of naíonraí groups were established with the support of Comhdháil Náisiúnta and Conradh na Gaeilge. An Comhchoiste Réamhscolaíochta Teo was set up in 1978 and was a joint committee of Na Naíonraí Gaelacha and Bord na Gaeilge for the support of preschooling through Irish. Its main focus was the foundation and development of childcare and preschool education services through the medium of Irish. An Comhchoiste Réamhscolaíochta Teo was replaced by Forbairt Naíonraí Teo as the national representative organization in 2003 and Comhar Naíonraí na Gaeltachta was established in 2004. Currently support is provided by Gaeloideachas (<www.gaeloideachas.ie>) for Irish-medium settings outside the Gaeltacht and by Na Naíonraí Gaelacha (<http://www.naionrai.ie/>) for naíonraí staff, while Comhar Naíonraí na Gaeltachta (<http://www.comharnaionrai.ie/>) supports services in Gaeltacht regions. See Chapter 4: History of Naíonraí and Irish-medium Early Years Education, for a fuller account of Irish-medium provision.
- *Irish Steiner Waldorf Early Childhood Association*: Starting with the first school in Germany in 1919, the Steiner philosophy recognizes in each child a unique emerging spirituality and considers that education should lead the child towards clarity of thought, strength of will and sensitivity of feeling. The Irish Steiner Kindergarten Association, now known as Bláthú Steiner Early Childhood Association, was

established in 1992. In 2021, there are thirteen Steiner Waldorf or Steiner Waldorf inspired preschools and national schools in Ireland. See: <https://www.blathu.org/>.

- *St Nicholas Montessori Society of Ireland*: In 1970, the St Nicholas Montessori Society was founded by Síghle Fitzgerald and started running courses in 1984. The Montessori qualification is not recognized by the Department of Education for mainstream teaching in primary schools; therefore, the vast majority of Montessori-qualified practitioners are based in early years settings, as resource teachers in national schools or as teachers in special schools. See: <https://smsi.ie/>. Unaffiliated to the NCVOs, the Association Montessori International Teachers (Ireland) has operated since 1946 and offers a range of courses through the Sion Hill Training College (<https://aatimontessoriireland.wordpress.com/>).

In addition to the organizations profiled above, numerous regional and local groupings played instrumental roles in the development of out-of-home ECEC services in Ireland that are beyond the scope of this chapter. These include the Cross Border Management Group, the Ballymun Childcare Working Group, the Border Counties Childcare Committee (now the National Childhood Network), the Cork Early Years Network and the Irish Childcare Policy Network (which became Start Strong in 2009).

Discussion and conclusion

This chapter has profiled the key departments, agencies and organizations that had a remit for or contributed to the development of childcare or ECEC services in Ireland in the twentieth century. It reveals the sterling efforts of many of the pioneers who lay the foundations of our vibrant current sector, women who fought against the dominant religious and popular discourses and societal norms to champion the rights of children to quality ECEC experiences. Their endeavours resulted in the provision of ECEC services and experiences to hundreds of thousands of young children and their families that were not provided for by the State. Their efforts forced the State to recognize its responsibilities in supporting young children and their families and gradually elicited small financial supports towards the running of what were essentially community, private and voluntary services. But like many pioneers in other spheres, it was not always a celebrated or rewarding space to occupy: there was often suspicion of out-of-home childcare and ECEC services, both of the parents who used them and of the preschool leaders who established them. They were the champions in a society that limited the horizons and expectations of women generally.

The 'cabin to crèche' revolution (Kennedy 1989: 10) from the 1960s onwards prompted and catalysed the growing organic and eclectic mix of ECEC provision supported by various organizations and agencies. Over time, the State, largely through the Department of Health and Health Boards, began to fund some of these organizations and agencies. This move was largely prompted as a response to fulfil the State's obligations, as prompted by both national and international developments, in supporting necessitous children and families affected by educational disadvantage or deprivation (Hayes 2002). Overall, these services operated within an unregulated and fragmented national policy landscape (O'Flaherty and Hayes 1997). By 2000, there was the equivalent of a patchwork quilt of national and local agencies and organizations that coalesced to provide an uneven range of services for children and their families. Many of these departments, agencies and organizations worked in isolation and insulation from one another, often competing territorially for the limited State funding or demand for services locally (Hayes and Kernan 2008). They largely operated in a system that was uncoordinated, underfunded, underregulated and unsupported. The real impetus for development emerged from interested and energetic individuals, significant community engagement, grass roots and local movements, and some philanthropic interventions.

Yet in spite of their efforts, the ECEC sector in 2000, and indeed in 2021, bears the hallmarks of the fragmentation of its origins in both policy and practice. ECEC policy is still dispersed among a myriad of State departments and agencies, characterized by a lack of harmonization and coordination (Walsh 2016). Despite recent policies focusing on the birth to 6 age range, the traditional divide between 'care' and 'education' or 'preschool' and 'school' is glaringly evident in the terms and conditions of early childhood professionals and teachers. Investment in the sector is fragmented across multiple funding streams, resulting in a complex and administratively burdensome landscape for providers to navigate. Cumulatively, this funding still remains paltry and parsimonious relative to international standards. Much remains to be achieved to build on the vision and endeavours of the founding pioneers of our current ECEC sector.

Bibliography

Carruthers, F. (2001). *The Organisational Work of Lady Ishbel Aberdeen, Marchioness of Aberdeen and Temair (1857–1939)*. Unpublished PhD Thesis, National University of Ireland Maynooth. Available at: <http://mural.maynoothuniversity.ie/5179/1/Frances_Carruthers_20140708154835.pdf>.

Commission on the Status of Women (1973). *Report to the Minister of Finance*. Dublin: Government Publications Office.

Coolahan, J. (2017). *Towards the Era of Lifelong Learning: A History of Irish Education 1800–2016*. Dublin: Institute of Public Administration.

Cowman, M. (2007). *Memoirs of Pre-school Services Ireland 1892–2007*. Dublin: St Catherine's Provincial House Blackrock.

Cremin, V. (1993). *The Liberty Crèche 1893–1993: A Hundred Years of Childcare in Inner City Dublin*. Dublin: Liberty Crèche.

Department of Education (1954). *Report of the Council of Education*. Dublin: The Stationery Office.

Department of Education (1965). *Investment in Education*. Dublin: The Stationery Office.

Department of Education (1989). *Statistical Report for 1988 89*. Dublin: The Stationery Office.

Department of Health (1980). *The Task Force on Child Care Services: Final Report to the Minister for Health*. Dublin: The Stationery Office.

Department of Health (1985). *Minimum Legal Requirements and Standards for Day Care Services for Children: Report of a Committee Appointed by the Minister for Health* (Unpublished).

Department of Health and Children (1997). *Child Care (Pre-School Services) Regulations 1996 and Child Care (Pre-School Services) (Amendment) Regulations, 1997 and Explanatory Guide to Requirements and Procedures for Notification and Inspection.* Dublin: Department of Health and Children. Available at: <https://assets.gov.ie/13135/8f7b2b9a0ef343289bf5a979af778 7d8.pdf>.

Douglas, F. (1994). *The History of the Irish Pre-school Playgroups Association.* Dublin: IPPA. Available at: <https://omepireland.ie/wp-content/uploads/ 2019/07/History-of-the-IPPA.pdf>.

Flood, E. and Hardy, C. (2013). *Early Care & Education Practice.* Dublin: Gill and McMillan. Chapter on the historical development of the ECEC Sector in Ireland available at: <http://www.gillmacmillan.ie/AcuCustom/Sitename/ DAM/056/Early_Care_Education_Practice_-_Look_Inside_Sample.pdf>.

Gilligan, R. (1991). *Irish Child Care Services: Policy, Practice and Provision.* Dublin: Institute of Public Administration.

Glendenning, D. (1999). *Education and the Law.* Dublin: Butterworths.

Government of Ireland (1937). *Constitution of Ireland.* Dublin: The Stationery Office. Available at: <http://www.irishstatutebook.ie/pdf/en.cons.pdf>.

Government of Ireland (1970). *Health Act, 1970.* Dublin: The Stationery Office. Available at: <http://www.irishstatutebook.ie/eli/1970/act/1/enacted/en/ html>.

Government of Ireland (1983). *Working Party on Child Care Facilities for Working Parents, 1983. Working Party on Child Care Facilities for Working Parents: Report to the Minister for Labour: March 1983.* Dublin: The Stationery Office.

Government of Ireland (1991). *Child Care Act, 1991.* Dublin: The Stationery Office. Available at: <http://www.irishstatutebook.ie/eli/1991/act/17/enacted/en/ html>.

Hayes, N. (2002). *Children's Rights – Whose Right? A Review of Child Policy Development in Ireland.* Dublin: The Policy Institute.

Hayes, N. and Kernan, M. (2008). *Engaging Young Children: A Nurturing Pedagogy.* Dublin: Gill and MacMillan.

Hayes, N., O'Flaherty, J. with Kernan, M. (1997). *A Window on Early Education in Ireland. The First National Report of the IEA Pre-Primary Project.* Dublin: Dublin Institute of Technology.

Hennessy, E. and Hayes, N. (1997). 'Early Childhood Services in Ireland', *International Journal of Early Years Education*, 5 (3), 211–224.

Holland, S. (1979). *Rutland Street: The Story of an Educational Experiment for Disadvantaged Children in Dublin.* Dublin: Pergamon.

Humphreys, A. (1966). *New Dubliners – Urbanisation and the Irish Family.* London: Routledge and Kegan Paul.

Irish Preschool Playgroups Association (1990). *IPPA Statistics for Year Ending 31 December 1989*. Dublin: IPPA.

Irish Preschool Playgroups Association (2004). *Annual Report 2003*. Dublin: IPPA.

Kennedy, F. (1989). *Family, Economy and Government in Ireland*. Dublin: Economic and Social Research Institute.

Kennedy, F. (2001). *From Cottage to Crèche: Family Change in Ireland*. Dublin: Institute of Public Administration.

Kernan, M. (2000). 'Early Education in Ireland: Emerging Policy', *Irish Educational Studies*, 19 (1), 175–188.

Kernan, M. (2005). 'Developing Citizenship through Supervised Play: The Civics Institute of Ireland Playgrounds, 1933–75', *History of Education*, 34 (6), 675–687.

McGee, P. (1990). 'Special Education in Ireland', *European Journal of Special Needs Education*, 5 (1), 48–63.

McKenna, A. (1970). *Training Preschool Personnel*. Dublin: OMEP Ireland.

National Children's Nurseries Association (2002). *Annual Report 2001*. Dublin: NCNA.

O'Flaherty, J. and Hayes, N. (1997). 'The IEA Pre-primary Project in Ireland', *International Journal of Early Years Education*, 5 (1), 47–56.

Singer, E. and Wong, S. (2018). 'Reflections of Pioneers in Early Childhood Education Research on their Collaboration with Practitioners in the Development of Theories and Innovative Practices', *Early Years*, 38 (2), 125–138. Available at: <https://doi.org/10.1080/09575146.2018.1440534>.

Singer, E. and Wong, S. (2021). 'Early Childhood Theories, Ideals and Social-political Movements, an Oral History Study of Pioneers in the Second Half of the Twentieth Century', *Early Child Development and Care*. Available at: <https://doi.org/10.1080/03004430.2020.1850445>.

United Nations (1989). *Convention on the Rights of the Child*. New York: United Nations.

Walsh, T. (2016). 'Recent Policy Developments in Early Childhood Education (ECE): A Jigsaw with too Many Pieces?', *An Leanbh Óg*, 10, 69–94. Available at: <http://mural.maynoothuniversity.ie/12836/1/TW_recent.pdf>.

Whyte, J. (1979). 'Church, State and Society 1950–1970'. In J. Lee (ed.), *Ireland 1945–1970*, pp. 73–82. Dublin: Gill and Macmillan.

NÓIRÍN HAYES

2 Mapping Irish policy development in early childhood education and care: A century of change?

Introduction

Unpicking the policy threads that interweave to comprise Irish policy in early childhood education and care (ECEC) across the century 1921–2021 is a complex task illustrating, among other things, the changing nature of the relationship between the State and family. For much of this period the early care of young children has been characterized as the responsibility of the family while their early education was regarded as a matter for school. This reflects the long shadow of a nationalistic and Catholic lens through which the Church has opposed State interference in family life, a situation still visible within the Irish Constitution.

   Formalized policy attention to ECEC began to emerge in the late 1990s. This stemmed from a confluence of factors including the recognition by government that the absence of childcare[1] acts as a barrier to the participation of women in the labour force, the increased demand for childcare from parents, unions and employers, and the recognition of the value of quality childcare to young children as a right. A combination of European Union (EU) funding, increased national demand and a growing awareness of the positive short and long-term benefits of ECEC on children and society provided both opportunity and funding for policy action. To

---

1   The terms 'ECEC' and 'childcare' are used interchangeably throughout this chapter and refer to services and settings providing for children under 6 years unless otherwise stated.

present the complex, entangled and somewhat confusing history of ECEC policy in Ireland over the century, this chapter is structured around three time periods: 1921–1970, 1971–1998 and 1999–2021. These time periods were selected as they each represent a particular approach to policy development with regard to ECEC.

1921–1970

A family affair

Ideologically, for much of the twentieth century, childcare was considered to be a private family issue, which did not necessitate State intervention, a gap that was filled in large part by the voluntary and private sector (Douglas 1994). During this period charitable organizations played an important role in developing and supporting services to families, particularly those living in urban poverty. Services included supervised playgrounds (Civics Institute) and day nurseries (Civics Institute and Daughters of Charity) (Cowman 2007, Douglas 1994, Kernan 2005). During the 1960s a growing interest in the value of play for young children led to the establishment of groups such as OMEP (Ireland), the World Organization for Early Childhood Education and the Irish Preschool Playgroups Association (IPPA). As membership expanded and in the absence of legislation, the IPPA established a registration system for members with conditions acting as a guide for good practice. Irish language preschools, the naíonraí, also flourished and in 1974 came together as Na Naíscoileanna Gaelacha to share experience, advice and training for members. These organizations were important agents in highlighting the importance of quality ECEC to children's development and to mothers' wellbeing. They were early influencers of policy through the astute inclusion of members on committees and invitations to departmental officials to speak at seminars and conferences. Through these contacts, the messages emerging from national and international research and practice began to influence thinking at both a practice and policy level.

State involvement in the care of children was initially targeted directly at neglected or 'at risk' children, but over time policy gradually moved towards a family support model to addressing the care of 'at risk' children. The *Health Act 1970* empowered the Department of Health to provide grants towards the operating costs of daycare centres. The bulk of this grant aid went to voluntary groups or charitable organizations providing sessional childcare/preschool care to children considered 'at risk' and who, without such interventions, would need residential care. The numbers of families and children availing of these services was relatively small and largely confined to disadvantaged urban areas in Dublin and Cork. At the same time, health professionals working with 'at risk' populations of children began to recognize the value of regular attendance at 'a well-run day centre where they receive proper care and attention and also have opportunities of learning to mix with other children' (Department of Health 1980: para. 10.1.3).

The role of education

The early years of the century saw substantial changes in the education system which impacted on perceptions of, and policy for, early childhood. The political events of the 1920s led to a shift from a progressive education towards identifying schools as sites for the implementation of the 'gaelicisation policy' of the new Irish Free State (O'Callaghan 2011). This narrow focus provided little opportunity for teachers to implement a progressive, child-centred curriculum resulting in Irish early education diverging from international trends. A review of the curriculum in the late 1940s brought about a shift in policy direction and teachers were encouraged to facilitate children's play and advised that infant teaching:

> if it is to be successful, must be based on the young child's instinctive urge to play, to talk, to imitate, to manipulate materials, to make and do things. (Department of Education 1951: 3)

In response to increasing evidence from the US and UK, the role of early education as a compensatory intervention to counteract the impact of disadvantage on preschool children drew the attention of the Department of Education. In 1969, the Department established the Rutland Street Project, which aimed to improve the life chances of young children in Dublin inner city through providing a curriculum to improve perceptual discrimination, extend children's knowledge of the world and assist language development (Holland 1979). It remained, for many years, the only preschool supported by the Department of Education. However, by the mid-1970s the Department was grant-aiding a number of voluntary groups to provide preschools for young Traveller children, maintaining the focus on supporting preschool education as an intervention for socially or educationally disadvantaged children.

1971–1998

Diverse policy drivers

By the 1970s, new policy drivers emerged and became significant in shaping the landscape we have today. The removal of the marriage bar in the civil service, alongside European-informed equality legislation, saw a gradual increase in the number of women working outside the home and leading to changes in family life. These changes led to calls from a number of different organizations and departmental sources for increased policy attention to childcare (Department of Equality and Law Reform 1994, Department of Health 1985, Department of Labour 1983, OMEP 1992). Maintaining its historic distancing from direct involvement in family affairs, the State reacted with a series of disconnected policy actions leading to the division of responsibility for ECEC across a number of government departments (Hayes 1995, Walsh 2016). This in turn created problems of coordination and delays in the development of services and maintained a clear distinction between childcare and early education 'with childcare part of the equality and work agenda and early education part of the strategy for combating educational disadvantage' (Hayes 2010: 67).

If one were to identify any government department with an expansion of childcare in the 1980s and 1990s, it would be the Department of Health which funded, to different degrees, community-based services for young children and their families considered to be 'at risk'. In some instances, this involved grant-aiding day nurseries in disadvantaged areas and/or supporting places in local community playgroups (Hayes 1995). Successive Ministers for Health recognized the role of day care services as a support measure for disadvantaged families and their children and the number of centres supported by grant aid increased from thirty in 1974 to eighty-seven in 1980 and 175 in 1982 (Department of Health 1985: 6). In terms of legislation, the publication of the *Child Care Act 1991* proved a crucial development for childcare policy in Ireland. Once the final sections had been signed into law in December 1996, the *Child Care (Pre-school Services) Regulations* (Department of Health and Children 1997) came into force and the Preschool Inspectorate was established. These regulations mark the first formalization of policy in ECEC, through the legislative control over services for children aged birth to 6, excluding the infant primary school classes. The regulations were particularly relevant as they gave wider responsibility to the State in the supervision of preschool services for all children rather than focusing only on those considered 'at risk' (Hayes 2016). Originally part of the Health Board system, the Inspectorate became part of the Child and Family Agency (Tusla) when it was formed in 2014. The regulations attend primarily to aspects of health and safety in settings and to the development of children. Over the years, the Inspectorate has expanded in numbers and in remit in line with the growth of ECEC and School Age Childcare (SAC) nationally and, in 2018, it launched a Quality and Regulatory Framework (Department of Children and Youth Affairs [DCYA] 2018) for all childcare services.

A busy policy space

Paralleling the evolving policy attention to childcare, the 1990s witnessed a period of unprecedented economic growth in Ireland due in part to a strategic partnership approach to economic policy development. Over time negotiations between government, employers, unions and the community pillar moved to a more explicit and defined social focus. The momentum that gathered from the 1980s into the 1990s ensured that childcare featured in negotiations culminating in *Partnership 2000* (Government of Ireland 1996) calling for the development of a national childcare framework. In response, an Expert Working Group was established by the Department of Justice, Equality and Law Reform (DJELR) in 1997. The membership of this group was wide-ranging and included representatives from across the sector and the Departments of Education and Science and Health and Children. The terms of reference were restricted to considering childcare as a service for parents at work and those in areas of disadvantage accessing work through training and/or education, signalling childcare as a labour market initiative rather than a service for young children and their families. The final report proposed a comprehensive, seven-year *National Childcare Strategy* (NCS) (Government of Ireland 1999a) for the management and development of the childcare sector and represented the first concerted attempt to develop a coherent and comprehensive government policy that specifically addressed childcare.

At this time within education, the principles underpinning the new primary school curriculum (Department of Education 1971) reflected a progressive ideology focusing on a child-centred approach to practice which encouraged active and discovery-learning and less formal teaching, particularly in the infant classes with an emphasis on learning through play. Evidence suggests, however, that in the main, teaching in the infant classes continued along traditional lines (O'Rourke and Archer 1987, Hayes et al. 1997). While the Department of Education supported a number of early childhood pilot initiatives such as the Early Start project (Ryan et al. 1998) and Traveller preschools, it did not take a policy position on early education *per se* (Hayes and Bradley 2006). By the 1990s, in light of accumulating evidence identifying the importance of early education in the lives of young children and, in particular, its mitigating role in combatting educational disadvantage, the Department turned its policy attention to considering ECEC. In

1998, a National Forum on Early Childhood Education was convened by the Minister for Education to provide for multi-lateral discussions among a wide range of groups, many of whom were also represented on the NCS Expert Working Group. The Forum produced a comprehensive report (Coolahan 1998) which went on to inform *Ready to Learn, White Paper on Early Education* (Government of Ireland 1999b). The White Paper was ambitious in its scope, recognized the importance of integrating care and education across the whole spectrum of early childhood education and care services, and addressed:

> the development of very young children in the home, supports to parents concerning how best to help their children learn, a wide range of supports for private providers and voluntary/community groups and a strategy to enhance the quality of infant education in primary schools. (DES 1999: vii)

In addition to national factors converging to drive policy developments on childcare, international influences also played a significant role. These included a commitment to expanding and developing certain children's services following a critical report from the United Nations (UN) Committee on the Rights of the Child arising from the first plenary hearing of Irish National Report on realizing the UN Convention on the Rights of the Child in 1996 (Kaoukji and Little 2007). Specifically the UN Committee recommended that the State adopt a comprehensive National Strategy for Children to incorporate the principles and provisions of the Convention (Children's Rights Alliance [CRA] 1998). Responding to the recommendation, the then Minister for Health and Children Brian Cowen TD announced the Government's commitment to develop a national children's strategy. The Strategy, *Our Children-Their Lives* (Government of Ireland 2000) laid the foundation for child policy in Ireland for ten years. In terms of ECEC policy, it noted that '[C]hildren's early education and developmental needs will be met through quality childcare services and family-friendly employment measures' (Government of Ireland 2000: 50).

1999–2021

Leveraging EU funding

The publication of the *White Paper on Early Childhood Education* and the *National Childcare Strategy* in 1999 marked a significant start to the millennium and State involvement in developing and supporting ECEC in Ireland. The reports provided a context within which to develop a cross-departmental approach to ECEC which would integrate care and education, an ambition identified explicitly in both reports. However, failure to create a mechanism for an integrated and coordinated response to the recommendations and outputs from both represents a missed opportunity for the development of a coherent and strategic policy approach, contributing to the fractured evolution of policy across the sector. Circumstances at the time privileged the NCS, specifically because the implementation of the strategy was linked to the National Development Plan (NDP) 2000–2006, providing the context within which to access substantial EU funding. This in turn led to the establishment of the *Equal Opportunities Childcare Programme* (EOCP) from 2000–2006 and its successor the *National Childcare Investment Plan* (NCIP) from 2006–2011, laying the foundation for continued, though less extensive, investment in the childcare sector in subsequent years.

The aims guiding the EOCP were to enhance the quality of childcare, increase the number of childcare places and introduce a coordinated approach to the delivery of childcare services. To facilitate integration and cross-departmental collaboration, a number of different oversight and advisory groups were established including a Childcare Directorate within the National Children's Office (NCO) of the DJELR, a National Co-ordinating Childcare Committee (NCCC) and thirty-three County/City Childcare Committees (CCCs). These bodies provided the infrastructure for implementing the strategy at national, regional and local level and continue in a more-or-less similar format today. The Childcare Directorate was responsible for the EOCP and engaged in inter-departmental policy work with two key departments, the Department of Health and Children on issues relating to regulation and inspection and the Department of Education and Science in relation to aspects of training, qualifications and quality practice.

A DES-commissioned report on ECEC in Ireland expressed concern with the policy split between education and care and criticized the fragmented and dispersed nature of responsibility for the sector, noting that 'no one Department or Agency had been given clear responsibility to lead integrated policy or to provide coherence across the various childhood bodies and services' (Organisation for Economic Co-operation and Development [OECD] 2004: 23). Efforts to address this continued over the next two decades. In 2005, an Office of the Minister for Children (OMC), with a Junior Minister attending Cabinet meetings, was established (becoming the Office of the Minister for Children and Youth Affairs [OMCYA] in 2008). The OMC was responsible for interacting with every department and every agency that could contribute to policy leading to better outcomes for all children. To encourage an integrated approach to ECEC policy, an Early Years Education Policy Unit (EYEPU) was established and co-located between the OMC and the DES. However, Langford cautioned that integrated policy development was challenging and that it would take time '... to gain acceptance for the notion that the best way to deliver policies and services for children is to get Government departments and agencies to work together strategically' (Kaoukji and Little 2007: 72). In 2011, a full Department of Children and Youth Affairs (DCYA) was established which included a childcare policy unit, which has grown over the years. The department was renamed the Department for Children, Equality, Disability, Integration and Youth (DCEDIY) in 2020, significantly broadening its remit and focus. Although the childcare unit was retained, it was retitled the Early Learning and Care and School Age Childcare Division. It is too soon to evaluate the implication of these name changes for ECEC policy over the long term.

A new funding stream became available to government when Atlantic Philanthropies was established in Ireland in 1987 and began to contribute to the development of services for children and youth in 2003 (Boyle 2016). Through working in partnership with government, it aimed to support the development of services directly, and indirectly through influencing policy. Though not without its challenges (Kaoukji and Little 2007) philanthropic investment in initiatives such as the Prevention and Early Intervention and Area Based Childhood projects had a significant impact in the growth of community services including ECEC (Hayes 2021). At the same time an interim report on the EOCP revealed that the performance of the programme, in terms of the number of childcare places and geographical distribution was disappointing, positing that this reflected the requirement to meet the dual objectives of increasing supply of childcare places for children of working parents while also promoting social inclusion through provision of affordable childcare (DJELR 2003). This observation illustrates a persistent tension at a policy level between regarding childcare as a service to parents while also regarding it as a form of intervention. In response to the report, funding was opened up to private-for-profit providers who could apply for funding up to a maximum of €100,000 per facility and a maximum of €500,000 for multiple services. This investment strategy privileged the development of large centre-based ECEC settings resulting in a robust response from the construction industry and private childcare chains. This trend continues despite evidence that Irish families prefer a wider choice of settings for young children including with relatives, childminders, centre-based care or a combination of all; parents report different preferences across different ages and family requirements (McGinnity et al. 2013). With such a strong policy focus on increasing places it is perhaps not a surprise that there was limited parallel investment in a strategic quality assurance programme or in supports to grow a skilled, professional and sustainable workforce.

A question of quality

In an effort to enhance quality, the EOCP had moved to '… stimulate the provision of quality childcare places, through the provision of grants for the childcare sector' (Langford 2006: 259). These grants were intended to strengthen what was a weak system and included financial support to the National Voluntary Childcare Organizations[2] charged with implementing a range of measures aimed at upskilling their members and creating a greater and better informed awareness of quality practice. In addition, responding to an increasing diverse population a group was established to develop diversity guidelines which led ultimately to the publication of the *Diversity, Equality and Inclusion Charter and Guidelines for Early Childhood Education and Care* (DCYA 2016).

The absence of a policy-led quality enhancement strategy linked to the expansion of places led to the uneven evolution of a sector of varied quality. The growth in demand for services, particularly in urban areas, saw an increase in private-for-profit businesses where the tension between costs and profits can compromise the quality of provision. This was highlighted in a televised documentary aired in 2013, which resulted in a renewed focus on inspection, regulation and quality supports. A central support was the establishment, in 2014, of a quality development and mentoring service, Better Start, with a regional reach through a network of mentors to facilitate and enhance the quality of practice in all ECEC settings. Although not established as part of the localized childcare structures, Better Start has, over time, developed strategic links to a number of CCCs.

It has been suggested that meaningful policy changes in relation to quality only became evident in the mid-2000s with the implementation of aspects of the *White Paper on Early Childhood Education* (Horgan et al. 2014). Although it failed to get the level of funding available to the NCS, the DES did establish the Centre for Early Childhood and Development (CECDE) which was responsible for addressing aspects of quality in ECEC while growing a research profile. The CECDE brought together a wide variety of players across the ECEC and early primary systems and established links with colleagues and researchers, nationally and internationally. Following extensive consultation across the ECEC system, it published *Síolta: The National Quality Framework for Early Childhood*

---

2   This group currently comprises Barnardos, Childminding Ireland, Early Childhood Ireland, Irish Steiner Kindergarten Association, National Childhood Network, National Parents' Council and St Nicholas Montessori Teachers' Association/ Society of Ireland.

Education (CECDE 2006). The DES also supported the National Council for Curriculum and Assessment (NCCA) to publish *Aistear*: *The Early Childhood Curriculum Framework* (NCCA 2009). Both *Síolta* and *Aistear* were developed in close collaboration with the early childhood sector and designed for those working with children from birth to 6 years. Both frameworks were sufficiently broad to be applied in any early learning setting from the home, across varied early childhood settings through to the infant classes of the primary school. The financial crisis of 2008 had a serious impact on these developments and slowed the pace of implementation. It led to the closure of the CECDE and limited the funding available for the national roll out and training mechanism necessary to realize *Síolta* and *Aistear* in practice. This, in turn, contributed to confusion about the relationship between the frameworks and the fractured application of the frameworks in practice. To ameliorate this, the NCCA, with the support of the DCYA and DES, developed an online practice guide integrating both *Síolta* and *Aistear* (NCCA 2016). All funded settings must now provide evidence of working within both frameworks and Better Start locates its mentoring work within the *Síolta/Aistear* principles.

Access and affordability

Despite developing a variety of funding schemes to support parents with the costs of childcare, affordability has remained a persistent difficulty. In 2006, at the height of the Celtic Tiger, the government moved to address affordability by introducing the Early Childcare Supplement (ECS) for all children under-6 years of age. This direct, non-taxable payment of €250 per quarter year, was available to parents for each eligible child to cover their childcare costs. There was no obligation to spend the money on ECEC and the scheme contributed nothing directly towards the sustainability of the ECEC sector itself. Following the 2008 financial crisis, the government announced the abolishment of ECS scheme while ring-fencing a portion of the budget to fund provision of a universal free pre-school year. The scheme, introduced in 2010, included all children in the year before school entry, for three hours per day, during school terms. Funding was directed through an Early Childhood Care and Education (ECCE) scheme available to both private and community services. It was the first universal early childhood scheme outside the infant classes of the primary school system but did not reflect the primary school system in terms of either investment or supports. The scheme, covering as it did the costs of a specified period of preschool for children over 3 years of age, proved universally popular with parents and in 2016 the DCYA introduced a second free preschool year. While a welcome contribution to the cost of childcare, the sessional nature of the ECCE scheme meant it was neither supportive of parents' participation in paid work nor did it make a significant impact on the costs of full-time childcare (Horgan et al. 2014). The State's clear preference for market-based responses meant that the care and education of young children remained a private, and costly, responsibility for parents.

In its *Irish Country Report*, the European Commission (EC 2015: 64) noted 'no progress on improving access to affordable and full-time child-care' pointing out that the costs of ECEC in Ireland were higher than in any other EU country. To address the issue of affordability, the DCYA set up an Inter Departmental Group (IDG) to 'identify and assess policy options for increasing the affordability, quality and supply of early years and school-age care and education services in Ireland' (DCYA 2018: 6). Taking account of the many different schemes directed at addressing the costs of childcare, the IDG recommended the design of a Single Affordable Childcare Scheme. In 2019, the DCYA introduced a National Childcare Subsidy scheme designed to replace the existing targeted childcare funding schemes which were 'administratively complex, inadequate in terms of accessibility and limited to those on specific social welfare payments or training programmes. By contrast, it suggested that the new, streamlined scheme should provide means-tested support towards childcare costs based primarily on income' (DCYA 2018: 7). This new system continues the tradition of funding parents to meet the costs of childcare rather than investing directly into the childcare system. It provides two types of childcare subsidy for children over 6 months of age:

- A universal subsidy for children under three years old. Children over three who have not yet qualified for the ECCE scheme are also eligible, which is not means tested
- An income-assessed subsidy for children up to fifteen years old, which is means tested (<https://www.ncs.gov.ie/en/faqs/>).

The impact of the National Childcare Scheme on the affordability of childcare and the sustainability of ECEC services has yet to be evaluated. It is noteworthy that the schemes brought in under this single measure do not include the funding for the ECCE scheme, a further strengthening of the care and education divide prevalent in Irish ECEC policy, an issue which is now explored.

The enigma of integrated ECEC policy

The introduction of a scheme to directly fund free preschool places signalled a change in policy direction in keeping with calls from many individuals and policy bodies over the years (Wolfe et al. 2013). Paradoxically, in being introduced as an educational, school readiness initiative, the ECCE scheme, as it was called, both heightened the conceptual split between care and education and restricted the integrated nature of care and education to services for children over 3 years of age. The focus on the pedagogical potential of these services led to a number of key policy actions which enhanced services for children over three but led, over time, to diminished support for settings serving children under three. For instance, the scheme incentivized settings to position more qualified staff with the older children and many of the available mentoring and quality supports were directed solely at preschool places. These included access to CPD programmes and/or additional funding through the Access and Inclusion Model (AIM) (details at <https://aim.gov.ie>), a scheme to support settings include young children with disabilities to attend preschool.

The ECCE scheme also brought greater attention to the developmental and educational nature of ECEC. In 2015, the DES commenced development of an inspection system to evaluate and support the educational features of ECEC. In cooperation with the DCYA, the DES employed a number of early years inspectors to carry out the Early Years Education Inspections (EYEIs) across those settings providing preschool places under the ECCE scheme. The EYEIs were designed to evaluate the nature, range and appropriateness of the early educational experiences of children. Inspections are informed by the principles of the *Aistear* and *Síolta* frameworks along with international research related to early childhood education and inspection (DES 2018). In 2019, the DES announced its intention to expand its inspections to cover all ECEC settings across the age range of 6 months to 6 years. The Early Years Education Inspections were developed to complement the Tusla inspections. However, the fact that there are two separate inspection schemes serves as another example of the structural split between care and education.

Amid growing concerns about the absence of a vision for a coherent, integrated ECEC system (Start Strong 2010), the Minister for Children and Youth Affairs announced the development of Ireland's first National Early Years Strategy. To this end, an Expert Advisory Group (EAG) was established to advise the Minister on matters relating to a strategy. The report of the EAG, *Right from the Start* (DCYA 2013) identified five issues that needed to be addressed in parallel over the lifetime of any strategy. These were to (i) increase investment, (ii) extend paid parental leave, (iii) strengthen child and family supports, (iv) insist on good governance, accountability and quality in all services and (v) enhance and extend quality ECEC services.

Taking account of the EAG recommendations, *First 5: A Whole of Government Strategy for Babies, Young Children and their Families (2019–2028)* (Government of Ireland 2018) was published. The strategy does not provide an explicit vision or strategy for ECEC as a specific service type and, unexpectedly replaces and redefines the term 'ECEC' with the term 'Early Learning and Care (ELC)'. By dropping the term 'education' and by removing the junior and senior infants from consideration in both the definition and the strategy itself (Government of Ireland 2018: 26), the change in language implicitly consolidates the distinction between early childhood education and early childhood care. The focus of the strategy is wide-ranging and addresses the various different service supports for families with children under 6 years. The strategy continues to maintain a distance from investing directly in ECEC and an ambiguity in tone is evident throughout exemplified in the emphasis on the importance of family. The following quote is particularly instructive:

> Given the importance of parental care in the first year and the evidence that shows prolonged periods in centre-based ELC can have a negative impact on children's cognitive and socio-emotional outcomes, particularly for younger children, paid parental leave and wider supports for parents to balance caring and work have been prioritised in this Strategy. With those notable caveats, ELC benefits all children, with the largest gains experienced by children from vulnerable groups, including low-income or immigrant households and those with less educated parents. These gains are most likely in settings when there is a diverse mix of young children. (Government of Ireland 2018: 87)

Among the objectives of *First 5* is that 'babies and young children have access to safe, high-quality, developmentally appropriate, integrated ELC (and school-age childcare), which reflects diversity of need' (Government of Ireland 2018: 143). Quality of provision and the affordability of services are identified as requiring immediate policy attention. In 2019, to address the quality objective, a Steering Group was established to develop a Workforce Development Plan. Drawing on the *EU Quality Framework for Early Childhood Education and Care* (EU 2019), the Workforce Development Plan will:

> set out plans to raise the profile of careers in ELC and SAC, establish a career framework and leadership development opportunities and will work towards building a more gender-balanced and diverse workforce. Consideration will also be given to broader ELC and school-age childcare workforce, including those in inspection, mentoring and training roles and support for those who facilitate practice placements. (DCEDIY 2019: 4)

To address affordability, an Expert Working Group was set up in 2019 by the DCEDIY to develop a new Funding Model for Early Learning and Care and School Age Childcare. This Expert Group will examine the current model of funding, its effectiveness in delivering quality, affordable, sustainable and inclusive services, and consider how additional resourcing can be delivered for the sector. As we await the DCEDIY reports on a new funding model and the workforce development plan, the DES, through the NCCA, is reviewing the primary school curriculum and has announced a consultation process to review and update *Aistear*. Working with teachers and early childhood educators, both the review and the consultation will link primary curriculum considerations with what children learn in the free preschool years, thus bedding the preschool experience into the wider educational frame. How these separate departmental policy initiatives on quality, affordability and curriculum relate to each other will have a profound impact on the future ECEC landscape. The commitment by government (Government of Ireland 2020: 80) to establish an agency, Childcare Ireland, to assist in the expansion of high-quality childcare, is an initiative which could have a profound impact on ECEC, acting as a context within which to integrate and develop the many different activities within and across the ECEC policy space.

Conclusion

Ireland has been slow to develop policies for ECEC and has faced both internal and external challenges. The trajectory shows a disinclination by the State to become directly involved in the care and education of young children, accompanied by a resistance to support or regulate this emerging field into the new millennium. Since 2000, however, we have seen what has been characterized as 'rapid policy change without transformation' (Wolfe et al. 2013: 123). Despite extensive investment and many reports and working groups, Ireland continues to work within a split system, consolidating the distinction between care and education. Services are expensive, staff are poorly paid and the regulatory and inspection systems are burdensome. The focus of most recent policy perpetuates the characterization of childcare as a service for parents and early education as a service to children from 3 to 6 years of age. There is little evidence of a holistic policy approach that recognizes the unique educational role of ECEC in the lives of all young children, in tandem with its role in supporting parents. Notwithstanding this, there is a continued interest and commitment to quality provision and professionalization among those working within the field. The Covid-19 pandemic shone a brief light on the centrality of childcare services to a functioning society and the lives of our youngest children, while also highlighting its fragile nature. This led to some new discussions and publications on alternative models of provision, including a move from the current market model to a public model of ECEC (Citizens Assembly 2021, INFORM 2020, Oireachtas Library and Research Service 2020). History has shown the power of national organizations and external influences to affect policy direction. These developments and conversations, building on the existing strengths within the system, can contribute to a renewed vision for an integrated high-quality, affordable and sustainable model of ECEC.

Bibliography

Boyle, R. (2016). Philanthropy Working with Government: A Case Study of the Atlantic Philanthropies' Partnership with the Irish Government. Dublin: IPA.

Centre for Early Childhood Development and Education (2006). Síolta – The National Quality Framework for Early Childhood Education. Dublin: CECDE/DES.

Children's Rights Alliance (1998). CRA Newsletter Issue 8. Dublin: CRA.

Citizens Assembly (2021). Recommendations of the Citizens' Assembly on Gender Equality. Available at: <https://www.citizensassembly.ie/en/news-publications/press-releases/recommendations-of-the-citizens-assembly-on-gender-equality.html>.

Coolahan, J. (1998). Report of the National Forum on Early Childhood Education. Dublin: The Stationery Office.

Cowman, M. (2007). Memoirs of Pre-school Services Ireland 1892–2007. Dublin: St Catherine's Provincial House Blackrock.

Department of Children and Youth Affairs (2013). Right from the Start: Report of the Expert Advisory Group on the Early Years Strategy. Dublin: The Stationery Office.

Department of Children and Youth Affairs (2016). Diversity, Equality and Inclusion Charter and Guidelines for Early Childhood Education and Care. Dublin: The Stationery Office.

Department of Children and Youth Affairs (2018). *Focused Policy Assessment of the Affordable Childcare Scheme.* Dublin: DCYA.

Department of Children, Equality, Disability, Integration and Youth (2019). *Workforce Development Plan for the Early Learning and Care (ELC), School Age Childcare (SAC) and Childminding Sector: Background Note and Terms of Reference for the Steering Group.* Available at: <https://assets.gov.ie/26650/a384c2888749488d8e93badc501507b3.pdf>.

Department of Education (1951). *An Naí-Scoil: The Infant School – Notes for Teachers.* Dublin: The Stationery Office.

Department of Education (1971). *Primary School Curriculum: Teacher's Handbook – Part 1 and 2.* Dublin: Department of Education.

Department of Education and Skills (2018). *A Guide to Early Years Education Inspection (EYEI).* Dublin: The Stationery Office.

Department of Equality and Law Reform (1994). *Working Group on Childcare Facilities for Working Parents. Report to the Minister for Equality and Law Reform.* Dublin: The Stationery Office.

Department of Health (1985). *Minimum Legal Requirements and Standards for Day Care Services for Children: Report of a Committee appointed by the Minister for Health.* Dublin: The Stationery Office.

Department of Health and Children (1997). *Child Care (Pre-School Services) Regulations 1996 and Child Care (Pre-School Services) (Amendment) Regulations, 1997.* Dublin: Department of Health and Children.

Department of Justice, Equality and Law Reform (2003). *A Review of Progress to End 2003 on the Implementation of the Equal Opportunities Childcare Programme 2000–2006.* Dublin: DJELR.

Department of Labour (1983). *Report of the Working Group on Childcare Facilities for Working Parents.* Dublin: The Stationery Office.

Douglas, F. (1994). *The History of the Irish Pre-school Playgroups Association.* Dublin: IPPA. Available at: <https://omepireland.ie/wp-content/uploads/2019/07/History-of-the-IPPA.pdf>.

European Commission (2015). *Country Report Ireland, including an In-Depth Review on the Prevention and Correction of Macroeconomic Imbalances.* Brussels: EC.

European Union (2019). *Council Recommendation on High Quality Early Childhood Education and Care Systems.* Brussels: EC.

Government of Ireland (1996). *Partnership 2000 for Inclusion, Employment and Competitiveness.* Dublin: The Stationery Office.

Government of Ireland (1999a). *National Childcare Strategy: Report of the Partnership 2000 Expert Working Group on Childcare.* Dublin: The Stationery Office.

Government of Ireland (1999b). *Ready to Learn – A White Paper on Early Childhood Education.* Dublin: The Stationery Office.

Government of Ireland (2000). *National Children's Strategy – Our Children-Their Lives*. Dublin: The Stationery Office.

Government of Ireland (2018). *A Whole of Government Strategy for Babies, Young Children and their Families 2019–2028*. Dublin: The Stationery Office.

Government of Ireland (2020). *Programme for Government: Our Shared Future*. Dublin: The Stationery Office.

Hayes, N. (1995). *The Case for a National Policy on Early Education: Poverty and Policy, Discussion Paper No. 2*. Dublin: Combat Poverty Agency.

Hayes, N. (2010). 'Childcare? Early Childhood Education and Care? Towards an Integrated Early Years Policy for Young Children in Ireland', *Early Years: An International Journal of Research and Development*, 30 (1), 67–78.

Hayes, N. (2016). 'Early Childhood Education and Care: A Neglected Policy Arena?' In M. Murphy and F. Dukelow (eds), *The Irish Welfare State in the Twenty-First Century*, pp. 193–214. London: Palgrave.

Hayes, N. (2021). 'Childcare Policy Development in Ireland: The Case of Early Childhood Education and Care.' In D. de Buitléir (ed.), *Achieving Impact in Public Service*. Dublin: Institute of Public Administration.

Hayes, N. and Bradley, S. (2006). 'The Childcare Question'. In B. Fanning and M. Rush (eds), *Care and Social Change in the Irish Welfare Economy*, pp. 163–178. Dublin: University College Dublin Press.

Hayes, N., O'Flaherty, J. and Kernan, M. (1997). *A Window into Early Education in Ireland: The First National Report of the IEA Pre-Primary Project*. Dublin: Dublin Institute of Technology.

Holland, S. (1979). *Rutland Street: The Story of an Educational Experiment for Disadvantaged Children in Dublin*. Oxford: Pergamon Press.

Horgan, D., Martin, S., Cunneen, M. and Towler, M. (2014). 'Early Childhood Care and Education Policy: Ireland Country Note', *New Zealand Research in Early Childhood Education Journal*, 17, 1–13.

INFORM (2020). *Act Now: Re-Imagining Early Childhood Education and Care in Ireland: A Discussion Paper*. Dublin: INFORM. Available at <https://www.dropbox.com/s/y10xuzfg2cnj7qv/INFORM_Act%20Now%20discussion%20paper%20for%20PfG.pdf?dl=0>.

Kaoukji, D. and Little, M. (2007). 'Interview with Sylda Langford: People, Relationships and Power Struggles – The View from the Director-General of the Irish Office of the Minister for Children', *Journal of Children's Services*, 2 (1), 67–75.

Kernan, M. (2005). 'Developing Citizenship through Supervised Play: The Civics Institute of Ireland Playgrounds, 1933–75', *History of Education*, 34 (6), 675–687.

Langford, S. (2006). 'Delivering Integrated Services and Policies for Children', *Journal of the Statistical and Social Inquiry Society of Ireland*, XXXVI, 250–260.

McGinnity, F., Murray, A. and McNally, S. (2013). *Mothers' Return to Work and Childcare Choices for Infants in Ireland, Growing Up in Ireland: National Longitudinal Study of Children.* Dublin: The Stationery Office.

National Council for Curriculum and Assessment (2009). *Aistear: The Early Childhood Curriculum Framework.* Dublin: NCCA.

National Council for Curriculum and Assessment (2016). *The Aistear/Síolta Practice Guide.* Dublin: NCCA. Available at: <https://www.aistearsiolta.ie/en/>.

O'Callaghan, J. (2011). 'Politics, Policy and History: History Teaching in Irish Secondary Schools 1922–1970', *Études Irlandaises*, 36 (1), 25–41.

Oireachtas Library and Research Service (2020). *Public Provision of Early Childhood Education: An Overview of the International Evidence.* Dublin: Houses of the Oireachtas.

Organisation for Economic Co-operation and Development (2004). *Thematic Review of Early Childhood Education and Care Policy in Ireland.* Paris: OECD.

Organisation Mondiale pour l'Education Préscolaire (Ireland) (1992). *Young Children in Ireland: The Feasibility of Establishing an Agency Focusing on the Welfare, Education, Development and Happiness of Young Children.* Dublin: OMEP.

O'Rourke, B. and Archer, P. (1987). 'A Survey of Teaching Practice in Infant Classrooms in Irish Primary Schools', *Irish Journal of Education*, 27, 53–79.

Ryan, S., O'hUalláchain, S. and Hogan, J. (1998). *Early Start Pre-School Programme – Final Evaluation Report.* Dublin: Education Research Centre.

Start Strong (2010). *Start Strong Children 2020: Planning Now for the Future.* Dublin: Start Strong.

Walsh, T. (2016). 'Recent Policy Developments in Early Childhood Education (ECE): A Jigsaw with too Many Pieces?', *An Leanbh Óg OMEP Ireland Journal of Early Childhood Studies*, 10, 69–94.

Wolfe, T., O'Donoghue-Hynes, B. and Hayes, N. (2013). 'Rapid Change without Transformation: The Dominance of a National Policy Paradigm Over International Influences on ECEC Development in Ireland 1995–2012', *International Journal of Early Childhood*, 45 (2), 191–205.

MAURA O'CONNOR

3 Provision for early childhood education
   through the infant classes of primary schools

Introduction

This chapter provides an historical analysis of the growth and development of early childhood education in Ireland from 1921–2021, focusing particularly on children in infant classes (first two years in primary [national] schools). It examines the concept of the young school-going child as expressed in policy documents and considers the intentions, actions and contexts of policymakers, educationalists and practitioners as they practised the art of curriculum design, implementation and evaluation in the period under review. The compulsory school age in Ireland is 6, however, nearly 40 per cent of 4-year-olds and virtually all 5-year-olds attend primary school with over 130,000 children in infant classes in 2019 (Department of Education 2020: 10). In general, early childhood care and education services are delivered outside the formal education system by a diverse range of private, community and voluntary organizations.

The chapter focuses primarily on five key policy changes that signalled five historical epochs in the evolution of infant education and practice in Ireland. The first epoch, which predates the 100 years under review, begins with the publication in 1900 of the *Revised Programme of Instruction in National Schools.* This revolutionary curriculum placed the young child at its core, and school life promised to be an enlightening period where children learned largely through play. The second epoch symbolizes the advent of political independence in 1922, when the educational policy of the Irish Free State accorded a privileged position to the teaching of the Irish language within the infant curriculum. The third epoch commences with the introduction in 1948 of a more child-centred curriculum developed alongside the all-Irish policy in the schools. The fourth epoch heralds the reintroduction in 1971 of a child-centred curriculum for all classes in primary schools using a bottom-up approach. The fifth epoch, beginning in 1999, marks the continuation of child-centredness placing greater emphasis on the agentic child who guides his or her own learning and the teacher portrayed as a curriculum developer as well as a curriculum implementer.

A backward glance, 1900–1921

Towards the end of the nineteenth century, in Ireland, it became evident to educationalists that the programme in primary schools with its emphasis on rote-learning in overcrowded classrooms was inappropriate to meet the needs of young children. In many schools the interests of the young child in infant classes were seldom, if ever, the primary concern of the teacher. In 1872, a system of payment-by-results was introduced whereby a sum of money was paid to the teacher for each pupil who passed an annual examination. A prescriptive programme for results-fees was outlined 'for infants over four and under six, and for those over six and under seven' (O'Connor 2010: 77). For many young children who had previously been largely ignored, this scheme meant an early introduction to literacy and numeracy.

The *Revised Programme* (Commissioners of National Education in Ireland [CNEI] 1901), which was implemented in primary schools from 1900 to 1922, heralded a whole new concept in Irish educational practice in relation to early childhood education. It signified for the first time in the history of Irish education that the interests of the infant as an individual were foregrounded and placed at the core of the curriculum. The new programme marked the beginning of State endorsement of child-centred principles. The infant curriculum was modelled on the principles underlying good Froebelian practice and was consistent with the Froebelian notion of quality Kindergarten practice, though modified to suit Irish conditions. While the focus in the revised curriculum remained on the 3Rs (reading, writing and arithmetic), much emphasis was placed on activity-based and experiential principles. Froebel's 'gifts' and 'occupations' were placed on the syllabus as well as drawing, singing, school discipline and physical drill, cookery, laundry and needlework. The programme stressed that the purpose of manual instruction was not a preparation for trades but 'rather to train the intelligence and observation, and to produce habits of neatness, dexterity, and carefulness in the child' (CNEI 1901: 72). The *Revised Programme* signalled a new departure from the old didactic curriculum of the nineteenth century. It promoted instead a more child-centred, heuristic approach by which young children were 'enabled to find out things for themselves, by being placed, so to speak, in the position of discoverers, instead of being merely told things' (*Ibid.*: 3).

The teachers of infant classes, many of whom were untrained, struggled without great success to introduce child-centred and activity-based learning into their classrooms. In 1903, an evaluation of the school system was carried out by an inspector from England, Mr F. H. Dale. When commenting on infant education, he complained that the training of the younger children was one of the weakest parts of Irish primary education (Dale 1904). Practically, child-centred curricula demanded resources (both human and material), but these were not sufficiently available for all young children and their teachers. Nevertheless, the first twenty years of the twentieth century witnessed a radical shift in curricular policy and a revolution in the pedagogies and learning experiences promoted for use in infant classes. The status and profile of infant education increased greatly with the publication of the *Revised Programme* providing early childhood with due recognition and an education that focused on the holistic development of the child was prioritized (O'Connor 2010: 181–184). Regrettably, this new-found enthusiasm was not to be encouraged in the New Irish State.

The educational policy of the Irish Free State, 1921–1948

The process of implementing the *Revised Programme* (CNEI 1901) was interrupted in the early 1920s with the onset of independence in Ireland. The main priority of the new Irish Free State government of 1922, in conjunction with the Catholic Church, was to foster a sense of national identity among its citizens. The Catholic religion and the promotion of the Irish language were recognized as the main characteristics of the new identity. In an independent Ireland, education was seen as a vehicle for nation-building, and curricular reform was prioritized by both State and Church. As early as 1920, at the Irish National Teachers' Organisation (INTO) Conference, a resolution was passed for the establishment of the first National Programme Conference. This was held between 1921 and 1922. While relevant stakeholders were invited to attend, it was not representative of all interested parties (Walsh 2012: 131–133).

As Akenson (1975: 44) declares, 'then came the shocker'. The Conference recommended that 'the work in the Infant Standards is to be entirely in Irish' (National Programme Conference 1922: 3). This was a rule that affected nearly 250,000 children whose home language in over 90 per cent of cases was English (Ó Cuív 1969: 162). In the new State, the infant programme was to include language lessons comprising of stories, dialogues, rhymes, recitations, nature lessons, object lessons and picture talks, handwork, drawing, kindergarten, arithmetic, singing and games (National Programme of Primary Instruction 1922: 15–16). If a teacher was unable to do this, it was stated that Irish should be used as much as possible as the language of the school. Consequently, the introduction of the child-centred curriculum was pushed to the background while a new status was accorded to the teaching of Irish and other concomitant aspects of the nation's Gaelic culture in the schools. Many teachers were displeased with this new requirement. As was explained by O'Connell (1968: 347), the question was not one of practicality, or the ability on the part of the teacher, but rather a fundamental educational principle was involved; should a young child receive his or her instruction in school through a language other than that of the home? The recommendations were accepted, despite opposition, and supporters of the Irish language were given an opportunity to exclude the use of English in the infant classes.

At the Second National Programme Conference in 1925–1926, a small concession was made which recommended that the work in the infant classes between the hours of 10.30 a.m. and 2.00 p.m. be entirely through Irish where the teachers were sufficiently qualified to teach it (National

Programme Conference 1926: 4). This modification was generally of little educational benefit to young children due to the late starting and early finishing times in schools. As a result, for the following twenty years young pupils were to be 'immersed in [the Irish] language at the infant stage and schooled thereafter in a curriculum in which the Irish language was the dominant feature' (Akenson 1975: 47).

By 1934, the government was discontented with the slow rate of improvement in relation to the language revival. To increase the proficiency of the pupils in the Irish language, certain modifications of the infant programme were outlined in the *Revised Programme of Instruction* (Department of Education 1934a) which was introduced in 1934. It was stressed in the curriculum that for infants, the aim of the programme was to train them to understand Irish, and to speak it as their natural language. At the same time teachers were formally instructed by means of a Department of Education regulation that the work in infant classes should be entirely through Irish (Department of Education 1934b). Thus, the small concession given in 1926 that allowed infant teaching and learning through English before 10.30 a.m. and after 2.00 p.m. was removed. A political and nationalistic motive and mood saw the English language once again diminished in infant classrooms at a time when it was the vernacular of the majority of the young children. The word 'kindergarten' was removed from the infant programme and the interests of the young children as individuals were to be sacrificed in favour of building national identity and nationhood in a new nationalistic State.

In the first two decades of the new State, Irish nationalism and culture replaced child-centredness at the centre of the curriculum. Great care was taken by the State and the Church 'to ensure the child would be moulded into an obedient Gaelic-speaking citizen' (O'Connor 2010: 260). The concept of the child as portrayed in the curriculum documentation from this era was that of one who needed to be filled with knowledge through 'strict discipline and the amassing of vast quantities of factual information' (*Ibid.*). Sound educational theory was to suffer in an endeavour to use the schools as the prime agents in effecting the wished-for Gaelic State. Teaching in the infant classes, consequently, was to be nation-centred as distinct from child-centred.

A child-centred curriculum aligned to the all-Irish policy, 1948–1971

While patriotic fervour and nationalistic demands led the development of an all-Irish programme for infant classes in 1922, 1926 and 1934, the nucleus of a conceptual framework for the reintroduction of a more child-centred curriculum was developing alongside the all-Irish policy in schools from the 1930s. In 1941, the INTO issued *The Report of the Committee of Inquiry into the use of Irish as a Teaching Medium of Children whose home Language is English* (INTO 1941). This report pointed to the conclusion that the majority of infant teachers believed that teaching children through Irish inhibited them intellectually and repressed their urge to express themselves. They believed further that some children were mentally and physically damaged by this 'draconian linguistic code', were placed 'in a linguistic straight jacket' and school life represented 'a life of repression, confusion and unhappiness' (*Ibid*.: 19).

A change of government in 1948 saw a new direction emerge for early childhood education. The new Minister for Education, General Richard Mulcahy, had been a leading critic of the pedagogies and methodologies promoted by the previous Fianna Fáil government in relation to the education of young children, and called for an investigation of the system of teaching infant classes through the medium of the Irish language. As part of the inquiry, members of the Inspectorate held meetings with teachers to discuss the implementation of the all-Irish programme in their schools. It is significant to note that this was the first time that infant teachers were consulted, and listened to, regarding curricular matters. This led to the publication in 1948 of the *Revised Programme for Infants* (Department of Education 1948).

The aim of the revised programme was 'to provide the atmosphere and background in which the child's whole personality may develop naturally and easily' (*Ibid*.: 5). It presented a new concept of what constituted early childhood education by stressing that 'cognisance' should be taken 'of the child's interests, activities and speech needs, and utilise them to the full in aiding and directing such development' (*Ibid*.). A more informed, natural approach to learning was proposed three years later in *An Naí-Scoil: The Infant School – Notes for Teachers* (Department of Education 1951). In the *Notes for Teachers* (1951), it was stated that 'Infant teaching if it is to be successful, must be based on the child's urge to play, to talk, to imitate, to manipulate materials, to make and do things' (*Ibid.*: 3). Teachers were encouraged to provide a stimulating learning environment wherein the holistic development of the child would be fostered and nurtured. While the Irish language was to remain as the medium of instruction in the infant classrooms, it was stressed that it should be integrated into 'nature activities' (*Ibid.*: 55), including children's 'games, their handwork, the pictures they draw or paint' (*Ibid.*: 5), as well as number, songs, dance and music (*Ibid.*: 46–47).

Infant teachers were supported in their attempts to implement the new programme by a group of female organizing inspectors, who travelled to schools and most major centres throughout Ireland presenting intensive summer courses. Here they endeavoured 'to imbue the infant teacher with an understanding of the best in infant teaching' (O'Connor 1997: 24) by sharing advice and guidance on the preparation of resources, classroom organization, teaching approaches and methodologies. The engagements of the organizing inspectors with infant teachers contributed to 'an awareness of the insights afforded by progressive infant school practice, and a knowledge, interest and enthusiasm for liberal education was cultivated and built up in the teaching community in Ireland' (*Ibid.*: 27).

The architects of the 1948 programme made creditable efforts to reconcile satisfactorily the Gaelic policy with progressive ideologies. In this way, they attempted to reinvent child-centredness to suit the new Irish context. The curriculum promoted a different view of the child, and this was to be reflected in child-centred methodologies and practice. It was a foreshadow of the liberal philosophy of the curriculum that was to come in 1971. Coolahan with O'Donovan (2009: 133) assert that the *Notes for Teachers* (1951) 'prefigured major curricular change to come twenty years later'. The wheels of change had been set in motion, and the next decade was to witness the laying of the foundation for the development of a new curriculum for all classes in primary schools.

A child-centred curriculum for all classes in primary schools, 1971–1999

The conceptualization of the young child in society evolved and changed during the 1950s and particularly in the 1960s, and this led to a realization of a need for educational developments and curricular reform to bring it in line with progressive thinking in relation to the child and child development. The need for curriculum innovation was voiced not only by educationalists, but also by economists, politicians and the general public. One of the major catalysts for change was the *Investment in Education* report (Department of Education 1965) compiled for the Organisation for Economic Cooperation and Development (OECD), which suggested that the Irish primary school did not orientate young people towards the social and work environment. The publication in England of the report of the Central Advisory Council for Education (1967) (commonly known as the Plowden Report) gave direction for educational innovation by endorsing a progressive approach to primary education. This report was reflected upon and discussed by educationalists and interested parties in Ireland. In the late 1960s, it was evident that a new focus was being placed on educational research and enlightened educational theory, and less so on the traditional discussion on the Irish language. The stage was being set for curricular reform, innovation and educational change.

The work of crafting the plans for a new curriculum was assigned to the Inspectorate of the Department of Education (Coolahan with O'Donovan 2009: 182). A large number of schools became involved in a pilot project directed towards assisting the process of drafting the curriculum. The *Primary School Curriculum* (Department of Education 1971), published in 1971, was underpinned by the ideology of child-centredness, integrated-discovery and activity-learning. The twin aims for primary education according to the principles of the curriculum were 'to enable each child to live a full life as a child and to equip him to avail himself of a further education so that he may go on to live a full and useful life as an adult in society' (Department of Education 1971: 12). Guidelines and approaches were suggested but teachers were encouraged to adapt the programme to suit the needs and environment of the school surroundings.

In the *Primary School Curriculum* (1971), the young child was per-ceived as the active agent in his or her own education. The teacher was no longer regarded as the one who imparted information, but rather one who guided and stimulated each child in the pursuit of knowledge by offering appropriate learning experiences. To develop 'self-reliance, confidence and flexibility of mind', both individual and group activities were recom-mended, and each child afforded the opportunity to 'experience the joy of discovery' while progressing at his or her 'own natural rate' (*Ibid.:*16). The subjects to be studied in the infant classes included Irish, English, mathem-atics, religion, music, art and craft, social and environmental studies and physical education. Infant teachers were requested to recognize that early childhood education, if it were to be successful, had to be based on the young child's 'natural urge to play, to investigate and create' (*Ibid.*: 283). It was stressed that 'free play activities form an important part of infant education' where 'the child is given an opportunity to become acquainted with a wide variety of materials which he can handle, mould, shape and play with to his heart's content' (*Ibid.*).

According to the *Primary School Curriculum* (1971), the infant school programme was to be extended upwards and outwards to incorporate all the classes of the primary school. It was suggested that the process should be gradual, systematic, organic, with no sharp wrench for the child between one stage of his or her development and the next. Unlike the *Notes for Teachers* (Department of Education 1951), this new curriculum incorpor-ated modern psychological and sociological ideas on education from the 1950s and 1960s which placed much emphasis on early childhood education and development. It was addressed to a wider audience, including parents, who as a result of such publications as *All Our Children* (Department of Education 1969) and *Your Child and Your School* (Department of Education 1970) had a better understanding of the value of approaches to educa-tion that differed greatly from those of former days. The pioneering work of infant teachers in Ireland was acknowledged in the *Primary School Curriculum* (1971). It stated therein that one of the most significant devel-opments after the publication of the *Notes for Teachers* in 1951, had 'been the application of these principles beyond the infant classes in a number of our schools' (Department of Education 1971: 15).

In theory, the child-centred approach to infant pedagogy as exemplified in the teaching of the younger classes was to be followed in the senior classes. In practice, the mainstreaming and infusion of child-centredness upwards to classes beyond infants proved challenging. While there was tacit support in principle by teachers, and the aims and principles of the programme were endorsed by them, many aspects of the curriculum's content and principles did not become common practice in classrooms. Reasons for this included poor provision for teacher training in new content and pedagogies, high pupil-teacher ratios, the predominance of small schools, the lack of appropriate educational aids and facilities, and inadequate inspection and advisory services (Walsh 2012: 332–342).

The continuation of child-centredness, 1999–2021

In the late 1980s and 1990s, a range of government policy documents including the *Review Body on the Primary Curriculum* (Review Body on the Primary Curriculum 1990) and the *Primary Education Review Body* (Department of Education 1990) were published which set the scene for new developments in primary education. The conceptualization of the young child in society changed greatly in the 1990s with early childhood education and care moving centre stage. Of particular importance, and no doubt the catalyst for developments that were to come, was the National Forum on Early Childhood Education in 1998 (Coolahan 1998). This forum provided the first opportunity in Ireland for diverse groups and organizations with an interest in early childhood education to unite. It explored a broad range of issues related to the provision of early childhood for children from birth to the age of 6. As a result of the Forum, initiatives focusing on the needs of young children were introduced and it provided the basis for the publication in 1999 of the first-ever White Paper on Early Childhood Education, *Ready to Learn* (Government of Ireland 1999). The White Paper recommended the development of national curriculum guidelines for the early years sector to ensure that early childhood provision would be 'structured, developmental, of high quality and designed to create in young children a readiness to learn' (*Ibid.*: 51).

In 1999, the child-centred *Primary School Curriculum* of 1971 was superseded by the revised *Primary School Curriculum* (National Council for Curriculum and Assessment [NCCA] 1999). This revised curriculum was developed by the NCCA and built on the principles and philosophy of the 1971 child-centred curriculum, with its aims, scope and content reformed, renewed and adapted to incorporate contemporary educational research and thinking. Like its predecessor, it was underpinned by an ideology of child-centred education and promoted active and discovery-learning methodologies. It adopted a holistic approach to learning where the social, emotional, physical, spiritual and intellectual dimensions of learning were highlighted.

The *Primary School Curriculum* (1999) was made available to teachers as twenty-three booklets. It outlined seven areas of learning, some of which were further subdivided to yield a total of twelve subject areas. The *Introduction Handbook* outlined the vision, goals, aims, principles, objectives, content and pedagogies. Each subject area of the curriculum was presented with a curriculum statement, a range of objectives, learning outcomes and planning guidelines, resource suggestions, sample lesson plans, together with exemplars and illustrations. For infant classes, the subjects to be studied included the core subjects Irish, English, mathematics, history, geography, science, visual arts, music, drama, physical education, social, personal and health education and religious education. The curriculum articulated not only the content to be covered and the outcomes to be achieved, but also a wide range of approaches to learning for young children focusing on play, active learning, integration and collaboration. The benefits of language as a teaching strategy for the development of cognitive, social and imaginative life was highlighted, and the need for the child to develop generic skills was seen as a crucial factor in the learning process. Assessment was regarded as an essential component of a successful teaching and learning process.

Unlike the previous curricula of the twentieth century, the *Primary School Curriculum* (1999) was developed over a prolonged period using a partnership-based approach with teachers playing a central role in its drafting. Its introduction was phased into schools over a number of years with guidance and support programmes offered to teachers to enable them to implement the curriculum in their classrooms and schools. At the close of the twentieth century, the child was conceptualized as a learner, and the teacher a 'caring facilitator and guide who interprets the children's needs and responds to them' (NCCA 1999: 20).

During the first two decades of the twenty-first century, the State played a more active role than heretofore in the education and care of young children. In 2002, the Centre for Early Childhood Development (CECDE) was established, and in that year also the Department of Education invited the OECD to conduct 'an intensive review' of early childhood policies and services. In its report in 2004, the OECD expressed concern in relation to the 'directive and formal' approaches it witnessed in infant classrooms and were critical of classroom management styles with teachers opting for 'whole class teaching, with children sitting quietly at tables' (OECD 2004: 54). The report recommended that greater advice and support should be given to teachers in relation to assessment, the integration of subjects, and how to move from a teacher-centred to a child-centred pedagogy. The review put forward the notion of a common quality framework for early education and care to cater for all young children, not only those of school-going age.

In 2009, *Aistear: The Early Childhood Curriculum Framework* (NCCA 2009) was published. It was the first curriculum framework designed for an Irish context and was developed for all children from birth to six across the range of early childhood settings. It described the types of learning that were important for children in their early years and offered ideas and suggestions as to how learning might be nurtured. Subjects were presented in an integrated thematic manner thereby allowing teachers and schools flexibility in planning, development, implementation and assessment (Daly and Foster 2012: 93–106). Learning through play, exploration, inquiry and experimentation were foregrounded with a particular focus on the conceptualization of the child as an active agent with rights to guide his or her own learning.

Aistear focused on the pedagogical role of the adult in children's learning and there was an expectation that the infant teacher would adopt this curriculum framework with its appropriate learning approaches and align it with the more prescriptive, subject-focused *Primary School Curriculum* (1999). While the latter set out a clear pathway for the child through stages of development in terms of acquiring specific skills and knowledge, the *Aistear* framework concentrated more on the development of attitudes, skills and learning dispositions. The interface between the *Primary School Curriculum* and *Aistear* was never clarified and this created tensions and dilemmas for infant teachers. Consequently, they struggled to accommodate the recommended teaching and learning approaches and methodologies. They complained that they were not given sufficient guidance or training in the new pedagogies and this 'contributed to multiple interpretations of what it means to use *Aistear* in a primary school context' (NCCA 2018a: 56). This was further complicated by the existence of 'very large numbers' of pupils in many infant classes resulting in 'a serious impediment to good practice' (Coolahan et al. 2017: 17).

In 2010, a universal free preschool year was offered to all children over 3 years of age, with a second year introduced in 2016. With many young children no longer beginning school at 4 years of age, as had been the norm in the past, the infant teacher once again needed to adapt and modify the junior infant programme to ensure continuity of curricula and developmentally appropriate learning experiences to effect positive transitions from preschool to primary school. In 2015, the *Primary Language Curriculum* (NCCA 2015) was introduced for Junior Infants to Second Class as part of the redevelopment of the *Primary School Curriculum* (1999). The presumption was that infant teachers would integrate this outcome-based language curriculum into their practice, align it with the content-objective curriculum in other subjects and then link it with the loosely defined *Aistear* framework outcomes. The absence of an essential supporting structure between the policy initiatives was problematic for infant teachers. Their concern was voiced to the NCCA during consultations in relation to a review of the *Primary School Curriculum* (1999) (NCCA 2018a).

Looking to the future

In February 2020, a *Draft Primary School Curriculum Framework for Consultation* (NCCA 2020) was published with the view to its introduction in all primary schools from 2024. It was the product of a range of research papers, much consultation and collaboration across a wide range of agencies, organizations and individuals with an interest in early childhood education. The framework sets out the proposed purpose, structure and content of the next curriculum. Its eight principles build on those of *Aistear* and the curriculum's seven key competencies aim to extend children's learning through *Aistear*'s four themes of wellbeing, identity and belonging, communicating and exploring and thinking. For infant classes in primary schools, it favours a rich and holistic curriculum with an integrated and thematic approach to learning across five broad and interconnected curriculum areas. It supports a variety of pedagogical strategies with assessment central to teaching and learning. It highlights the importance of nurturing positive dispositions in children alongside the development of skills, attitudes, values, knowledge and understanding. Strong connections between preschool and primary school are prioritized in the redeveloped curriculum to accommodate 'smooth transitions' for the learning journeys of young children (Walsh 2021: 36). The use of the *Mo Scéal: Preschool to Primary School Reporting Template* (NCCA 2018b) is recommended to 'tell the story of a child's learning and development in preschool' (NCCA 2020: 19) and thereby ensure continuity of learning and learning experiences into the infant classes.

In the third decade of the twenty-first century, the infant teacher in the primary school is afforded increased agency and flexibility to create child-centred and playful environments where young children engage in a variety of pedagogical interactions and strategies that encourage independence, creativity and collaboration. The balance of power has shifted, and once again the young child and his or her educational needs are the nucleus of the curriculum, just as they had been in the *Revised Programme* of 1900.

Conclusion

As we reflect on the conceptualization of early childhood education in Ireland from 1921–2021, what emerges clearly is that during this period different ideologies of early childhood pedagogy were foregrounded and backgrounded as the religious, political, social, economic and philosophical landscapes shifted and shaped each other. The conceptualizations of the school-going child and child-centredness as portrayed within curricula were defined and redefined throughout the period and impacted significantly on what the child learned and how the curriculum was delivered. The *Revised Programme* of 1900, based on child-centred principles, initiated a revolution in thinking with regard to infant education. The reforms in infant school practice, which followed the advent of Independence, saw the interests of the young child being sacrificed in favour of citizenship in a new nationalistic State. Any pedagogy which did not support this course of action was deemed by the State and the Church to be of little educational value. In the late 1940s, a new direction emerged in early childhood education when an attempt was made to re-invent child-centredness to suit the Irish context. An amalgam of the two was achieved in 1948 when a reconstructed national curriculum based on child-centredness and Irish culture focused on the learning styles of the young child and led to the publication of the *Revised Programme for Infants* (Department of Education 1948). As had been the case at the turn of the century, the individuality of the young child was once again recognized, and his or her abilities and interests were placed at the centre of the learning process.

The wheels of change had been set in motion, and the 1971 and 1999 child centred curricula built on and developed the principles and philosophies of the 1948 curriculum. In the twenty-first century, government-led policy changes have been underpinned by numerous research studies that have consistently highlighted the positive influence of quality early childhood education and the benefit it confers on children's social, emotional, physical and cognitive development (Walsh 2016). Added to this has been government recognition that quality early childhood education and care is an essential public service and makes a positive contribution to workers in the labour market and issues around family poverty.

The history of curricular provision for young children has demonstrated that converting curricular policy into classroom practice is not easily accomplished. Repeatedly, a clarion call from teachers throughout the century has been a request for support. The lack of pedagogical guidance and assistance left them unsure of what was expected of them at many critical junctures in the development of early childhood policy and practice in primary schools. To ensure the successful enactment of the re-developed primary school curriculum, ongoing professional development, guidance and support will have to be provided for teachers to assist them in providing challenging learning experiences that offer young children the opportunity to grow and develop their full potential as competent and confident learners.

The narrative of early childhood education in Ireland has demonstrated that the voices of the teachers of young children were not always heard and they found themselves being expected to evolve and extend their practices to respond to differing priorities, in many instances with little guidance, and against their better judgement. The vital importance of the infant teacher as a professional is recognized and acknowledged to a much greater extent today, but it must be consolidated, and it is crucial that infant teachers play a significant role as curriculum developers as well as curriculum implementers to ensure that all children can benefit from high-quality education and care.

Bibliography

Akenson, D. H. (1975). *A Mirror to Kathleen's Face – Education in Independent Ireland 1922–1960*. London: McGill-Queen's University Press.

Central Advisory Council for Education (England) (1967). *Children and Their Primary Schools– A Report of the Central Advisory Council for Education (England). Volume 1: Report*. London: Her Majesty's Stationery Office.

Commissioners of National Education (1901). *Sixty-seventh Report of CNEI for 1900*, Appendix I [Cd. 704] XXI.

Coolahan, J. (ed.) (1998). *Report of the National Forum for Early Childhood Education.* Dublin: The Stationery Office.

Coolahan, J. with O'Donovan, P. (2009). *A History of Ireland's School Inspectorate, 1831–2008.* Dublin: Four Courts Press.

Coolahan, J., Drudy, S., Hogan, P., Hyland, A. and McGuinness, S. (2017). *Towards a Better Future: A Review of the Irish School System.* Dublin: IPPN and NAPD.

Dale, F. H. (1904). *Report of Mr. F.H. Dale, His Majesty's Inspector of School, Board of Education on Primary Education in Ireland.* Printed for His Majesty's Stationery Office by Alexander Thom and Co. (Limited) Abbey Street [Cd.1981].

Daly, M. and Foster, A. (2012). '*Aistear*: The Early Childhood Framework.' In M. Mhic Mhatúna and M. Taylor (eds), *Early Childhood Education and Care: An Introduction for Students in Ireland*, pp. 93–106. Dublin: Gill and McMillan.

Department of Education (1934a). *Revised Programme of Primary Instruction.* Dublin: The Stationery Office.

Department of Education (1934b). *Revision of Rules and Regulations for National Schools.* Dublin: The Stationery Office.

Department of Education (1948). *Revised Programme for Infants.* Dublin: The Stationery Office.

Department of Education (1951). *An Naí-Scoil: The Infant School – Notes for Teachers.* Dublin: The Stationery Office.

Department of Education (1965). *Investment in Education – Report of the Survey Team Appointed by the Minister for Education in October 1962 – Annexes and Appendices.* Dublin: The Stationery Office.

Department of Education (1969). *Ár nDaltaí Uile – All our Children.* Dublin: Department of Education.

Department of Education (1970). *Your Child and Your School.* Dublin: Department of Education.

Department of Education (1971). *Primary School Curriculum: Teacher's Handbook – Part 1.* Dublin: Department of Education.

Department of Education (1990). *Report of the Primary Education Review Body.* Dublin: The Stationery Office.

Department of Education (2020). *Projections of Full-time Enrolment: Primary and Secondary Level 2020–2038.* Dublin: The Stationery Office.

Government of Ireland (1999). *Ready to Learn – A White Paper on Early Childhood Education.* Dublin: The Stationery Office.

Irish National Teachers' Organisation (1941). *Report of Committee of Inquiry into the Use of Irish as a Teaching Medium to Children Whose Home Language Is English*. Dublin: INTO.

National Council for Curriculum and Assessment (1999). *Primary School Curriculum*. Dublin: NCCA.

National Council for Curriculum and Assessment (2009). *Aistear: The Early Childhood Curriculum Framework*. Dublin: NCCA.

National Council for Curriculum and Assessment (2015). *Primary Language Curriculum*. Dublin: NCCA.

National Council for Curriculum and Assessment (2018a). *Primary Developments: Consultation on Curriculum Structure and Time*. Dublin: NCCA.

National Council for Curriculum and Assessment (2018b). *Mo Scéal: Preschool to School Reporting Template*. Dublin: NCCA.

National Council for Curriculum and Assessment (2020). *Draft Primary School Curriculum Framework for Consultation*. Dublin: NCCA.

National Programme Conference (1922). *National Programme of Primary Instruction*. Dublin: The Educational Company of Ireland.

National Programme Conference (1926). *Report and Programme Presented by the National Programme Conference to the Minister for Education*. Dublin: The Stationery Office.

O'Connell, T. (1968). *100 Years of Progress – The Story of the Irish National Teachers' Organisation 1868–1968*. Dublin: Dakota Press.

O'Connor, M. (1997). 'Eileen Irvine: An Educational Pioneer', *An Múinteoir: The Irish Teachers' Journal*, 6 (2), 23–24.

O'Connor, M. (2010). *The Development of Infant Education in Ireland, 1838–1948: Epochs and Eras*. Bern: Peter Lang.

Ó Cuív, B. (ed.) (1969). *A View of the Irish Language*. Dublin: The Stationery Office.

Organisation for Economic Co-operation and Development (2004). *Thematic Review of Early Childhood Education and Care Policy in Ireland*. Paris: OECD.

Review Body on the Primary Curriculum (1990). *Report of the Review Body on the Primary Curriculum*. Dublin: Department of Education.

Walsh, T. (2012). *Primary Education in Ireland, 1897–1990: Curriculum and Context*. Bern: Peter Lang.

Walsh, T. (2016). 'Recent Policy Developments in Early Childhood Education (ECE): A Jigsaw with too Many Pieces?', *An Leanbh Óg*, 10, 69–94.

Walsh, T. (2021). 'The Redeveloped Primary School Curriculum: An Opportunity for Continuity and Coherence in Early Childhood Education'. In B. Mooney (ed.), *Ireland's Education Yearbook 2020*, pp. 34–37. Dublin: Education Matters.

MÁIRE MHIC MHATHÚNA AND MAIRÉAD MAC CON IOMAIRE

4 Early childhood education and care provision through the medium of the Irish language

Introduction

This chapter will give an overview of the history of naíonraí or Irish-medium preschool settings in Gaeltacht[1] and non-Gaeltacht areas from their beginnings in the 1960s to date. The material for this chapter is based on desk research, interviews with the founding member of the naíonra movement and the personal involvement of the chapter authors. The rationale for establishing naíonraí will be described and the role of the pioneers who led the movement in the 1970s and 1980s will be analysed in light of their principles and philosophy. These principles are visible in the structures they set up to manage and promote naíonraí and in the resources they commissioned. These resources included children's songs and rhymes based on the oral tradition, suitable for the urban environment as well as rural areas, and the provision and mediation of children's books in Irish. A number of support agencies were set up and evolved over time, sometimes willingly, sometimes not. The current roles of support agencies in both the North of Ireland and the Republic will be examined and challenges facing the sector will be identified. Finally, proposals for the future direction of immersion early childhood education and care (ECEC) through the Irish language will be made, including the need for specialized training,

---

1   Irish-speaking areas mainly on the western seaboard.

Table 1. Naíonra statistics

Details	Gaeltacht Naíonraí registered with Comhar Naíonraí na Gaeltachta	Non-Gaeltacht Naíonraí registered with Gaeloideachas
Number of naíonraí	59	180
Number of sessions	74	283
Number of children	2,000	5,515
Number of staff	189	500
Co-location on primary school site	10	98
Children with languages other than Irish or English	20	129
Children with additional needs	33	163

evaluation of current practice, and cooperation among all participants and stakeholders.

To set the context, the number of preschool services currently working through Irish is 373 (10 per cent of the total) and of these 78 per cent are private and 22 per cent are community based (Pobal 2019). There are more services located in rural areas (67 per cent) than urban (33 per cent), a figure that reflects the rural siting of many Gaeltacht naíonraí. There is an equal amount of community (51 per cent) and private settings (49 per cent) in Gaeltacht areas. Comhar Naíonraí na Gaeltachta is the Gaeltacht naíonraí support agency, while Gaeloideachas is the support agency for naíonraí outside the Gaeltacht. An overview of the key statistics for both organizations is provided in Table 1.

As a number of Irish words are used throughout this chapter, Table 2 provides a translation of these as an easy reference guide.

Table 2. Translations of Irish words used in the chapter

Irish word	English translation
Breac-Ghaeltacht	Partly Irish-speaking area
Comhairleoirí	Practice advisors for practitioners in naíonraí
Dianchúrsa	Week-long intensive course in Irish
Gaeltacht	Irish-speaking areas mainly on the western seaboard
Gaeltacht naíonraí	Naíonraí located in Irish-speaking areas
Naíonáin	Infant children
Naíonra/naíonraí	Group providing early learning experiences to young children through the medium of Irish. Naíonraí is the plural term.
Naíscoil/naíscoileanna	Infant or nursery school through the Irish language. Naíscoileanna is the plural term.
Stiúrthóir	Directress or practitioner in a naíonra setting

Beginnings

The first naíonraí were established in Shannon (Co. Clare), Athlone (Co. Westmeath), Dublin and Cork towards the end of the 1960s. The term 'naíonra' was coined to denote a group providing early learning experiences to infants (naíonáin) or children (3–5 years) through the medium of the Irish language (Ó Buachalla 1979) and is now used to describe an Irish language immersion preschool. People in the Irish language community were concerned about the standard of Irish in the education system as the Irish-medium preparatory colleges for primary teaching were closed in 1961 and the number of schools teaching through Irish was reducing (Dunne 2020, Ó hUiginn 1980). Teaching through the medium of Irish in the infant classes of primary schools was also reducing steadily from the 1960s (O'Connor 2010) and Irish language supporters and activists wanted to develop new approaches to promoting Irish within the education system.

The development of Welsh-medium playschools in Wales, *cylchoedd meithrin*, provided an impetus to develop a similar movement in Ireland. The Welsh playgroups were founded in the mid-1960s to provide opportunities for children to learn Welsh in such settings and over sixty groups were in operation by 1970 (Baker and Prys Jones 1998). Leaders in the Irish language organizations Conradh na Gaeilge, Comhdháil Náisiúnta na Gaeilge and Comhdháil Cheilteach an nÓg invited speakers from Wales to talk about this development. Dr Trefor Morgan, a Welsh businessman and activist, spoke at a meeting in Dublin in 1966 about the potential of the language-focused playgroups to act as a catalyst for wider language development in the community. Many of those present were active members of Conradh na Gaeilge and the organizations tasked their local organizers to establish naíonraí around the country.

Another inspirational lecture was given by Dr Jac L. Williams, Professor of Welsh at the University of Aberystwyth, Wales the following year and published as a pamphlet, *Bilingualism Today* (Williams 1967). The pamphlet explained how young children could begin acquiring Welsh as a second language in Welsh language preschools. The director of Comhdháil Náisiúnta na Gaeilge, Col. Eoghan Ó Néill, travelled to meetings around the country speaking about this new idea. A new voluntary organization, Na Naíscoileanna Gaelacha, was established in 1974 under the auspices of Conradh na Gaeilge to provide assistance to people setting up or working in naíonraí at that time (Ó Murchú 1979a). Contact with Wales continued and Dan L. James, Lecturer in Education at the University of Aberystwyth, gave a lecture on second language acquisition approaches in minority-language preschools in 1976. The name of Na Naíscoileanna Gaelacha organization was changed to Na Naíonraí Gaelacha in 1979 to better reflect the natural acquisition of Irish rather than formal teaching (Uí Chonghaile 2012). An overview of the many organizations involved in the promotion and support of Irish language preschool education is provided in Table 3.

Table 3. Irish language organizations involved with Naíonraí

Organization	Dates	Activities
Conradh na Gaeilge	1893–present	Maintenance and development of the Irish language through a branch network throughout the country
Comhdháil Náisiúnta na Gaeilge	1943–2014*	Coordinating umbrella body for voluntary Irish language organizations
Comhdháil Cheilteach na nÓg	1902–present	Youth wing of the Celtic Congress, an inter-Celtic cultural organization
Gaeltarra Éireann, now Údarás na Gaeltachta	1957–present	Gaeltacht industrial agency
Bord na Gaeilge, from 1999 Foras na Gaeilge	1978–present	All-Ireland public body to promote the Irish language and Ulster Scots
Na Naíscoileanna Gaelacha, name amended in 1979 to Na Naíonraí Gaelacha	1974–present	Voluntary advocacy group for naíonraí
An Comhchoiste Réamhscolaíochta, from 2003 Forbairt Naíonraí Teo.	1978–2014*	Agency to promote and manage Irish-medium preschooling
Seirbhísí Naíonraí Teo., from 2004 Comhar Naíonraí na Gaeltachta	1997–present	Gaeltacht naíonraí support agency
Gaelscoileanna, from 2014 Gaeloideachas	1973–present*	National support organization for Irish-medium education at all levels

*Due to a major reorganization of Irish language organizations in 2014 by Foras na Gaeilge, their funding body, many smaller groups closed or were subsumed into larger organizations. Forbairt Naíonraí Teo. (FNT), for example, was subsumed into Gaelscoileanna, which in turn changed its name to Gaeloideachas to reflect its broader remit.

Early developments

As the numbers of naíonraí grew, the committee of Na Naíonraí Gaelacha saw that a more formal, permanent structure was required to manage the development and support for naíonraí, over and above what a voluntary organization could do. The limited funding provided by Conradh na Gaeilge and Gaeltarra Éireann (now Údarás na Gaeltachta, the Gaeltacht development authority) for Gaeltacht naíonraí up to that time was insufficient to manage a national organization. They submitted a business plan to Bord na Gaeilge (now Foras na Gaeilge) which outlined the need for a development officer, a publication plan to provide a handbook and resources, and suggestions for training in immersion pedagogy. A joint committee, An Comhchoiste Réamhscolaíochta, was established between Bord na Gaeilge and Na Naíonraí Gaelacha in 1978 (Uí Chonghaile 2012).

The first Gaeltacht naíonra was established in 1978 in An Cheathrú Rua, Connemara, at the invitation of Gaeltarra Éireann. Many of the management staff coming to work in new factories in the area were not native Irish speakers and it was felt that giving their children a grounding in Irish from the beginning would promote the use of the language in the home and help prepare children for schooling in Irish. A small grant was paid to cover the running costs of this naíonra and the first practitioner/stiúrthóir, Mairéad Mac Con Iomaire, worked in the naíonra on a voluntary basis. Naíonraí soon spread to other Gaeltacht regions and the Gaeltacht naíonraí joined forces with An Comhchoiste Réamhscolaíochta when it was founded in 1978 to support naíonraí across the country. Among those promoting Gaeltacht naíonraí in Gaeltarra Éireann (later Údarás na Gaeltachta) were senior management figures including Seosamh Ó hÓgartaigh, Pádraig Ó hAoláin and Mícheál Ó hÉanaigh. They provided leadership, support and grants to the fledging naíonra movement in the Gaeltacht. The gender divide, evident in the people involved in the early stages of the *naíonra* movement reflects the social mores of the time, with many women working in the home but contributing to wider society through voluntary work and the men in this case contributing ideas and advice based on their employment experience.

Údarás na Gaeltachta established Seirbhísí Naíonraí Teo. in 1997 to assist Gaeltacht naíonraí committees manage payroll procedures for the eighteen staff working in naíonraí. Over time, the voluntary committees managing Gaeltacht naíonraí had become increasingly reluctant to oversee employment procedures for staff. This type of business model was probably influenced by the Údarás's experience of supporting other Gaeltacht companies. They provided a grant to assist the administration of the service and employed Mairéad Mac Con Iomaire as manager. It quickly became clear that policies and procedures needed to be developed and that curriculum guidance was needed for the expanding Gaeltacht naíonraí services. A handbook of policies and procedures for the services (Seirbhísí Naíonra Teo. 1997) was published in 1997, followed by the *Loinnir* (Mac Con Iomaire 2006) curriculum guide in 2006. A toy library was set up in each of the main Gaeltacht regions, where staff could borrow toys and equipment for a set period of time. Údarás na Gaeltachta established the company Comhar Naíonraí na Gaeltachta in 2004 to take over and expand the responsibilities of Seirbhísí Naíonraí Teo. Staff were now directly employed by Comhar Naíonraí na Gaeltachta and standardized pay and conditions of employment were developed across the Gaeltacht regions. Comhar Naíonraí na Gaeltachta's remit now covers other kinds of provision such as crèches, afterschool services, parent and toddler groups and breakfast clubs (Comhar Naíonraí na Gaeltachta 2021).

Founding principles

The naíonra movement was founded on strong linguistic principles from the beginning, focusing on early total immersion approaches to second language learning. This grew out of understandings about first language acquisition by young children, the psychology of early language learning and awareness of second language learning theories (Ó Murchú 1980). According to Baker and Wright (2021), immersion education can succeed very well if delivered effectively in additive language contexts as an optional choice, the children's home language is respected, teachers are competent bilinguals and the focus is on delivering the mainstream curriculum through the second language. Societal and historical factors also play a role with issues of identity, culture and second language proficiency influencing choice.

The principles of ECEC were also important, especially learning through play (Ó Murchú 1979b). Blaise et al. (2016) show how broad the field of play and learning now is and Wood (2014) describes how the ideas behind play and pedagogy have changed over time and how child-initiated play, adult-guided play and a more outcome-focused version of educational play can guide practitioners and researchers. A balanced child-initiated approach with elements of adult-guided language input to play and learning was adopted by the naíonraí as the emphasis was on providing opportunities for learning Irish as a second language in the context of children's overall development.

Pioneers in the naíonra movement

As part of research for a chapter on children's literature in Irish (Mhic Mhathúna and Mac Con Iomaire 2013), a large number of people who had participated in establishing and developing naíonraí were contacted. Written replies to a questionnaire were received from some participants and some of the main players or pioneers attended a focus group held in Dublin in 2012. Those who contributed included, in alphabetical order, Máire Feirtéar, Mairéad Mac Seanlaoich, Máire Mhic Niallais, Treasa Ní Ailpín, Bríd Ní Choincheanainn, Aingeal Ó Buachalla, Helen Ó Cíosáin, Helen Ó Murchú, Peig Uí Chaollaí and Neilí Ó Neachtain. A semi-structured discussion schedule was drawn up and the ensuing discussion included the recollections and reminiscences of the participants, as well as reasons for their participation. The authors of this chapter were also part of the movement from the mid-1970s. Many others were actively involved as practitioners, researchers or supporters. It is noteworthy that the practical development of naíonraí, the on-the-ground work, was led almost entirely by women, which gave the movement a nurturing, child-focused character, fuelled by the women's strong belief in the importance of the Irish language and the value of high-quality ECEC.

These beliefs crystalized as an interest in providing early years education through the medium of Irish. Happily, many of them had organizational experience in groups such *as Na Teaghlaigh Ghaelacha* (an organization for Irish-speaking families) or Conradh na Gaeilge, and they were active members of Irish-medium primary school committees as teachers or parents. Their overriding objective was to provide opportunities for young Irish-speaking children to meet outside the home and to facilitate the acquisition of Irish for other children. Several participants had attended the lectures by Jac. L. Williams and Dan L. James on the Welsh-medium preschools and were enthused by the approach adopted in Wales. They were also interested in the Irish Preschool Playgroups Association (IPPA) movement and some had attended training courses provide by the IPPA and St Nicholas Montessori Society. Interestingly, the naíonraí adopted the Montessori term for practitioner 'directress' and translated this into Irish as stiúrthóir (plural form is stiúrthóirí).

Children attending the first naíonraí had different language backgrounds. Some of the children in Gaeltacht areas were proficient speakers of the language and lived in strong Irish-speaking areas. Other Gaeltacht children lived in English-dominant areas and still others in Breac-Ghaeltacht areas with little or no Irish in the community. The majority of children outside the Gaeltacht were English-speaking but their parents were interested in them acquiring Irish at a young age (Hickey 1997). This meant that practitioners in the strong Gaeltacht areas could concentrate on language enrichment while those in other areas provided opportunities for second language acquisition.

The role of the pioneers

The pioneers played many roles during the early years of the naíonraí. Some were practitioners, some comhairleoirí or practice advisors and others were writers and authors. Some people had multiple roles and also served as committee members of Na Naíonraí Gaelacha and An Comhchoiste Réamhscolaíochta. Both organizations received considerable help and advice from senior figures in Irish language groups including Maolsheachlainn Ó Caollaí, president and Seán Mac Mathúna, general secretary of Conradh na Gaeilge in the 1970s. Liam Ó Dochartaigh, education officer of Bord na Gaeilge also contributed as did Caoimhín Ó Marcaigh, editor-in-chief of An Gúm publishing house.[2] Many others in the Irish language community also advised informally.

The Comhchoiste Réamhscolaíochta set about organizing the work on a structured basis. It initiated an insurance scheme, provided support and advice to practitioners through the practice advisors and organized short training courses. A week-long intensive course (An Dianchúrsa) was organized to show practitioners how language-focused early years education could be provided and a twenty-hour programme was provided for trainee primary school teachers. These programmes provided basic information about the immersion approach in the early years. A handbook for naíonra practitioners *Lámhleabhar do Stiúrthóirí Naíonraí* [Handbook for naíonra practitioners] was published in 1979 (An Comhchoiste Réamhscolaíochta 1979) and a second edition followed in 1985. Deirdre Uí Ghrádaigh edited a third edition of the Handbook in 2005 (Uí Ghrádaigh 2005), which included additional emphasis on storytelling as a vehicle for language learning. Hickey (1997) had previously noted the challenge of presenting stories to young children in a language they were only beginning to learn and Uí Ghrádaigh (2005: 119–123) offered a clear rationale for presenting stories to children in Irish and procedures for mediating the stories using props and story sacks. She also advised making books highly visible in the setting and ensuring that ethnic and cultural diversity featured in the selection of books.

It is noteworthy that these publications were in Irish, intended to both advance understanding of the content and to normalize the use of relevant terminology and discussion in the Irish language. Training videos

2   Irish-medium publishers under the aegis of the Department of Education from 1926 to 1999 when its functions were transferred to Foras na Gaeilge.

on various aspects of practice were also commissioned, a pioneering practice at the time.

An evaluation of how children were making progress in learning Irish and their overall development was undertaken in 1982 by Síle Ní Aodhagáin, *Staidéar Treorach ar na Naíonraí in Éirinn* [Pilot study on naíonraí in Ireland] (Ní Aodhagáin 1982). This study emphasized the importance of training, as more progress in Irish was made by children in naíonraí with practitioners who had completed the Dianchúrsa. Helen Ó Murchú, the first chairperson of An Comhchoiste Réamhscolaíochta concurred with this finding and suggested that a year-long training programme should be initiated as well as shorter in-service programmes (Ó Murchú 1985).

Philosophy and approach

The overarching aim of the naíonraí was to develop children's abilities through the medium of Irish, be they native speakers of Irish or acquiring Irish as a second language (Ó Murchú 1979a). Their educational approach was learning through play, mirroring the natural path of first language acquisition and focusing on children's communicative needs in the context of the naíonra. Siobhán Ní Mhuirthile of Mary Immaculate College Limerick and other members of the Comhchoiste Réamhscolaíochta led the development of play-based approaches to second language learning of Irish. This was an innovative approach and as one of the pioneers said '*Bhíomar ag tionscnamh cur chuige nua i suíomh nua is ag foghlaim de réir mar a bhíomar ag dul ar aghaidh*' [We were introducing a new approach in a new context and learning as we went on]. The practitioners were advised not to think in terms of teaching Irish formally but to focus on communicating with the children and stimulating communication between the children. Communication in the target language was key but this was to be based on selected vocabulary and appropriate interactive strategies (Mhic Mhathúna 1996). One strategy was to link appropriate songs and rhymes to regular activities, thus providing opportunities for repeated vocabulary and use in defined contexts, without the need for translation. Examples of traditional and newly composed rhymes and songs were provided in the Handbook for sand and water play, routines and fun (An Comhchoiste Réamhscolaíochta 1979: 59–61).

Children's songs and rhymes

There is a wealth of traditional songs and rhymes for children in Irish (see, e.g., *Cniogaide Cnagaide* edited by Williams, 1988) but new rhymes in the Irish tradition/style were needed for the urban context of naíonraí and for children who were beginner learners of the language. As one pioneer said, '*Níl a thuilleadh aistriúcháin ar Humpty Dumpty ag teastáil*' [We don't need any more translations of Humpty Dumpty]. Treasa Ní Ailpín, a primary teacher and native Irish speaker, was already composing songs and rhymes in the traditional style for her young family in Dublin. These were published in two collections, *Sonas agus Só* (Ní Ailpín 1977) and *Timpeall an Tí* (Ní Ailpín 1979) and provided exemplars of how traditional forms could be transposed into an urban environment. She then wrote many more rhymes to accompany the naíonra activities and these were published in *Amhráin do Pháistí* (Ní Ailpín, Ó Dubhghaill agus Ó Háinle 1980) and *Maidin sa Naíonra* (Ní Ailpín, Ní Dhorchaí and Mac Con Iomaire 1991) both as booklets and – new for the time – cassette tapes. These were republished as CDs in 2005 (Ní Ailpín and Breathnach 2005). An important aspect of these publications was that they provided examples of Irish rhythm and phonology in a music style appropriate for young children (Mac Liam 1981).

Traditional rhymes were also a great resource for Gaeltacht naíonraí. Mairéad Mac Con Iomaire published two collections of children's rhymes that she had collected from her father, *Scéilín, Scéilín* [Story, Story] (Mac Con Iomaire 1978) and *Dreoilín, Dreoilín, Rí na n-Éan* [Wren, wren, king of the birds] (Mac Con Iomaire 1984). The rhymes described nature and the rural environment in rich, idiomatic language suitable for Gaeltacht children. The Comhchoiste Réamhscolaíochta published a booklet and cassette tape of traditional children's songs entitled *Damhsa na gCoiníní* [The rabbits' dance] (An Comhchoiste Réamhscolaíochta 1984). This was republished in 2005 (Forbairt Naíonraí Teo. 2005). Practitioners were advised to recite the rhymes on a regular basis with the children, though Hickey's research (Hickey 1997, Hickey et al. 1999) in Gaeltacht and non-Gaeltacht settings showed that this did not happen very often.

Drawing on linguistic theory about context-specific language use, Hickey (1997) advised practitioners to assist the children in going beyond the immediate context of the songs and rhymes and to model the use of the vocabulary and phrases in other naíonra activities. The songs and rhymes provided a store of formulaic utterances that could be transferred to other contexts when they had been acquired and reduced the burden of language learning (Ellis 2008, Wray 2004). The Comhchoiste Réamhscolaíochta published a series of wall friezes with the words and illustration of the rhymes (now out of print) to act both as examples of environmental print in Irish and as reminders to practitioners to use them.

Books and stories

A growing number of children's books in Irish were available in the 1970s and 1980, produced mainly by An Gúm/Government Publication. A number of these were original texts commissioned by An Gúm and others were translations from English and other languages (Ní Chuilleanáin 2012). Browne and Nolan publishers also published schoolbooks in Irish, some of which were suitable to read to young children. The pioneers thought that these books were very useful in developing emergent literacy in Irish and listed several books that were particularly suitable. Some of the books, however, contained a mismatch between the context/illustrations and the complexity of the language, especially for young second language learners. The pioneers said that Irish-speaking parents and practitioners were pleased that children's books were available in Irish but that many were not overly critical of the content or language level books beyond that. Nic Congáil (2012) credited the naíonra movement with providing a context and market for the development of wider genres books in Irish for young children, particularly those with simple illustrations and text.

It was also recognized that reading books to young children in their second language in group settings is quite a challenge (Hickey 1997). The benefits are obvious – emergent literacy, oral language development, participation in group activity – but it is difficult to maintain children's interest in a story through a language they are only beginning to learn. The *Lámhleabhar* [Handbook] (An Comhchoiste Réamhscolaíochta 1979) advised reading the story in a lively fashion and basing the telling on the illustrations. Practitioners should simplify the language and use short sentences when pointing to the relevant part of the illustration. Children did not necessarily have to understand every word but could get the overall gist of the story. Practitioners were advised to use or create repeated phrases in the story, thus providing opportunities for children to join in with these phrases. When children with different levels of Irish were in the same naíonra group as in the Gaeltacht, it was particularly challenging to provide input at multiple levels and to ensure the story sessions were enjoyable and beneficial for all. However, the pioneers thought that children really enjoyed stories told in this manner. One pioneer said, '*Ba chuma cén teanga a bhí ag na páistí, d'éist siad i gcónaí le geáitsíocht*' [It didn't matter which language the children had, they always listened to an active reading].

Peig Uí Chaollaí, one of the first naíonra practitioners in Dublin in the 1970s, developed an innovative approach to story reading by using large format illustrations from a story (similar to 'big books' today) and developing a formulaic but interactive style of telling the story with these illustrations (Mhic Mhathúna 2010). Through repeated telling of the same story over an extended period of time, children understood the storyline and could gradually play a more active part in the telling, eventually being able to make connections between episodes in the story and their own experiences, all through Irish. Other practitioners made use of puppets and drama to present stories to the children using many of the same techniques. These techniques were demonstrated at the Dianchúrsa training sessions and other events and practitioners were encouraged to base the puppet plays on books or stories the children were familiar with.

Gaeltacht children could also benefit from the storytelling tradition in their area and Gaeltacht practitioners were more open to storytelling as well as story-reading. Some practitioner-based stories on the seasons or local events, others on everyday events in the naíonra, children's pets or outings with the children, for example. They based stories on pictures sourced from local publications or stories in English and told the story to the children in Irish. Finding suitable stories in the local dialect was also an issue, particularly in Donegal as practitioners wanted to present stories and songs to children in the dialect variant they would hear in their local area. This situation has improved in more recent times as CDs and online versions of suitable songs for young children have been issued by Gaeltacht singers and musicians. *Rabhlaí Rabhlaí*, a compendium of traditional rhymes in the Corca Dhuibhne dialect was produced in 1998 (Ó Cathasaigh and Doyle 1998), followed by a second collection *Tidil Eidil Éró* in 2009 (Ó Cathasaigh and Doyle 2009). *Gugalaí Gug*, (Ryan and Mac Dhonnagáin 2005) a modern version of traditional songs and rhymes in the Connacht dialect was published in 2005. Donegal singers and musicians Nellie Nic Giolla Bhríde and Doiminic Mac Giolla Bhríde produced *Ící Pící*, a book and CD of newly composed songs for children in 2010 (Nic Giolla Bhríde and Mac Giolla Bhríde 2010) and Eoghan Mac Giolla Bhríde edited *Báidín Fheidhlimidh*, a compendium of traditional songs for children in the Donegal dialect in 2012 (McGee and Brennan 2012). It is noteworthy that idiomatic nonsense words were often used for titles, giving an immediate flavour of the dialect. Two CDs for very young children, *Sicín Mise go Sona Sásta* [I'm a happy little chicken] (Ní Mhuircheartaigh and Mac Gearailt 2014) and *Ardaigh an Laiste* [Lift up the Latch] (Ní Mhuircheartaigh and Mac Gearailt 2016) were produced in 2016 by Tús Maith, a support agency for speaking Irish in the home in the Kerry Gaeltacht.

It was difficult to find suitable accommodation for Gaeltacht naíonraí in the 1970s and 1980s. Many sessions were held in large community halls which were difficult to heat. For many years practitioners had to set up the naíonra every morning and then clear everything away at the end of the session, a draining use of energy and organization which limited the use of the space for displays of children's work etc. Most Gaeltacht communities now have purpose-built buildings while three new buildings adjacent to primary schools are almost completed (R. Mac Pháidín, personal communication 4th May 2021).

Current roles of support organizations

A number of support agencies provide support and services for naíonraí across the country. Comhar Naíonraí na Gaeltachta is one of the largest organizations in the country providing early years services, be they through English or Irish, on a community basis. The two main aims of the organization are to provide:

- High-quality community-based early years services through the Irish language in the Gaeltacht
- Support services to relevant Gaeltacht committees who have a service-level agreement with Comhar Naíonraí na Gaeltachta.

From the very beginning, Comhar Naíonraí na Gaeltachta recognized the vital importance of working closely with Gaeltacht communities and of providing community-based services rather than private services. Comhar Naíonraí na Gaeltachta has established local offices in each Gaeltacht region, with locally based advisors in each area. Almost 180 staff were working in naíonraí in 2020 and a further ten people in other roles in the organization. A wide range of services is provided, including the development of policies and procedures, in-service training, management services, local practice advisors, publications and participation in research. Recent research projects have included *Borradh: Scéim Pleanála Teanga* [Borradh Language Planning Project] between 2007 and 2013 (Comhar Naíonraí na Gaeltachta 2008, 2009, 2012) and participation in the Preschool to Primary School Transitive Initiative, now published as *Mo Scéal* (National Council for Curriculum and Assessment [NCCA] 2018).

Changes in supports for the naíonra sector outside the Gaeltacht

The ECEC sector, along with many others, suffered cutbacks during the recent economic recession. The cutbacks in relation to naíonraí outside the Gaeltacht were severe as core Foras na Gaeilge funding for FNT ceased in 2014 following a reorganization of the funded Irish language sector. FNT subsequently closed in 2015 when Pobal, acting on behalf of the Department of Children and Youth Affairs (DCYA), also withdrew its funding of FNT staff and services to support naíonraí. Foras na Gaeilge had discontinued a substantial subsidy scheme for naíonraí during the recession in 2013. This meant that dedicated support for *Aistear* (An Chomhairle Náisiúnta Curaclaim agus Measúnachta 2009) and *Síolta* (An Lárionad um Fhorbairt agus Oideachas na Luath-Óige 2006) through Irish was not being made available by any organization.

However, limited funding from Foras na Gaeilge for Irish language support and immersion education in naíonraí continues to the present time. Part of the funding previously provided to FNT by Foras na Gaeilge was reallocated to Gaelscoileanna, a member organization for Irish-medium schools. The organization was renamed Gaeloideachas to reflect its wider role which, as of 2014, includes the provision of support services for naíonraí outside Gaeltacht areas. Gaeloideachas provides a range of advisory and support services for naíonraí, including support for immersion education, online Irish language learning resources for staff as well as limited professional development, grants for setting up new naíonraí and advocacy. Newsletters are produced monthly for each part of the sector including parents and during the Covid-19 pandemic, Gaeloideachas commissioned a series of posters and video animations in Irish regarding social distancing, cough etiquette and handwashing. They provided links to many Irish language resources during this time including storytelling in Irish by well-known Irish writers and authors. Contact details of all naíonraí registered with Gaeloideachas are available on the website <www.gaeloideachas.ie>.

However, Gaeloideachas does not provide on-the-ground support to practitioners or monitor the use of Irish in these services, and neither does any other organization. Limited support through the Irish language is available from Better Start, the national quality development service for ECEC but overall, the provision of Irish-medium support is now much weaker than when the practice advisors from An Comhchoiste Réamhscolaíochta and FNT provided mentoring and advisory services through visiting naíonraí outside the Gaeltacht on a regular basis.

While naíonraí benefit from national supports, it is significant that the Department of Children, Equality, Disability, Integration and Youth (formerly DCYA) no longer funds any voluntary organizations to provide dedicated support through Irish to naíonraí, nor is any of the funding provided by that department to support the ECEC sector conditional on services and resources also being made accessible to naíonraí in Irish, their working language. The issue of using Irish as a working language in the naíonra sector is significant, both as an ideological principle and as a mediator of experience. On a personal note, much of the preparatory work for this chapter was completed through Irish, with both authors drawing on documentation, knowledge and experience gained in the sector through the Irish language.

Northern Ireland

The first naíscoil (infant or nursery school through the Irish language) was established in Belfast in 1978 and in 2020 there were fifty-six services/naíscoileanna in operation, many with links to local Irish-medium primary schools. Mhic Aoidh (2019) acknowledges that one of the developments flowing from the Good Friday Agreement (1998) was government support for Irish immersion education, which funded the expansion of the naíscoileanna.

Altram is a community-based organization, founded in Belfast in 1990, to promote high-quality early years education through Irish to children and their families. It offers support and in-service training to the *naíscoileanna* through its core team of three early years specialists and other support workers (Altram 2020). It also provides advice and guidance to management committees. The organization is funded by the Department of Education (Northern Ireland), through Comhairle na Gaelscolaíochta and by the Health and Social Care Board. Similarly, to naíonraí in other parts of Ireland, the need for specific training in immersion pedagogy was recognized in evaluations of the Irish-medium sector in Northern Ireland (Conway 2017, RSM McClure Watters et al. 2016). The Council for the

Curriculum Examinations and Assessment (CCEA) published a guide to ECEC which includes a short section on Irish-medium nursery education (CCEA 2018: 15–16).

Challenges and future directions in Irish-medium early years education

Many issues in regard to ECEC apply equally well to Irish-medium and English-medium settings (Mhic Aoidh 2019). However, based on research, readings and experience, the authors of this chapter consider that a number of specific issues apply to Irish-medium immersion education on a whole-island basis and indeed to immersion early years education further afield.

Specialized training: Particular high-level skills are required of practitioners, in both ECEC and immersion pedagogy in the early years. They need to understand how second languages are acquired incrementally, how language learning can be facilitated through supportive interactions in a play-based approach and how the language of children with Irish as their first language can be enriched and extended. Practitioners need to have a repertoire of skills that allows them to see the language learning opportunities in all aspects of ECEC work, both planned and incidental. To do this well, practitioners should be highly competent speakers of the target language, Irish in this case, and be able to relate to children in the appropriate register through supportive relationships. This means that children will be offered a rich educational experience as well as opportunities for language learning. The relationship between the child and the adult is key to making this happen as combining early years expertise with language skills is a complex task (Mhic Aoidh 2019).

Many researchers, including Hickey and de Mejía (2016), have recognized the need for specialized training at pre-service and in-service levels to develop these competencies in practitioners but few degree level programmes in Ireland offer input on understanding second language learning and developing strategies to promote this type of learning (Qualifax 2021). Currently, the number of immersion practitioners is relatively small, which makes it economically and socially difficult to provide specialist training programmes, however much needed they are. ECEC training at all levels from certificate to degree and postgraduate study should be made available online through Irish to serve dispersed Irish language communities in the Gaeltacht and other areas. This in turn would ensure a pool of graduates eligible to provide professional support in areas such as leadership, mentoring, advocacy and inspection services. Continuous Professional Development (CPD) training should be provided on current topics and new developments and accredited in line with other CPD training for the ECEC sector.

National policies: It is a feature of minority-language education at all levels that the immersion curriculum follows the majority language curriculum and that all national policies apply to minority-language settings (Baker and Wright 2021, Tedick et al. 2011). *Aistear* (An Chomhairle Náisiúnta Curaclaim agus Measúnachta 2009), *Síolta* (An Lárionad um Fhorbairt agus Oideachas na Luath-Óige 2006) and *An Chéad 5* [*First 5*] (Rialtas na hÉireann 2018) policy documents are all available in both Irish and English and support materials are available in both languages. The Irish language is the working language of naíonraí and national ECEC services should be made available through Irish at the same time as English-medium policies, procedures and supports. This may mean that a dedicated officer in the relevant government departments is tasked to oversee these developments.

Inspection: ECEC services are subject to four different inspection regimes in the Republic, but only the Department of Education inspections are carried out through Irish in Gaeltacht regions. Inspections by Tusla, the Child and Family Agency, Environmental Health and Pobal should be carried out in Irish in services working through Irish. The reports from these inspections in Irish-medium settings should also be made available in Irish as happens with the Department of Education reports. The Department of Education (Northern Ireland) states that there is a team of education inspectors in Northern Ireland who have proficiency in Irish and who understand the principles and practices of early years immersion education

(Department of Education 2020). There should be an Irish language condition applied to government grants for ECEC services in the Gaeltacht to encourage the use of Irish in all settings.

Evaluations: A planned series of self and external evaluations should be carried out in naíonraí on a systemic basis to map children's language learning in these contexts and ascertain which factors and strategies are most conducive to language learning.

Cooperation: Services provided by naíonraí support organizations are shaped to suit the educational, regulatory and social environments in which they operate. However, greater cooperation and collaboration between the organizations across the country would be beneficial in identifying good practice, sharing of common experiences and pooling of resources in programme planning and research. This could include outreach to parents, acknowledging their role in choosing immersion early education and identifying ways they can both offer and receive support from naíonraí.

Finally, as noted by other authors in this book, a national agency is required to oversee all aspects of ECEC in Ireland. This should serve practitioners who wish to work through Irish as well as English and other languages. This would raise the status of ECEC, facilitate coordination across the myriad of government departments and agencies and provide coordinated services to young children, their families and those who work with them in the ECEC sector.

Bibliography

Altram (2020). Seirbhísí Speisialtóra Luathbhlianta [Early Years Specialist Services]. Available at: <https://www.altram.org/seirbh%C3%ADs%C3%AD-speisi alt%C3%B3ra-luathbhlianta>.

An Chomhairle Náisiúnta Curaclaim agus Measúnachta (2009). *Aistear: Creatchuraclam na Luath-Óige*. Baile Átha Cliath: CNCM.

An Comhchoiste Réamhscolaíochta (1979/1985). *Lámhleabhar do Stiúrthóirí Naíonraí*. Baile Átha Cliath: An Comhchoiste Réamhscolaíochta.

An Comhchoiste Réamhscolaíochta (1984). *Damhsa na gCoiníní* [Dance of the Rabbits]. Baile Átha Cliath: An Comhchoiste Réamhscolaíochta.

An Lárionad um Fhorbairt agus Oideachas na Luath-Óige (2006). *Síolta. An Chreatlach Náisiúnta Cáilíochta d'Oideachas na Luath-Óige.* [*Síolta. The National Quality Framework for Early Childhood Education*]. Baile Átha Cliath: LFOLÓ.

Baker, C. and Prys Jones, S. (1998). *Encyclopedia of Bilingualism and Bilingual Education*. Clevedon: Multilingual Matters.

Baker, C. and Wright, W. (2021). *Foundations of Bilingualism and Bilingual Education*, 7th ed. Bristol: Multilingual Matters.

Blaise, M., Edwards, S. and Brooker, L. (2016). Theoretical Perspectives on Play and Learning. In L. Brooker, M. Blaise and S. Edwards (eds), *The Sage Handbook of Play and Learning in Early Childhood*, pp. 5–8. London: Sage.

Comhar Naíonraí na Gaeltachta (2008). *Borradh 1: Mé Féin* [Borradh 1: Myself]. Gaillimh: Comhar Naíonraí na Gaeltachta.

Comhar Naíonraí na Gaeltacha (2009). *Borradh 2: An Timpeallacht* [Borradh 2: The Environment]. Gaillimh: Comhar Naíonraí na Gaeltachta.

Comhar Naíonraí na Gaeltacha (2012). *Borradh 3: Drámaíocht, Caint agus Spraoi* [Borradh 3: Drama, Talk and Fun]. Gaillimh: Comhar Naíonraí na Gaeltachta.

Comhar Naíonraí na Gaeltacha (2021). *Services*. Available at: <http://comharnaion rai.ie/seirbhisi.php>.

Conway, G. (2017). *Na Luathbhlianta Gaeilge. Tuarascáil ar an Earnáil. Achoimre Fheidhmeach* [Irish-medium Early Years State of the Sector Report. Executive Summary]. Belfast: Altram.

Council for the Curriculum, Examinations and Assessment (2018). *Curriculum Guidance for Preschool Education*. Belfast: Department of Education.

Department of Education (Northern Ireland) (2020). *Department of Education Response. Research on the Outcomes of Pre-school Irish Medium Education*. Belfast: Department of Education.

Dunne, C. (2020). *Learning and Teaching Irish in English-Medium Schools Part 1: 1878–1971*. Available at: <https://ncca.ie/media/4796/learning-and-teaching-irish-in-english-medium-schools-1878-1971-part-1.pdf>.

Ellis, R. (2008). *The Study of Second Language Acquisition*, 2nd ed. Oxford: Oxford University Press.

Forbairt Naíonraí Teo. (2005). *Damhsa na gCoiníní* [Dance of the Rabbits]. Baile Átha Cliath: Forbairt Naíonraí Teo.

Hickey, T. (1997). *Early Immersion Education in Ireland: Na Naíonraí/An Luath-Thumadh in Éirinn: Na Naíonraí*. Dublin: Institiúid Teangeolaíochta Éireann.

Hickey, T., with Ó Cíosáin, H. and Ní Ghallchóir, A. (1999). *Luath-oideachas trí Ghaeilge sa Ghaeltacht* [Early Childhood Education through Irish in the Gaeltacht]. Gaillimh: Údarás na Gaeltachta.

Hickey, T. and de Mejía, A-M. (2016). *Immersion Education in the Early Years.* London: Routledge.

Mac Con Iomaire, M. (1978). *Scéilín, Scéilín* [Story, Story]. Gaillimh: Seirbhísí Naíonraí (Gaeltachta) Teo.

Mac Con Iomaire, M. (1984). *Dreoilín, Dreoilín Rí na nÉan* [The Wren, the Wren, King of the Birds]. Gaillimh: Seirbhísí Naíonraí (Gaeltachta) Teo.

Mac Con Iomaire, M. (2006). *Loinnir, Clár Oibre do Naíonraí na Gaeltachta* [Loinnir, Work Programme for Gaeltacht Naíonraí]. Gaillimh: Seirbhísí Naíonraí (Gaeltachta) Teo.

Mac Liam, S. (1981). 'Léirmheas ar *Amhráin do Pháistí* [Review of Amhráin do Pháistí] by Treasa Ní Ailpín, Brian Ó Dubhghaill and Íde Ó Háinle', *Teagasc na Gaeilge,* 2, 144–145.

McGee, D. and Brennan, D. (2012). *Báidín Fheidhlimidh.* Gaoth Dobhair: Éabhlóid.

Mhic Aoidh, E. (2019). 'Factors Which Impact on Transitions from Irish-medium Naíscoil to Bunscoil', *Teanga Special Edition 10: Multilingualism in the Early Years,* 207–227. <https://doi.org/10.35903/teanga.v10i0.79>.

Mhic Mhathúna, M. (1996). 'Is liomsa é leon'. Ról na bPáistí agus na Stiúrthóirí i Sealbhú na Gaeilge in Naíonraí ['That's My Lion'. The Role of Children and Practitioners in the Acquisition of Irish in Naíonraí], *Oideas,* 44, 113–125.

Mhic Mhathúna, M. (2010). 'Arís is Arís Eile: Scéalta mar Áis Teanga sa Naíonra [Again and Again: Stories as Language Resource in Naíonraí]', *Oideas,* 55, 31–42.

Mhic Mhathúna. M. agus Mac Con Iomaire, M. (2013). Litríocht na nÓg sna Naíonraí: Na Luathbhlianta. [Children's Literature in the Naíonraí : The Early Years]. In C. Nic Lochlainn agus Ríona Nic Congáil (eds), *Laethanta Gréine & Oícheanta Sí,* pp. 173–196. Baile Átha Cliath: Leabhar Comhar.

National Council for Curriculum and Assessment (2018). *Mo Scéal.* Available at: <https://ncca.ie/en/early-childhood/mo-sc%C3%A9al>.

Ní Ailpín, T. (1977). *Sonas is Só* [Happiness and Ease]. Baile Átha Cliath: An Gúm.

Ní Ailpín, T. (1979). *Timpeall an Tí* [Around the House]. Baile Átha Cliath: An Gúm.

Ní Ailpín, T. (1991). *Maidin sa Naíonra* [Morning in the Naíonra]. Baile Átha Cliath: An Comhchoiste Réamhscolaíochta.

Ní Ailpín, T. agus Breathnach, M. (2005). *Maidin sa Naíonra* [Morning in the Naíonra]. Baile Átha Cliath: Forbairt Naíonraí Teo.

Ní Ailpín, T., Ó Dubhghaill, B. agus Ó Háinle, Í. (1980). *Amhráin do Pháistí* [Songs for Children]. Baile Átha Cliath: An Comhchoiste Réamhscolaíochta.

Ní Aodhagáin, S. (1982). *Staidéar Treorach ar an Naíonraí in Éirinn.* [Pilot Study on Naíonraí in Ireland]. Baile Átha Cliath: An Comhchoiste Réamhscolaíochta Teo.

Ní Chuilleanáin, O. (2012). 'Tosaíocht Aistriúcháin ar Litríocht na nÓg go Gaeilge: An staid Reatha [The Prevalence of Translation in Literature for Children in Irish]'. In R. Nic Congáil (ed.), *Codladh Céad Bliain: Cnuasach Aistí ar Litríocht na nÓg*, pp. 127–149. Baile Átha Cliath: Leabhair Comhar.

Ní Mhuircheartaigh, B. and Mac Gearailt., P. M. (2014). *Sicín Mise go Sona Sásta.* Baile an Fheirtéaraigh: Oidhreacht Chorca Dhuibhne.

Ní Mhuircheartaigh, B. and Mac Gearailt, P. M. (2016). *Ardaigh an Laiste.* Baile an Fheirtéaraigh: Oidhreacht Chorca Dhuibhne.

Nic Congáil. R. (2012). Réamhrá [Introduction]. In R. Nic Congáil (ed.), *Codladh Céad Bliain: Cnuasach Aistí ar Litríocht na nÓg*, pp. 11–21. Baile Átha Cliath: Leabhair Comhar.

Nic Giolla Bhríde, N. and Mac Giolla Bhríde, D. (2010). *Ící Pící.* Gaoth Dobhair: Éabhlóid.

Ó Buachalla, A. (1979). 'Stiúrthóirí agus Naíonraí. [Practitioners and Naíonraí]'. In An Comhchoiste Réamhscolaíochta, *Lámhleabhar do Stiúrthóirí Naíonraí*, pp. 12–13. Baile Átha Cliath: An Comhchoiste Réamhscolaíochta.

Ó Cathasaigh, R. (2009). *Tídil Eidil Éro.* Limerick: Aonad Forbartha Curaclam, Colásite Mhuire gan Smál and Baile an Fheirtéaraigh, Oidhreacht Chorca Dhuibhne.

Ó Cathasaigh, R. and Doyle, D. L. (1998). *Rabhlaí Rabhlaí.* Limerick: Aonad Forbartha Curaclaim, Coláiste Mhuire gan Smál, Ollscoil Luimní and Baile an Fheirtéaraigh, Oidhreacht Chorca Dhuibhne.

O'Connor, M. (2010). *The Development of Infant Education in Ireland, 1838–1948: Epochs and Eras.* Bern: Peter Lang.

Ó hUiginn, C. (1980). 'Comhthéacs na Timpeallachta [The Environmental Context]', *Teagasc na Gaeilge*, 1, 51–57.

Ó Murchú, H. (1979a). 'An Naíscolaíocht agus an Ghaeilge. [Preschool education and the Irish Language]'. In An Comhchoiste Réamhscolaíochta, *Lámhleabhar do Stiúrthóirí Naíonraí*, pp. 5–7. Baile Átha Cliath: An Comhchoiste Réamhscolaíochta.

Ó Murchú, H. (1979b). An Súgradh. [Play]. In An Comhchoiste Réamhscolaíochta. *Lámhleabhar do Stiúrthóirí Naíonra* [Handbook for Naíonra Practitioners], pp. 14–19. Baile Átha Cliath: An Comhchoiste Réamhscolaíochta.

Ó Murchú, H. (1980). 'Réamhscolaíocht trí Ghaeilge [Preschooling through the Irish Language]', *Teagasc na Gaeilge*, 1, 19–33.

Ó Murchú, H. (1985). 'Smaointe ar an Réamhscolaíocht [Reflections on Preschooling]', *Teagasc na Gaeilge*, 4, 87–105.

Pobal (2019). *Early Years Sector Profile 2018–19*. Available at: <https://www.pobal. ie/app/uploads/2019/12/Annual-Early-Years-Sector-Profile-Report-AEY SPR-2018-19.pdf>.

Qualifax (2021). *Programmes in Early Childhood Education at NFQ Levels 6, 7, 8*. Available at: <https://www.qualifax.ie/index.php?option=com_wrap per&view=wrapper&Itemid=16>.

Rialtas na hÉireann (2018). *An Chéad 5. Straitéis Uile-Rialtais do Naíonáin, Leanaí Óga agus a dTeaghlaigh 2019–2028 [First 5. A Whole of Government Strategy for Babies, Young Children and Their Families 2019–2028]*. Baile Átha Cliath: Rialtas na hÉireann.

RSM McClure Watters (Consulting), Mhic Aoidh, E., Ní Thuairisg, L. agus Nic Íomhair, A (2016). *Research on the Educational Outcomes of Preschool Irish Medium Education*. Belfast: Department of Education.

Ryan, J. and Mac Dhonnagáin, T. (2005). *Gugalaí Gug*. Galway: Futa Fata.

Seirbhísí Naíonra Teo. (1997). *Polasaithe & Nósanna Imeachta Naíonra (Gaeilge)*. Gaillimh: Seirbhísí Naíonra Teo.

Tedick, D., Chrisdtian, D. and Fortune, T. W. (eds) (2011). *Immersion Education. Practices, Policies, Possibilities*. Bristol: Multilingual Matters.

Uí Chonghaile, M. (2012). 'Na Naíonraí. [The Naíonraí]'. In M. Mhic Mhathúna and M. Taylor (eds), *Early Childhood Education and Care. An Introduction for Students in Ireland*, pp. 154–160. Dublin: Gill and Macmillan.

Uí Ghrádaigh, D. (ed.) (2005). *Lámhleabhar do Stiúrthóirí Naíonraí*, 3rd ed. [Handbook for Naíonra Practitioners]. Baile Átha Cliath: Forbairt Naíonraí Teo.

Williams, Jac. L. (1967). *Bilingualism Today*. Baile Átha Cliath: Comhdháil Náisiúnta na Gaeilge.

Williams, N. (1988). *Cniogaide Cnagaide. Rainn traidisiúnta do pháistí* [Cniogaide Cnagaide. Traditional Rhymes for Children]. Baile Átha Cliath: An Clóchomhar.

Wood. E. (2014). 'The Play-pedagogy Interface in Contemporary Debates'. In L. Brooker, M. Blaise and S. Edwards (eds), *The Sage Handbook of Play and Learning in Early Childhood*, pp. 145–156. London: Sage.

Wray, A. (2004). *Formulaic Language and the Lexicon*. Cambridge: Cambridge University Press.

CARMEL BRENNAN AND ARLENE FORSTER

5 Early childhood education and care curriculum provision and the development of *Aistear*

Introduction

This chapter reviews the history of curriculum development in the early childhood education and care (ECEC) sector in Ireland over the last century. It brings together a practice and policy perspective, in recognition of the organic, practice-based origins of the sector and the more recent involvement of State and academic institutions in policy formation. The term 'curriculum' as used in this chapter refers to the philosophies, aims and programmes that have been part of the ECEC sector since the 1960s. We trace the evolution of curriculum through three significant phases beginning with the informal contexts of the first preschool playgroups and then the subsequent changing rhetoric of curriculum in response to the formalization of the sectors in the 1990s. The end of the twentieth century heralded the third phase prompting the first national debate about ECEC and paving the way for the development of the *Aistear* curriculum framework (NCCA 2009) and links with the primary school system. Reflecting the authors' experiences and direct involvement in curriculum work, the chapter, at times, augments documentary evidence with experiential and autobiographical accounts. Finally, the chapter offers reflections on a possible next phase in our curriculum journey as the sector contributes to reconceptualizing curricula across the education system.

Two parallel traditions

The roots of the ECEC sector in Europe can be found in nineteenth-century developments focussed on providing protective services to children of the poor and early education services to the better off, as evidenced by the projects of Montessori, Steiner and Froebel. Later, during and the post-Second World War, there was a new focus on providing daycare services for the children of women entering the labour force. In Ireland, the influence of the European movement was most strongly felt, for a brief period, in the review of the primary curriculum at the turn of the twentieth century (Walsh 2005), and later in the playgroup movement, which was born more from a perceived need to create safe social spaces for children to play together rather than educational needs. Following Independence in 1922, the primary school curriculum diverged philosophically and became strictly education focussed (*Ibid.*) and the playgroup movement of the late 1960s, keen to distinguish itself from schooling, followed a very separate trajectory to the school system.

These separate systems were also noted in Sweden (Dahlberg and Taguchi 1994 cited in Moss 2013: 230), with the ECEC sector reflecting the 'child as nature' tradition, where the focus is on the natural, innate drives and abilities of the child developing along a biological trajectory in contrast to compulsory school education, where the child is positioned as 'reproducer of culture and knowledge'. Moss (2013) suggests that for both sectors to grow and find a meeting place with each other and with the extended education community, we must first recognize both traditions and their cultural systems, since this cultural affiliation can be a huge barrier to change. The introduction of *Aistear: The Early Childhood Curriculum Framework* (NCCA 2009), more than ten years ago, has created an opportunity for new encounters (Moss 2013) and for shared values and objectives across the wider education system. This review of the development of the ECEC curriculum is intended as a contribution to that change.

Phase 1: The preschool playgroup movement

The ECEC sector in Ireland is only 50 years old, although a significant cohort of 3-year-olds were attending primary school at the end of the nineteenth century and consequently, the Belmore Commission, charged with a review of the curriculum in 1898, engaged with the progressive kindergarten philosophers of the time in Europe, particularly Froebel, and developed a Kindergarten model with an emphasis on play and flexibility for young children (Walsh 2005). Furthermore, Montessori came to Waterford in 1926 and again in 1934 to visit pilot Montessori-based infant primary classrooms but her philosophy met with strong opposition from Rev Professor Timothy Corcoran S. J., a very dominant educationalist of the time. He guided a return to 'strict authoritarian teaching' (*Ibid.*: 258), strongly opposed Montessori's child-centred approach and succeeded in excluding her methods from the State school system (Walsh 2012: 140–142), although not from the voluntary/private ECEC sector. By 1992, there was more than 200 Montessori schools in the country, mainly in the cities. Corcoran's influence lived on in the primary schools for almost fifty years, until the new curriculum of 1971 'returned to the child-centred, heuristic and discovery-learning ideals of the 1900 Revised Programme' (Walsh 2005: 265). The ECEC sector that took root in the late 1960s was keen to differentiate itself from the school sector.

The nationwide ECEC system came in the form of the preschool playgroup movement which started in New Zealand in the 1940s and slowly wound its way to England, where the Preschool Playgroup Movement (PPA) was established in 1962, and on to Ireland where the Irish Preschool Playgroups Association (IPPA) formed in 1969. By 1970, the IPPA had 130 members and by 1982 the membership had passed 1,000 (Douglas 1994).

The movement in England met with the already established work of pioneers such as Susan Isaacs and the McMillan sisters, whose projects were underpinned by the European philosophies of Montessori, Steiner and especially Froebel with his celebration of play for the multiple possibilities and open-ended experiences it offers children and his commitment to engaging with families. They translated these theories into practice in culturally attuned ways in their nurseries. Like Froebel, they wanted their settings to reflect the nurture and learning of family life, while at the same time offering children new and stimulating activities beyond those available at home (Isaacs 1952). Drawing on Froebel and Steiner, they promoted children's free play and first-hand experiences, and the connection with nature and the outdoors and they emphasized the importance of social interaction, inquiry and discovery. Isaacs, like Froebel, particularly valued imaginative, open-ended play, which she saw as a vehicle for the expression of children's unconscious feelings and thoughts and a generator of higher-order thinking skills, thus bringing together her care and education agenda. This value on care and education through play, as well as the involvement of parents, became core principles of the work of the PPA and their affiliated playgroups. Brenda Crowe, herself a Froebel nursery teacher, and National Advisor to the PPA, authored two publications *Playgroup Activities* (Crowe 1971a) and *The Playgroup Movement: A Report by the National Adviser of the Pre-school Playgroups Association* (Crowe 1971b) published by the PPA and these became the guiding manuals of the early movement in Ireland. Both publications offered practical guidance and advice on setting up and running a playgroup, the focus being on practice rather than philosophy.

From the beginning, the IPPA was affiliated to the PPA and its influence was immense in bringing practice based on Froebelian and Montessori philosophies to the Irish playgroup movement. IPPA founding members attended PPA seminars on training, disseminated the PPA publications, availed of Montessori training facilitated by the St Nicholas Montessori Centre in London and Dublin, and organized a 1970/1971 Winter series of talks in Dublin, delivered by such significant pioneers as Sr Marion, from the Froebel Department at Sion Hill, and the aforementioned Brenda Crowe from the PPA. Later, in 1975, Lady Plowden, Chair of the 1967 Plowden Report came to Ireland to speak at the IPPA annual general meeting, promoting these child-centred philosophies and drawing much publicity (Douglas 1994). These talks, courses and associations informed the IPPA basic introductory training courses.

While the first playgroup leaders may not have been familiar with the philosophers, according to Irene Gunning, a playgroup leader of the 1970s and later CEO of the IPPA and Early Childhood Ireland, three strong principles – play, process, and partnership with parents – drove their practice (personal communication 2020). They believed that play is a natural learning mechanism of the child, engaging them emotionally and cognitively, that they learn in the process of doing, that the process should be trusted and that partnership with parents enhances the experience of the child both at home and in the playgroup. Summarizing the approach, Gunning, quoted in the Irish Times (Wayman 2009), says, 'The playgroups had a very holistic approach ... Play is learning; education and care co-exist in play.' This relationship between child, playleader, parent and play was also captured in the first logo of the organization in 1970.

The play curriculum

The play-based approach to curriculum, adopted from the PPA in Britain, and implemented with varying degrees of success in playgroups in Ireland is described by Brenda Crowe (1973: 43):

> Ideally ... the room will be prepared, and the playgroup leader will be waiting at the door to greet the children ... The following activities will be awaiting the children: water play, wet and dry sand, clay and/or playdough, woodwork, painting, well equipped home corner complete with dressing up clothes and possibly dough for cooking, books, table toys, bricks, push and pull toys, large junk from which to make cars, boats etc., climbing and balancing apparatus and tables offering an inviting range of odds and ends, glue, scissors, paint etc. which encourage children to experiment freely and imaginatively, in two or three dimensions combining several skills.

Similar practice in Ireland is reflected in the 1993 Information Packs published by the IPPA (IPPA 1993) and the Northern Ireland PPA (NIPPA 1993), particularly in the sections on equipment and play and the role of the Playleader, as well as in the experience of the first-named author of this chapter, who worked as a playgroup leader and advisor at that time. Douglas conducted research on IPPA member services in Cork from 1986 to 1990, using equipment and activities checklists that also reflect this practice (Douglas 1994). Together, these sources suggest, that with some variation and flexibility, the routine in playgroups followed a pattern. The children arrived in the morning and gathered around the leaders to settle in and chat. They then played in the home corner, the sand, water and under tables, and they painted, moulded playdough and played tabletop games and jigsaws, usually indoors, for the morning. A mid-morning lunch was prefaced by the call to tidy up and followed by outdoor play and indoor singing, dancing, storytelling and craft activities. Morning play was led by the children with the adult as co-player at times. Post lunch activities tended to be adult led. While practice followed this recognizable pattern, it remained informal, undocumented and unregulated until the mid-1990s.

Playgroup leaders were very determined to differentiate their playgroups from schools and strongly rejected the use of such terms as teacher, curriculum, subjects or testing. These were replaced with terms such as play leader, activities, play corners (home, construction, nature music, etc.) and observation. They were an unqualified workforce, providing a basic service in their neighbourhoods, funded by parents in the main and they did not want to be compared to schools. Their commitment to play was their mantra. The ECEC sector's identity has been strongly framed by both these values and antipathies.

IPPA training

Playgroup leaders looked to the IPPA, in the main, for training. It predominantly came in two forms – through training programmes and local branch meetings. In sociocultural terms, these meetings might be called a 'Community of Practice' (Lave and Wenger 1991), sessions where educators share their experiences and look to one another for advice and support. The practical, oral approach was also embedded in the IPPA introductory training. The ten-session course drew on adult learning principles, particularly that effective learning was experiential (Rogers 1969). Typically, each session included an opportunity to play with materials (sand, water, playdough, blocks etc.) followed by a discussion about the experience and the benefits. Again, the focus was on practical support for organizing activities. These courses were provided in almost every night school in the country, such was the demand and enthusiasm for the work (Douglas 1994).

Babies and toddlers

This training focussed on sessional services for the preschool age group, 3–5 years. The National Children's Nursery Association (NCNA), founded in 1988 and representing the growing daycare sector, brought a focus to babies and toddlers. From the beginning they recognized the connection between care and learning, establishing a quality indicator as supporting children's learning while meeting their needs for care and attention (NCNA 1998). However, in many ways, the existence of both organizations represented a divide between the age groups that continues to this day. As suggested by the *White Paper on Early Childhood Education* of 1999 (Government of Ireland 1999), discussed later, the concept of the integrated nature of education and care, particularly for the under threes, continued to be contentious (Hayes 2007).

Phase 2: Moving towards a more formal sector

The 1990s brought a new phase in the ECEC sector in Ireland. The introduction of the Early Start intervention project for 3- to 5-year-olds in 1994 impacted in two significant ways. Firstly, it introduced a focussed, intervention style curriculum (Hayes and Bradley 2006), supported by the Department of Education, and staffed by primary teachers and childcare assistants, as a model of good practice in the sector. Secondly, inadvertently, it also led to the establishment of the National Council for Vocational Awards (NCVA) Level 2, now renamed as Quality and Qualifications Ireland (QQI) Level 5, as the minimum qualifications for the early childhood sector. A survey of the educational attainment of the ECEC workforce in 2007/2008 found that 41 per cent of staff had attained this qualification (DES 2009). Course requirements were established by the NCVA, and hence theoretical input, curriculum models and pedagogic strategies became part of the ECEC parlance. Piaget was largely the underpinning theorist. His theories had enjoyed a resurgence in the mid-1960s in North American early childhood programmes such as Headstart and Highscope and greatly influenced the National Association for the Education of Young Children (NAEYC) position on curriculum, framed as Developmentally Appropriate Practice (DAP) (Bredecamp 1987). Known as constructivism, in recognition that the child constructs their own learning, the theory brought a new emphasis to child-centred learning and children's play, but it also brought fixed ideas about children's capabilities or inabilities in the early stages of development. The Piagetian tendency was to assess children against universal normative milestones in terms of physical, intellectual, language, emotional and social development (known by the acronym PILES). Educators tried to identify areas in which children were challenged and then implement strategies for improvement. The consequent conflicts between theory and practice were identified by Carswell (2002) in his research into the preschool playgroups and the ECEC educators' interpretation of their role, commissioned by the IPPA.

While Carswell found that preschool educators propounded a Piagetian theory of the child as an individual, innately driven, self-constructing learner, he identifies the prevalent view among them of the 'needy, dependant' child (*Ibid*.: 8). He also found that while they voiced a strong commitment to free play and supporting children's intrinsic learning trajectories, they organized their everyday programmes along adult predetermined guidelines, with many adult led or 'extrinsically motivated' (*Ibid*.: 9) activities, and towards predetermined learning objectives, including school readiness. These practitioners describe the growing conflict between the traditional 'free play' approach and their new responsibilities in teaching the child how to behave, how to reach developmental milestones in PILES and how to construct valued domains of knowledge. The training and 'quality' programmes of the new millennium involved an attempt to address these confusions.

Phase 3: State involvement in the ECEC curriculum

The third phase, at the end of the century, brought a new awareness of the significance of early childhood to lifelong learning and wellbeing. It prompted both national debate and statutory investment in quality improvement in the sector. From the perspective of State involvement and policy formulation, 1998 marked a turning point with the *National*

Forum for Early Childhood Education taking place under the stewardship of Professor John Coolahan (Coolahan 1998). Established by the then Minister for Education and Science, Micheál Martin, the Forum saw, for the first time, a gathering of key stakeholders from across the voluntary, private and public sectors, including primary school representatives, to discuss a wide spectrum of issues, including curriculum. While discussions clearly demonstrated diverse perspectives on the detail of how ECEC might be and should be supported, common ground emerged in the broad agreement that the State had a vital role to play in ensuring that every child would have access to and benefit from rich learning experiences in their formative years.

This was reflected in the proposals relating to curriculum which were subsequently set out in *Ready to Learn*, the resultant White Paper on Early Childhood Education (Government of Ireland 1999). While the White Paper defined the early childhood period as being from birth to six with the upper limit marking the commencement of mandatory schooling, these proposals referred mainly to the first 4 years of a child's life and reinforced the care and education divide with care continuing to be seen as the priority for children under 3 and with education gaining importance from 3 years onwards. This is clearly captured in the White Paper's call for a 'specimen' curriculum for preschool children which would 'provide more specific detail on content and methodology' (*Ibid.*: 57). In the case of children under three, the White Paper echoed the Forum's concern regarding the relative absence of curriculum material supporting appropriate and playful experiences for very young children. Addressing this, it called for the development of 'a less formal curriculum … The emphasis at this level will be on how children learn and how parents can help their children to learn' (*Ibid.*: 57).

The White Paper acknowledged the extensive work of many organizations in the sector, including the development of a range of curriculum materials being used by practitioners. The importance of respecting this diversity of provision was emphasized, as was the diversity of underpinning philosophies which, in the main, reflected the work of early childhood pioneers such as Montessori, Froebel, Dewey and Steiner. It is of note that, from a curriculum perspective, the White Paper gave little attention to children between 4 and 6 years, a period when, at the time, almost all 5-year-olds and close to half of all 4-year-olds were enrolled in the primary school system. This may have been partly due to the ongoing work at that time in developing a revised primary curriculum (*Ibid.*) and which included a curriculum for junior and senior infants, the first two-year groups in primary school.

Work and influence of the national voluntary organizations

The year 1999 also marked the beginning of a significant period for the curriculum-based work of the national voluntary organizations, supported by grants from the European Social Fund to develop training and quality programmes. The organizations looked abroad for inspiration and research evidence which further heralded a new era of curriculum thinking in the sector. Informed by, among others, the competent child and the pedagogy of listening approach of Reggio Children in Italy, Te Whariki and the learning story approach to assessment in New Zealand (Carr 2001), and the work of Dahlberg et al. (1999) on quality, they began to focus on the cultural and competent child. The publications *Power of Play: A Play Curriculum in Action* (Brennan 2004) and *Nurture through Nature* (IPPA 2006) and the hundreds of stories generated by educators through various fora (see <www.earlychildhoodireland.ie>), reflect this shift. They tell stories of the play of competent, proactive children as they demonstrate, share and develop their understanding, skills and dispositions in play, indoors and outdoors. They recognize the funds of experience and knowledge (Hedges 2012) they bring from home, the expertise of children in their own lives, the experimentation with roles and relationships and their developing identities, all part of the 'cultural intelligence' (Trevarthen 2011) that had rarely been named in the education field before. They also demonstrate the power of story as a tool for making children's competencies and learning visible to all the important people in their lives.

These stories, at the same time, celebrate the work of educators and families in making these experiences available to children. They foreground the values and practices of early childhood educators and demonstrate what is possible. In this way, the educators become curriculum makers, bridging the gap between practice and theory. The sharing of these learning stories serves to spotlight good practice and support peer mentoring in developing curriculum. In many ways, the work of the national voluntary organizations paved the way for *Aistear: The Early Childhood Curriculum Framework*. Already, this sector had established an unwavering commitment to the child's right to play, an image of the young child as competent and proactive, and the central importance of family, community and relationships in the child's life.

The role of the National Council for Curriculum and Assessment (NCCA)

The *Education Act* 1998 (Government of Ireland 1998) expanded the remit of the NCCA to include advising the Minister for Education and Science on curriculum for early childhood education. Conscious of its strong identity and association with primary and post-primary education, and of the potential for this to generate concern within the early childhood sector about the potential 'schoolification' of practice, the Council prioritized relationship-building. The NCCA spent early 2001 meeting with and learning from stakeholders, including practitioners. This approach enabled the Council to build a profile as an organization whose work was based on partnership, informed by research and evidence from practice, and rooted in a respect for the uniqueness of the sector. This was pivotal in gaining the sector's trust and in laying foundations for open and authentic deliberation and engagement.

Four months were devoted to working with stakeholders and reviewing curriculum documents and resources used within the sector. These included *Project EYE* (Project EYE 2000); *Early Childhood (2 ¹⁄₂–6)* (St Nicholas Montessori College 1996); *Towards Quality Daycare* (NCNA 1998); *The IPPA Border Counties High Scope Project 1997–1999* (IPPA 1999), as well as examples of practice spotlighting the importance of play, creativity and story. In addition, curricula used internationally, including *Te Whariki* (New Zealand Ministry of Education 1996), the *Final Draft Framework: Early Years Band* (South Australian Curriculum Standards and Accountability [SACSA] 2001), the *Curriculum Framework for Children 3 to 5* (Scottish Council on the Curriculum 1999), the *Preschool Curriculum Guidelines* (Queensland School Curriculum Council 2001) and the *Curriculum for Pre-school* (Sweden, Ministry of Education 1998) were analysed.

This work helped to shape the *Early Childhood Framework for Learning: Background Paper* (NCCA 2001). Responding to the curriculum proposals in *Ready to Learn*, drawing on the sector's strong practice tradition which had grown organically since the late 1960s and taking account of the evolving thinking about the purpose of ECEC, the Background Paper diverged from the White Paper's proposals and signalled a more ambitious and integrated approach to curriculum development. This approach emerged from the sector's hopes and aspirations for a curriculum that would validate and embrace the rich tapestry of traditions and philosophies that characterized the sector. Likewise, stakeholders wanted a curriculum that would espouse the image of children as capable and competent learners; that would successfully integrate care and education; elevate and spotlight the importance of this phase of a child's learning; and recognize the integrity of the period for a child's joy and fulfilment rather than serving as an antechamber or preparation for what followed in later years.

These aspirations reflected a converging and meshing of practice and policy, each shaping and informing the other. Recognizing that practitioners and the voluntary organizations supporting their work had much to offer through their expertise, experience and commitment, the NCCA advised the Minister for Education and Science on the importance of an inclusive and consultative approach to developing what would become the State's first curriculum framework. Having issued its advice in April 2001, the NCCA was asked to progress work on the framework for the whole early childhood period, representing a significant departure from what had been envisaged two years earlier in the White Paper. The work had further significance in that it reflected new and emerging thinking about curriculum itself, signalling a move from detailed, prescribed curricula to more open curriculum frameworks, and placing more emphasis on the role of practitioners as 'curriculum makers' (Priestley and Philippou 2018).

Influences on curriculum thinking

The eight years that followed represented a coming together of key influences and traditions – NCCA's curriculum development experience
and partnership model; the rich, diverse tradition of ECEC that had
evolved in Ireland; international curriculum policy developments; and
key findings from research on child development and learning. Research,
international practice and policy trends as well as thinking within organizations in the sector had started to take account of an emerging sociocultural perspective shaped by Bronfenbrenner's (1979) ecological model
of human development. Ideas from influential thinkers such as Vygotsky
(1986), Rogoff (1990), Bruner (1996) and Bruce (2001) were converging
to create an image of children as capable, confident and active beings,
living and learning in partnership with the significant adults and children
in their lives.

    This vision became influential in shifting the driver for State interest
and investment in ECEC from a gender equality agenda to one focused
on children's rights and high-quality experiences. Prior to this, State involvement had been motivated largely by an interventionist perspective
with those children 'at risk' being the priority and then by a gender equality
focus (Hayes 2002). Ultimately and importantly, the powerful image of
competent children enabled stakeholders across the sector to unite in their
support for a single, overarching curriculum framework.

    This consensus facilitated the NCCA's establishment of the Early
Childhood Technical Working Group in 2003 whose members comprised
leading researchers and academics in Ireland (Daly and Forster 2009). Their
multi-disciplinary expertise and experience helped shape the consultative document, *Towards a Framework for Early Learning: Draft Proposals*
(NCCA 2004). The consultation with children which followed included
a ground-breaking portraiture study positioning children's voices at the
heart of curriculum development (NCCA 2007). Drawing on the work
of Lawrence-Lightfoot and Hoffmann Davis (1997), the purpose of the
study was to tune in and understand what children liked doing, where they
liked to be and who they liked to be with. The study highlighted key messages such as the importance of holistic learning and development through

play and first-hand experiences, relationships, the crucial role of parents, the power of communication, the importance of a sense of identity and belonging, and the benefits of observing and listening to children. This consultation was another milestone in the architecture of the curriculum framework as it enabled agreement on the purpose, philosophical under-pinnings and structure of the framework thereby shaping the direction of the NCCA's curriculum development work over the next four years.

Developing Aistear

The NCCA established the Early Childhood Committee in 2004. Unlike the Technical Working Group, this committee drew its member-ship from across the sector and included representatives of the many or-ganizations centrally involved in ECEC (Daly and Forster 2009). This structure gave critical voice to the sector in crafting the values, ideas and thinking which ultimately underpinned the curriculum framework. Feedback from the consultation in 2004 highlighted the importance of documenting the theory 'behind' *Aistear*. In response, the NCCA com-missioned four research papers. Written by ECEC experts in Ireland, this represented another element of partnership with the sector. The papers explored the relationship between education and care (Hayes 2007), early learning and development (French 2007), play (Kernan 2007) and formative assessment (Dunphy 2008). These papers informed the inten-sive and extensive discussion, deliberation and debate that took place during *Aistear*'s development.

At times, this engagement brought contestation. In particular, ter-minology commanded considerable attention. Words such as curriculum, assessment, teacher, teaching and even play, conveyed different mean-ings and presented particular challenges for stakeholders reflecting the coming together of two different philosophies and traditions (Dahlberg and Taguchi 1994 cited in Moss 2013). Some of this reflected the challenge of bringing stakeholders together from the whole early childhood period, including those working in the primary school system. Up to this point, there had been few opportunities for this diverse group to meet, to build relationships, to work together and, most importantly, to understand each other's traditions, philosophies and values. Yet even with such tensions, there was a shared commitment to building a curriculum framework which would ultimately enrich young children's experiences irrespective of which physical setting they were in. This commitment provided a common ground from which *Aistear* ultimately emerged.

Development work on *Aistear* coincided with Ireland's participation in one of the OECD's Starting Strong Reviews (OECD 2004) in which the quality of ECEC practice in Ireland generated mixed reviews. Another milestone influencing the NCCA's work was the publication of *Síolta, The National Quality Framework for Early Childhood Education* (Centre for Early Childhood Development and Education 2006). Drawing on an extensive research base (Duignan and Walsh 2004, Fallon 2005, Schonfeld et al. 2004), some of which also shaped *Aistear*, *Síolta*'s standards on Curriculum, Play, Interactions and Parents and Families had particular relevance.

Aistear

Overall, eight years of development work incorporating high levels of engagement with the sector and an unwavering commitment to high-quality experiences for children, culminated in the publication of *Aistear: The Early Childhood Curriculum Framework* in October 2009. As a national curriculum framework developed in the first decade of the new millennium, *Aistear* is shaped by the social, political and educational thinking of that time. Twelve principles prioritize early childhood as a unique and critical stage in the educational journey, children's relationships with others and the interactional nature of early learning and development. The principles espouse an image of children as competent, curious and active, and present learning as essentially social, interactional and involving meaning-making. They present the significant adults in children's lives, including practitioners and parents, as facilitators of learning.

Aistear signalled a new way of thinking about how learning is described and presented in a curriculum. This involved moving away from seeing young children's learning in terms of developmental domains to using a more holistic and integrated approach supported in Ireland's first *National Children's Strategy* (Government of Ireland 2000). This was achieved in *Aistear* using four interconnected and interdependent themes: Wellbeing, Identity and Belonging, Communicating, and Exploring and Thinking. These themes and their broad aims and learning goals provided a structure for describing the types of experiences that are important for children. It was hoped that this approach would also encourage and enable a better integration of care and education, and the use of a nurturing pedagogy as explored by Hayes (2007).

Towards curriculum implementation

Hopes ran high that an implementation strategy and appropriate resources would support practitioners in translating *Aistear* into practice. The reality proved different. An economic crash followed by a deep recession resulted in a period of austerity impacting children's lives (Devine 2015). Recognizing the need to support the sector in this challenging environment, the NCCA and Early Childhood Ireland collaborated on an initiative aptly named *Aistear in Action*. Drawing on the work of Witherell and Noddings (1991), Carr (2001) and Wilson (2011), the initiative gathered practitioners' stories of using *Aistear* to develop and enrich the curriculum they provided for children during the 'free preschool year'.[1] It was hoped that these stories, like those used in the previous decade to spotlight rich practices, would, in turn, provide insights into the process of curriculum development within services and, through these, support other practitioners.

As part of the initiative, practitioners shared their experiences of using *Aistear*. Through this, they developed a shared understanding of the

---

1   Reflecting the introduction of the Early Childhood Care and Education Scheme (ECCE) in 2010, the *Aistear in Action* initiative focused on the preschool year. See <https://www.gov.ie/en/publication/d7a5e6-early-childhood-care-and-educat ion-ecce-or-free-preschool/#early-childhood-care-and-education-ecce> for information on ECCE.

complexity of their work which further motivated them to engage with *Aistear* in more meaningful and sophisticated ways. The initiative high-lighted important messages about supporting and enabling curriculum change, and the role of reflective practice and mentoring as part of this. This is captured in the words of one service participating in the initiative, 'We have come to see the true value in an emergent curriculum; we have become more reflective in our practice and are looking at what we are doing to see the true value for the children … We have learned to step back, slow things down' (NCCA and Early Childhood Ireland 2013: 20).

Months after the initiative, Minister Fitzgerald, the then Minister for Children and Youth Affairs, launched *Right from the Start*, the report of the Expert Advisory Group on the Early Years Strategy (Department of Children and Youth Affairs 2013). The report highlighted the need to develop a national plan for the phased, supported and simultaneous implementation of *Síolta* and *Aistear*. It was hoped that this plan would help the roll out of the two frameworks across the sector, including in all services and at the levels of inspectors and those involved in further and higher education programmes.

Curriculum implementation proceeded in a slow, piecemeal fashion largely on foot of, and supported by, the efforts and commitments of organizations at regional and national levels. While this work enabled some settings to build familiarity with, to interrogate and to make sense of *Aistear*, the new curriculum framework continued to exist in name only for many settings. Furthermore, in the case of primary schools where many 4- and 5-year-olds were educated, teachers faced the challenge of working with the principles and pedagogies of *Aistear* alongside the Primary School Curriculum (DES 1999). This tension was reflected in Gray and Ryan's study (2016) in which they reported concerns about teachers' ability to teach curriculum subjects through play and noted the primary curriculum as a barrier to the successful implementation of *Aistear* in infant classes. Some teachers benefited from the *Aistear* Tutor Initiative, a collaboration initiated in 2010 between the then Association of Teacher Education Centres in Ireland (ATECI) and the NCCA (Uí Chadhla, Forster and Hough 2014). This initiative provided continuing professional development (CPD) which many teachers availed of and which, in turn, supported the development of play pedagogy, based on *Aistear*, in primary schools.

Drawing on the learning from *Aistear in Action* and concerned by the fragmented approach to implementation, the NCCA wrote to the Minister for Education and Skills calling for the prioritization of a comprehensive, coordinated approach to implementing *Aistear*. The period that followed saw the NCCA, on foot of a request from the Ministers for Education and Skills, and Children and Youth Affairs, developing the online *Aistear Síolta Practice Guide* (NCCA 2016) to provide practical assistance to settings as they worked with *Aistear* and *Síolta*. This online resource (available at: <https://www.aistearsiolta.ie/en/>) became a key reference point for the work of the newly established Better Start, Quality Development Service. Established by the Department of Children and Youth Affairs (DCYA), the Service supported practitioners' curriculum work by providing professional mentoring and coaching, CPD and expert early learning and care advice. In 2016, the *National Síolta Aistear Initiative* was established to provide targeted supports aimed at raising the quality of children's experiences. The initiative is grounded in the two national frameworks and provides tailored CPD responding to settings' needs and to national priorities.

Eleven and a half years on from its publication and *Aistear* has helped shape children's experiences in early childhood as well as the early years of primary. This upwash effect has been most visible in shaping thinking about the transition from preschool to primary school, especially from the perspective of supporting continuity of experiences and progression in children's learning. This thinking is reflected in the *Draft Primary Curriculum Framework* (NCCA 2020). Setting out directions for the re-development of the primary curriculum, this draft framework proposes moving from subjects in the early years of primary to broader, more integrated curriculum areas which connect with *Aistear*'s themes. In addition, the draft framework promotes the importance of appropriately playful learning opportunities for children in these years. This upward influence of *Aistear* acknowledges and celebrates the playful practice of practitioners across the early childhood sector, including primary school teachers working in infant classrooms.

Future directions

In conclusion, the history of ECEC curriculum in Ireland outside the primary school system is relatively short, primarily spanning the last five decades. Yet, it tells the story of a sector growing from a solid practice base and being shaped by emerging thinking about children's competences and innate drive to interact in, and to make sense of, their world. It is also a story of the meeting of two curriculum traditions in the process of developing Ireland's first curriculum framework for early childhood. Important factors bridging these traditions include young children's lived experiences, their innate curiosity and desire to make sense of their world, which fuels their imagination, creativity and explorations, and adults' central role in facilitating and enriching this.

This image of the young child as competent and proactive, and the companion image of practitioners scaffolding learning, marks a changing conceptualization of curriculum. An important dimension of this new understanding of curriculum is the dynamic interplay between practice, research and policy, each informing and shaping the others. This vision of curriculum positions practitioners as curriculum makers working with complex ideas as they respond to, and take account of, children's 'here and now'. Such a conceptualization calls for a new relationship in curriculum that focuses, not on readiness to progress onwards, but on the strengths of both the ECE and compulsory school education systems (OECD 2001) and is about 'a strong and equal partnership' (*Ibid.*: 128) between ECEC and compulsory school education. Realizing such a vision, however, is challenging and likely to require strategic and creative thinking about initial professional education and CPD, funding and resourcing, employment conditions, policy alignment, and ongoing collaboration and partnership with the whole sector.

As we look ahead, it will be important to check in with *Aistear* in light of developments since 2009 and ascertain where and what updates may be helpful. Relevant developments since 2009 include practitioners' and children's experiences of working with the framework, evolving philosophies, research, changing societal values and a much changed policy landscape. This landscape includes the redevelopment of the primary curriculum for the first time since 1999. The updating of *Aistear*, commenced in 2021, together with the redevelopment of the primary curriculum will help to ensure greater curriculum synergy and connections, thereby better supporting young children's learning as they journey through early childhood and into primary school. In turn, this will help to ensure that *Aistear* continues to support appropriately rich and engaging learning experiences for all children.

Bibliography

Bredecamp, S. (ed.) (1987). *Developmentally Appropriate Practice in Early Childhood Programs Serving Children from Birth through Age 8*. Washington, DC: NAEYC.

Brennan, C. (ed.) (2004). *Power of Play: A Play Curriculum in Action*. Dublin: IPPA.

Bronfenbrenner, U. (1979). *The Ecology of Human Development*. Cambridge: Cambridge University Press.

Bruce, T. (2001). *Learning through Play: Babies, Toddlers, and the Foundation Years*. London: Hodder and Stoughton.

Bruner, J. (1996). *The Culture of Education*. Cambridge: Harvard University Press.

Carr, M. (2001). *Assessment in Early Childhood Settings: Learning Stories*. London: Paul Chapman.

Carswell, D. (2002). *Child's Play: An Exploration into the Quality of Childcare Processes*. Dublin: IPPA.

Centre for Early Childhood Development and Education (2006). *Síolta, The National Quality Framework for Early Childhood Education*. Dublin: CECDE.

Coolahan, J. (1998). *Report on the National Forum for Early Childhood Education*. Dublin: The Stationery Office.

Crowe, B. (1971a). *Playgroup Activities*. London: Pre-school Playgroups Association.

Crowe, B. (1971b). *The Playgroup Movement: A Report by the National Adviser to the Pre-school Playgroups Association*. London: Pre-school Playgroups Association.

Crowe, B. (1973). *The Playgroup Movement*. London: Allen and Unwin Ltd.

Dahlberg, G., Moss, P. and Pence, A. R. (1999). *Beyond Quality in Early Childhood Education and Care: Postmodern Perspectives*. London: Falmer Press.

Daly, M. and Forster, A. (2009). 'The Story of *Aistear*: The Early Childhood Curriculum Framework: Partnership in Action', *An Leanbh Óg, The OMEP Ireland Journal of Early Childhood Studies*, 3 (1), 55–72.

Department of Children and Youth Affairs (2013). *Right from the Start. Report of the Expert Advisory Group on the Early Years Strategy*. Dublin: Government Publications Office.

Department of Education and Science (1999). *Primary School Curriculum*. Dublin: DES.

Department of Education and Science (2009). *Developing the Workforce in the Early Childhood Care and Education Sector: Background Discussion Paper*. Available at: <https://www.education.ie/en/schools-colleges/information/early-years/eye_background_discussion_paper.pdf>.

Devine, D. (2015). The Austerity Generation: It's a Perilous Time to Be a Child in Ireland. *The Irish Times*, March 2. Available at: <https://www.irishtimes.com/news/education/the-austerity-generation-it-s-a-perilous-time-to-be-a-child-in-ireland-1.2118715>.

Douglas, F. (1994). *The History of the Irish Preschool Playgroups Association*. Dublin: IPPA. Available at: <https://omepireland.ie/wp-content/uploads/2019/07/History-of-the-IPPA.pdf>.

Duignan, M. and Walsh, T. (2004). *Insights on Quality: A National Review of Policy, Practice and Research Relating to Quality in Early Childhood Care and Education in Ireland 1990–2004*. Dublin: CECDE.

Dunphy, E. (2008). *Supporting Early Learning and Development through Formative Assessment*. Background paper to the Framework for Early Learning. Commissioned by the NCCA. Available at: <https://ncca.ie/media/1112/how-aistear-was-developed-research-papers.pdf>.

Fallon, J. (ed.) (2005). *Early Childhood in Ireland: Evidence and Perspectives*. Dublin: CECDE.

French, G. (2007). *Children's Early Learning and Development*. Background paper to the Framework for Early Learning. Commissioned by the NCCA. Available at: <https://ncca.ie/media/1112/how-aistear-was-developed-research-papers.pdf>.

Government of Ireland (1998). *Education Act*. Dublin: The Irish Statute Book.

Government of Ireland (1999). *Ready to Learn: White Paper on Early Education*. Dublin: The Stationery Office.

Government of Ireland (2000). *National Children's Strategy – Our Children – Their Lives*. Dublin: Government Publications Office.

Gray, C. and Ryan, A. (2016). '*Aistear* vis-à-vis the Primary Curriculum: The Experiences of Early Years Teachers in Ireland', *International Journal of Early Years Education*, 24 (2), 188–205.

Hayes, N. (2002). *Children's Rights – Whose Right? A Review of Child Policy Development in Ireland*. Dublin: The Policy Institute, Trinity College Dublin.

Hayes, N. (2007). *Perspectives on the Relationship Between Education and Care in Early Childhood*. Background Paper to the Framework for Early Learning. Commissioned by the NCCA. Available at: <https://ncca.ie/media/1112/how-aistear-was-developed-research-papers.pdf>.

Hayes, N. and Bradley, S. (2006). *A Decade of Reflections. Conference Proceedings*. Dublin: CSER/DIT. Available at: <https://www.academia.edu/5979425/A_Decade_of_Reflection_Early_Childhood_Care_and_Education_in_Ireland_1996_2006?email_work_card=view-paper>.

Hedges, H. (2012). 'Teachers' Funds of Knowledge: A Challenge to Evidence-based Practice', *Teachers and Teaching*, 18 (1), 7–24. DOI: 10.1080/13540602.2011.622548

Irish Preschool Playgroups Association (1993a). *Information Pack*. Dublin: IPPA.

Irish Preschool Playgroups Association (1993b). *The IPPA Border Counties High/Scope Project 1997–1999*. Dublin: IPPA.

Irish Preschool Playgroups Association (2006). *Nurture through Nature*. Dublin: IPPA.

Isaacs, S. (1952). *The Educational Value of the Nursery School*. London: Headly Brothers Ltd.

Kernan, M. (2007). *Play as a Context for Early Learning and Development*. Background paper to the Framework for Early Learning. Commissioned by the NCCA. Available at: <https://ncca.ie/media/1112/how-aistear-was-developed-research-papers.pdf>.

Lave, J. and Wenger, E. (1991). *Situated Learning. Legitimate Peripheral Participation*. Cambridge: University of Cambridge Press.

Lawrence-Lightfoot, S. and Hoffmann Davis, J. (1997). *The Art and Science of Portraiture*. San Francisco: Jossey-Bass.

Moss, P. (2013). The Relationship between Early Childhood and Compulsory Education: A Properly Political Question. In P. Moss (ed.), *Early Childhood and Compulsory Education: Reconceptualising the Relationship*, pp. 2–50. Oxon: Routledge.

National Children's Nurseries Association (1998). *Towards Quality Daycare*. Dublin: NCNA.

National Council for Curriculum and Assessment (2001). *Early Childhood Framework for Learning: Background Paper*. Dublin: NCCA.

National Council for Curriculum and Assessment (2004). *Towards a Framework for Early Learning: Draft Proposals*. Dublin: NCCA.

National Council for Curriculum and Assessment (2007). *Listening for Children's Stories: Children as Partners in the Framework for Early Learning, A Portraiture*

Study. Dublin: NCCA. Available at: <https://ncca.ie/media/4086/how-aist
ear-was-developed-a-portraiture-study.pdf>.

National Council for Curriculum and Assessment (2009). *Aistear: The Early Childhood Curriculum Framework.* Dublin: NCCA.

National Council for Curriculum and Assessment (2016). *Aistear Síolta Practice Guide.* Dublin: NCCA. Available at: < https://www.aistearsiolta.ie/en/>.

National Council for Curriculum and Assessment (2020). *Draft Primary Curriculum Framework.* Dublin: NCCA. Available at: <https://ncca.ie/media/4870/en-primary-curriculum-framework-dec-2020.pdf>.

National Council for Curriculum and Assessment and Early Childhood Ireland (2013). *Aistear in Action Initiative: Final Report, A Collaboration between NCCA and Early Childhood Ireland.* Dublin: NCCA/ECI. Available at: <https://ncca.ie/media/2019/aia_report.pdf>.

New Zealand Ministry of Education (1996). *Te Whariki: Early Childhood Curriculum.* Wellington: Learning Media.

Northern Ireland Preschool Playgroup Association (1993). *Policy and Practice Guidelines for Running a Crèche.* Belfast: NIPPA.

Organisation for Economic Cooperation and Development (2001). *Starting Strong: Early Childhood Education and Care.* Paris: OECD.

Organisation for Economic Cooperation and Development (2004). *Thematic Review of Early Childhood Education and Care Policy in Ireland.* Paris: OECD.

Priestley, M. and Philippou, S. (2018). 'Curriculum Making as Social Practice: Complex Webs of Enactment', *Curriculum Journal,* 29 (2), 151–158.

Project E.Y.E. (2000). *Project E.Y.E., An Irish Curriculum for the Three to Four Year Old Child.* University College Cork: Early Years Unit, Education Department.

Queensland School Curriculum Council (2001). *Preschool Curriculum Guidelines.* <www.gld.gov.au/preschool>, accessed February 2001 to support the development of *Aistear: The Early Childhood Curriculum Framework.*

Rogers, C. R. (1969). *Freedom to Learn.* Columbus, OH: Merrill.

Rogoff, B. (1990). *Apprenticeship in Thinking: Cognitive Development in Social Context.* Oxford: Oxford University Press.

Schonfeld, H., Kiernan, G. and Walsh, T. (2004). *Making Connections: A Review of International Policies, Practices and Research Relating to Quality in Early Childhood Care and Education.* Dublin: CECDE.

Scottish Council on the Curriculum (1999). *Curriculum Framework for Children 3 to 5.* Dundee: SCCC.

South Australian Curriculum Standards and Accountability (SACSA) (2001). *The Final Draft SACSA Framework: Early Years Band.* <http://www2.nexus.edu.au/ems/sacsa/downloads/finaldraft/early_years/e_learners.html>, accessed in February 2001 to support the development of *Aistear: The Early Childhood Curriculum Framework*.

St Nicholas Montessori College (1996). *Early Childhood (2 1/2–6)*. Dublin: St Nicholas Montessori College.

Sweden Ministry of Education (1998). *Curriculum for Pre-school*. Available at: <http://www.skolverket.se/english/publ.shtml>.

Trevarthen, C. (2011). 'What Is It Like to Be a Person Who Knows Nothing? Defining the Active Intersubjective Mind of a Newborn Human Being', *Infant and Child Development*, 20, 119–135.

Uí Chadhla, N., Forster, A. and Hough, M. (2014). 'The *Aistear* Tutor Initiative – A Collaboration between the National Council for Curriculum and Assessment and the Association of Teachers' Education Centres in Ireland', *An Leanbh Óg OMEP Journal*, 8, 201–213.

Vygotsky, L. (1986). *Thought and Language*. Revised and edited by Alex Kozulin, Cambridge, MA: MIT Press.

Walsh, T. (2005). 'Constructions of Childhood in Ireland in the Twentieth Century: A View from the Primary School Curriculum 1900–1999', *Child Care in Practice*, 11 (2), 253–269.

Walsh, T. (2012). *Primary Education in Ireland 1897–1990: Curriculum and Context*. Bern: Peter Lang.

Wayman, S. (2009). 'A Time to Let Them Play', *Irish Times*, 7 April 2009. Available at: https://www.irishtimes.com/news/health/time-to-let-them-play-1.739844>.

Wilson, T. (2011). *Redirect The Surprising New Science of Psychological Change*. Boston, MA: Little Brown and Company.

Witherell, C. and Noddings, N. (1991). *Stories Lives Tell: Narrative and Dialogue in Education*. New York: Teacher College Press.

6 The road less travelled: The journey
    towards establishing a graduate-led early childhood
    education and care workforce in Ireland

Introduction

In Ireland, the State has traditionally held responsibility for children's education with children's care considered the private responsibility of the family. Consequently, in spite of growing recognition that both care and education are essential for a child's holistic development and, should be provided in a complementary seamless fashion (Government of Ireland 1999), a deeply entrenched split system of 'care and education', often exacerbated by policy decisions, prevails to the present day.

Although the infant classes in primary school date back to the foundation of the national education system in 1831, the State had limited involvement in children's early education outside of primary school. With the exception of some State-funded preschool provision for children in areas of disadvantage, there was no system of early childhood education and care (ECEC) outside of formal schooling in Ireland up to the late 1990s. Thus, while teacher education in primary schools has been an all-graduate profession since 1974, the need for pre-service qualifications and continuous professional development for those working in the ECEC sector (i.e., with children from birth to 6 years) outside the school system has, historically, been overlooked. Yet, across the world, ECEC is associated with a broad range of positive outcomes for individuals and society, including labour market activation/consolidation, education, economic and social benefits (i.e., improved child health and wellbeing) (European Commission [EC] 2019). It is also associated with increased success in employment, social

integration and reduced criminality in adulthood (Melhuish et al. 2015).
Clearly, the complexity of working with young children is increasingly recognized and the early childhood workforce is considered central to realizing
universally accessible, high-quality ECEC provision (EC 2014, International
Labour Organization [ILO] 2014, Urban et al. 2012). In particular, well-
qualified staff whose initial and continuing training enables them to fulfil
their professional role is essential (EC 2014, 2019, ILO 2014, Organisation
for Economic Cooperation and Development [OECD] 2019).

This chapter, which explores the journey towards establishing a
graduate-led workforce, discusses and critiques a number of influencing
issues and the seminal events along the way. These issues and events are
presented, in chronological order, in so far as possible. The chapter begins
with the historical evolution of the sector, followed by a spotlight on the
rise of ECEC, including commentary on the macro level of governance
of the sector, investment and the early education and care divide. It then
discusses the Model Framework for Education, Training and Professional
Development, the National Framework of Qualifications and the Workforce
Development Plan. The Early Childhood Care and Education (ECCE)
Scheme, which resulted in the most significant change in qualification profiles thus far, is addressed as are the establishment of mandatory training
requirements and the reforming of ECEC awards. A conclusive summation
is preceded by reference to achieving a graduate-led workforce.

Historical evolution of ECEC

The Irish Constitution, Bunreacht na hÉireann (1937), reflected societal
mores concerning the roles and responsibilities of women in the home as
reflected in Article 41.2:

> The State recognises that by her life within the home, woman gives to the State
> a support without which the common good cannot be achieved. The State shall,
> therefore, endeavour to ensure that mothers shall not be obliged by economic ne-
> cessity to engage in labour to the neglect of their duties in the home. (Government
> of Ireland 1937: 164)

Scannell (1988) suggests two possible interpretations of the provision: (1) it is a tribute to women's work in the home and a guarantee that no mother will be forced to work outside of the home, (2) it implies that the natural vocation of woman is in the home. Alongside Article 41.2, the marriage bar, introduced in 1932, required women working in the civil service and wider public and semi-State sectors to leave employment upon marriage. As the marriage-bar was not lifted until 1973, the majority of children were cared for at home (primarily by the mother), until they attended primary school.

At the foundation of the Irish State, however, a new dawn of progressive ideas highlighting the importance of early childhood and with a focus on early childhood education emerged. In 1943, the Dominican Sisters founded the Froebel College of Education in Dublin, premised upon the educational philosophy of Friedrich Froebel (1782–1852), founder of the Kindergarten movement. Froebel believed that children have inborn knowledge and skills and are innately creative beings (French 2007). Froebel emphasized the importance of play, active learning, nature, movement and happiness (Nolan 2012). The Department of Education agreed to recognize this training, which meant that graduates of the Froebel College of Education were eligible to work as primary school teachers. In 2013, the Froebel Department of Primary and Early Childhood Education at Maynooth University was formally established.

Maria Montessori (1870–1952), an advocate for independent learning, the use of sensory materials, child-sized equipment and furniture and freedom of choice for children, visited the first Montessori school in Ireland, led by Sr Gertrude Allman in Waterford in 1927. As Montessori schools multiplied throughout the country, the Dominican College, Dublin provided the first training course in 1943; followed by the St Nicholas's Montessori Training centre in 1970 (Mhic Mhathúna and Taylor 2012). As the Department of Education does not recognize this degree for mainstream primary teaching, graduates of these courses tend to work in early childhood settings or special and inclusive settings.

The *Vocational Education Act 1930* enabled the establishment of Vocational Schools and Technical Colleges and provided opportunities for professional development, which occurs after second level schooling but which is not part of the third level system. There are many Further and Adult Education and Training providers with a wide variety of schools, organizations and institutions involved in the delivery of ECEC courses.

In 1979, the then Dublin Institute of Technology (now the Technological University Dublin [TU Dublin]) established the first one-year general certificate course in early childhood, with University College Cork establishing the first three-year degree programme in 2000. The section on *Reforming Early Childhood Education and Care Awards* below explains that all undergraduate degree programmes are now of four years' duration. Currently, eighteen Higher Education Institutions (HEIs) offer undergraduate programmes in ECEC.

In areas designated as socio-economically disadvantaged, the then Department of Education and Science (DES) launched the Early Start PreSchool Pilot Project in 1994. Although established as 'a one year targeted intervention for three-year-old children considered most at risk of not reaching their potential within the education system' (OECD 2004: 32), Early Start remains a pilot to this day. As such, forty Early Start preschools continue to operate within primary schools in Ireland, with a fully qualified teacher and a childcare assistant. Hayes (2005) indicates that the establishment of the Early Start project unsettled the status quo causing the wider early education sector to review its position. Furthermore, outside of areas designated as disadvantaged, the State overlooked the right of *every* child to quality preschool provision.

Two events, however, underpinned a significant focus upon the ECEC sector from 1999 onwards; Ireland's ratification of the United Nations Convention on the Rights of the Child (UNCRC) (United Nations 1989) in 1992 and the convening of the National Forum for Early Childhood Education in 1998 (Coolahan 1998).

A spotlight on early childhood education and care (ECEC)

When Ireland ratified the UNCRC, it signalled a greater realization by the State of children's rights. While it reaffirms the parents' role in the upbringing and education of the child, the UNCRC stipulates that State parties shall 'take all appropriate measures to ensure that children of working parents have the right to benefit from childcare facilities and services for which they are eligible' (United Nations 1989: Articles 18.2 and 18.3). Nonetheless, the need for quality ECEC did not come to national attention until 1998, when Professor John Coolahan convened and chaired the National Forum for Early Childhood Education. The Forum provided the first opportunity in Ireland for diverse groups and organizations[1] to explore a broad range of issues related to the provision of ECEC for children from birth to 6 years (Coolahan 1998). The Forum report contributed to *Ready to Learn*, the White Paper on Early Childhood Education (Government of Ireland 1999a). Focussing upon quality ECEC for children aged birth to 6 years, the White Paper notes the inextricable link between care and education. Its stated aim is to:

> support the development and educational achievement of children through high quality early education, with a particular focus on the disadvantaged and children with special needs. The Paper sets out a comprehensive strategy to raise and maintain standards in respect of professional competencies, curriculum and methodologies. (*Ibid.*: 5)

Significantly, *Ready to Learn* asserts that 'the task of ensuring that high-quality education and care services are made available to young children depends, in a crucial way, on the quality and training of the personnel involved … ' (*Ibid.*: 9). Referring to the ad hoc manner in which the system of training and qualifications for early childhood workers had developed, the White Paper notes certain weaknesses in the existing system relating to 'inconsistency in standards, lack of consumer awareness regarding the skills developed by training programmes and difficulties regarding progression between levels of qualification' (*Ibid*: 9).

To redress the weaknesses, it proposed the development of a strategy including the designation of suitable qualifications and the establishment of clear routes of progression. Noting the validity of expertise gained through

---

1   Service providers, parents, teachers, teacher educators, care workers, statutory and voluntary agencies and social partners.

experience, the White Paper indicated that any changes regarding qualifications in ECEC generally must be phased in over time and require regular review, evaluation and revision of policy developments relating to qualifications. It is questionable, however, whether the State intended that the training and qualifications of staff would continue to develop in an ad hoc manner for a further seventeen years following the publication of the White Paper.

As the State sought to address the childcare needs of working mothers following unprecedented economic growth from the mid-1990s, the establishment of a physical childcare infrastructure took precedence over training and qualifications. As increasing numbers of women entered the labour market, the State sought to invest in the development of ECEC settings, beginning in 1999/2000. The absence of comprehensive macro level governance of the sector between 1999 and 2020 (Fig 1) perpetuated the delay in addressing the continued ad hoc development of staff training and qualifications.

To create a more integrated response to various child policy issues, the government created a post of Junior Minister for Children, with the first appointed in 2005. In keeping with a recommendation within *Ready to Learn,* an Early Years Education Policy Unit (EYEPU) was established in the DES (co-located within the Office of the Minister for Children and Youth Affairs). Five years later, when responsibility for the sector transferred to the newly established Department of Children and Youth Affairs (DCYA), a full Ministerial post was established.

Figure 1: Overview of macro-level governance of the ECEC sector, 1999–2020. The focus in Figure 1 is on the non-school ECEC sector.

Investing in an ECEC infrastructure

Following the publication of the *National Childcare Strategy* (Government of Ireland 1999b), the Department of Justice Equality and Law Reform (DJELR) established a National Childcare Coordinating Committee (NCCC) to advance implementation of the Strategy. The DJLER negotiated funding for *childcare* through the equality measures of the European Structural Funds (ESF), resulting in the Equal Opportunities Childcare Programme (EOCP 2000–2006). Funding under the EOCP supported local communities to increase childcare places in areas designated as disadvantaged and funded the creation of new childcare places to assist employees reconcile work and family commitments. A core objective was that the State would contribute to eliminating inequalities and promote equality between men and women (National Development Plan/ Structural Cohesion Fund 2003). Overall, the EOCP sought to improve the quality and quantity of childcare provision in Ireland from both an equal opportunities and disadvantaged perspective.

In the community/not for profit sector, while staffing grants to the sum of €190 million supported staff salaries for 1,280 full-time staff and 1,568 part-time staff, professional qualifications were not required. Moloney (2014) argues that in spite of creating 33,582 new childcare places nationally, the EOCP achieved limited progress as regards ECEC quality and did not advance policy objectives relating to professional qualifications. According to Hayes (2005), the initial development and expansion of ECEC in Ireland was underpinned by twin policy agendas relating to labour force equality and educational inequality, led by the *National Childcare Strategy* (Government of Ireland 1999b) and the White Paper (Government of Ireland 1999a), respectively. While both policies related to the same population of children, they were implemented separately, 'with childcare part of the equality and work agenda and early education part of the strategy for combating educational disadvantage' (Hayes 2010: 67). Thus, a clear distinction between childcare and early education was maintained, leading to inordinate disparities in relation to quality enhancement and training and qualifications across the sectors.

Dichotomy between care and education

Indicative of the deeply entrenched dichotomy between childcare and early education, which prevailed in Ireland at the time of the EOCP, the task of enhancing the quality of ECEC provision rested primarily with the State-funded National Voluntary Childcare Collaborative (NVCC), comprising eight national non-governmental organizations,[2] and the City and County Childcare Committees (CCCs) established through the EOCP. The NVCC and the CCCs offered guidance, resources, networking and training opportunities to those working with young children. Indeed, the distinction between the sectors permeated the OECD (2004) thematic review of ECEC in Ireland, which identified considerable disparity between the qualifications of teachers employed in the statutory primary school sector and those employed in the non-statutory (community, voluntary and private) services.

It also noted diverse approaches to ECEC, 'from a highly formalized, subject oriented school teaching approach to a play based, informal approach with little learning taking place' (OECD 2004: 60). *Aistear*[3]: *The Early Childhood Curriculum Framework* for children from birth to 6 years of age across the range of early childhood settings was developed (NCCA 2009) and, together with *Síolta*[4], *The National Quality Framework* (CECDE 2006), provides clear guidance regarding the scope and nature of professional practice in ECEC (DES 2010). Overall, however, the State prioritized issues of access and affordability, giving scant attention to the preparation of early childhood teachers working outside the primary school system, or the quality and duration of initial early childhood teacher preparation programmes (Moloney in press). Nonetheless, between 1998 and 2002, many

2   Irish Preschool Playgroups Association, Forbairt Naíonraí Teo, National Children's Nurseries Association, Childminding Ireland, St Nicholas Montessori Society of Ireland, Irish Steiner Kindergarten Association, Children in Hospital Ireland and Barnardos.
3   *Aistear* is the Irish word for journey.
4   *Síolta* is the Irish word for seeds.

initiatives contributed to progressing education and training in the ECEC sector. For instance, the National Children's Nurseries Association (NCNA) developed and facilitated a National Diploma in Nursery Management in UCD, while FÁS[5] offered the Childcare Traineeship Programme, as well as Childcare Supervisor courses. In the absence of a comprehensive State-led approach to staff training, these various initiatives played an invaluable role in supporting the professional development of staff and enhancing the quality of ECEC provision. As discussed in the following section, an EU funded childcare project led to one of the most significant developments in the history of ECEC in Ireland, the *Model Framework for Education, Training and Professional Development* (DJELR 2002), which has stood the test of time to the present day.

Model framework for education, training and professional development

Hayes explains how:

> an EU funded childcare project – the DIT/NOW OMNA early childhood training project – offered an opportunity for the sector to come together and review childcare services, identify training requirements and develop, ultimately, a model framework for training and education for early years staff. (Hayes 2005: 8)

On completion of the OMNA project (OMNA 2000), the team from the Centre for Social and Educational Research (CSER) at TU Dublin was appointed as Technical Assistance to the Certification Bodies Sub-group of the NCCC to consult on and develop a framework for training in the ECEC sector (DJELR 2002). Although ECEC policy initiatives

---

5   An Foras Áiseanna Saothair (Irish) referred to in English as the Training and Employment Authority and commonly known as FÁS, was a state agency in Ireland with responsibility for assisting those seeking employment.

generally focus upon children aged birth to 6 years, the Model Framework (DJELR 2002) addressed the education and training of those responsible for the care and education of children between birth and 8 years, thus reflecting certain international definitions of ECEC as encompassing the period from birth to 8 years (see <https://omepworld.org/identity-2/>). However, while the practice frameworks *Síolta* (CECDE 2006) and *Aistear* (NCCA 2009) refer to and support practice in infant classes in primary school, the Model Framework does not explicitly address primary teacher education (DES 2010).

The Model Framework (DJELR 2002: 11) identified five occupational profiles and associated skills/attributes depending on the role of the childcare practitioner, ranging from Basic Practitioner to Expert Practitioner. Experience, as well as education and training, were recognised as valid routes to the achievement of the various practitioner profiles.

The Model Framework (DJELR 2002: 12) also identified six core knowledge areas for ECEC practitioners as follows:

- Personal professional development
- Social environment
- Health, hygiene, nutrition and safety
- Education and play
- Communication, administration and management
- Child development.

Each area was presented as equally important, interdependent and interrelated, forming the basis for the organisation and development of education, training and qualifications for the ECEC profession.

Notwithstanding the publication of the Model Framework, the State did little to support further development of occupational role profiles or consolidate statutory qualification requirements. Consequently, no less than 500 qualifications remain acceptable to work with young children aged birth to 6 years in Ireland (details available at <https://www.gov.ie/pdf/?file=https://assets.gov.ie/137069/92c267cc-b02f-4d6d-8c6c-7cd2b0df7ddd.pdf#page=null>). This anomaly foregrounded the introduction of professional award criteria and guidelines for the sector in 2019 (see section on Reforming ECEC awards).

National Framework of Qualifications (NFQ)

The *Qualifications (Education and Training) Act* (Government of Ireland 1999c) gave responsibility for developing and validating sectoral stand-ards across all levels of the NFQ to four Awarding Bodies, i.e., the Further Education and Training Awards Council (FETAC), the Higher Education and Training Awards Council (HETAC), the Institutes of Technology (IOT) and the Universities. The NFQ is a 10-level, single framework for the development, recognition and awarding of qualifica-tion in Ireland (see <https://nfq.qqi.ie/>).

In 2012, the *Qualifications and Quality Assurance (Education and Training) Act* (Government of Ireland 2012) established an independent State Agency, Quality and Qualifications Ireland (QQI)[6], which took over the functions of these four bodies. Among its many roles, QQI pro-motes, maintains and develops the NFQ. As the occupational profiles set out in the Model Framework preceded the development of the NFQ, it was not possible to map the occupational profiles onto the framework in 2002. They have since been validated against the NFQ and against *Síolta* and *Aistear.* Consequently, the DES (2010) indicated they should form the basis for the development of award standards at all levels of the NFQ. While the DES suggestion remained aspirational until the publication of award criteria and guidelines in 2019, it is apparent that the need to address the issue of qualifications had been recognized by the State as evidenced by the publication of a Workforce Development Plan (WDP) in 2010.

Workforce Development Plan (WDP)

The publication of the WDP for ECEC defined early childhood as the period from birth to 6 years and recommended supporting the early

6   Quality and Qualifications Ireland is the national agency responsible for qualifica-tions and quality assurance in further education and training and higher education in Ireland.

childhood workforce to achieve qualifications appropriate to their occupational role and profile. It set out ambitious objectives and actions, including a recommendation that the occupational profiles set out in Model Framework (DJELR 2002), together with *Síolta* and *Aistear*, should inform the development of national awards in ECEC at all levels of the NFQ. It also addressed the requirement to meet the needs of practitioners in the workplace through flexible delivery, recognition of prior learning (RPL); quality and relevant courses, and clear progression pathways to enable learners to progress from one level of qualification to another (DES 2010). While the WDP generated much discussion in relation to qualification requirements, it was the introduction of the ECCE in 2010 that resulted in the most significant change in qualification profiles thus far.

The Early Childhood Care and Education (ECCE) Scheme

Ireland's National Partnership Agreement, *Towards 2016* (Government of Ireland 2006a) referenced the fact that childcare policy would ensure progress towards reaching the Barcelona targets[7] of making childcare available to 90 per cent of children aged between 3 years and mandatory school age. However, issues of affordability for parents predominated. In 2005, therefore, the State introduced an *Early Childcare Supplement* (ECS) of €1,104 per annum for each child under the age of 6 years to reduce the cost of childcare. From its inception in 2005 to its withdrawal in 2009, the ECS cost €480 million per annum.

The announcement of the abolition of the ECS and its replacement with a universal *Free Preschool Year* in 2010 demonstrated for the first time the State's commitment to recognize the value of early education, albeit in strictly economic terms (due to a saving of €310 million per annum in

---

7   In 2002, the Barcelona European Council set objectives with regard to the availability of high quality and affordable childcare facilities for preschool children, through two targets, i.e., ninety per cent of children from age three until mandatory school age and thirty-three per cent of children under three.

2009). While initially, children could avail of one year of free preschool provision, the State extended the Free Preschool Year[8] to two years in 2016, enabling children aged between 2 years and 8 months and 5 years and 6 months to avail of fifteen hours per week for thirty-eight weeks of the year in the two years before starting school.

From the outset of the ECCE scheme, those working directly with children were required to hold a Level 5 qualification in ECEC. Since December 2016, ECEC room leaders must hold a full NFQ Level 6 qualification. In return, the setting receives standard capitation of €69 per week for each participating child. In settings where the room leader holds a Level 7 or Level 8 Bachelor's degree and has '*three years paid post-qualification experience*' (emphasis added) … ' (DCYA n.d.), the State pays a higher capitation of €80.25 per participating child per week. The requirement for a practitioner to have three years paid experience (having already undertaken a three or a four -year degree), does not exist elsewhere in the Irish education system and creates an additional obstacle for graduate employment and, may act as a disincentive to graduates to enter the sector (Moloney and McKenna 2018).

Payment of a higher capitation is clearly an attempt by the State to create an association between qualifications and programme quality and to incentivize Level 7 and 8 graduates to work in the sector (Moloney 2015). Yet while the number of graduates working in the sector has increased from 11 per cent in 2011 to 22 per cent in 2018[9], annual turnover stands at 23 per cent (Pobal 2019). Furthermore, the higher capitation results in a 'messy patchwork' of qualifications across the birth to 6 years age cohort (Moloney 2021).

Critically, an unintended consequence of the ECCE scheme is that the most qualified staff are likely to be working with children aged 3 to 5 years. Pobal (2019) indicates that a staff member with an NFQ Level 8 or higher is twice as likely to care for children aged 3 to 5 years. Additionally, the DES only undertake early years education focussed inspections in settings participating in the ECCE scheme. This, coupled with the generally lower

8   Hereafter referred to as the ECCE scheme.
9   The most up to date figures available at the time of writing.

qualifications of those working with younger children, leads to questions about the rights of babies and toddlers to quality ECEC.

In Ireland, 3,542 children from birth to 1 year and 30,060 from 13 months to 36 months attend ECEC settings (Pobal 2019). Infant mental health and neuroscientific evidence points to the importance of nurturing education and care for babies and toddlers (French 2018a). Training and qualifications affect staff ability to provide responsive, nurturing, sensitive care and education to enhance babies' development and learning; the higher the qualification, the better the experience for the young child (Melhuish et al. 2015).

There is no financial incentive to encourage degree level graduates to work with babies and toddlers in the Irish ECEC sector. Given the immense learning and development during the first three years, babies are likely to remain in the care of the least qualified practitioners in the current policy landscape (French 2018b). While the ECCE scheme could be construed as recognizing all children's right to ECEC, the reality is that it has consolidated the age-old care/ education divide. It has therefore aligned those working with children aged 3 to school-going age with education, while those working with infants and toddlers are associated with care. The introduction of a mandatory qualification requirement in 2016 has at least ensured that staff working with infants and toddlers have a minimum level of training.

Mandatory training requirement

The first 'nod' towards a qualification requirement emerged through the *Childcare (Pre-school Services) Regulations, 2006* (Government of Ireland 2006b, Moloney 2021), which recommended that 'at least 50 per cent' of staff should hold a 'qualification appropriate to the care and development of children' and that 'qualified staff should rotate between age-groupings' (Government of Ireland 2006b: 39). Although large numbers of staff obtained a Level 5 qualification between 2006 and 2016

(Pobal 2019), the fact is that the situation where only fifty per cent of staff needed a qualification prevailed until the enactment of Part III (4a) of the *Childcare (Early Years Services) Regulations, 2016* in January 2018 (Government of Ireland 2016). The introduction of a mandatory qualification requirement occurred therefore in a context where those working with children (from 3 to 5 years) had been required to hold a qualification as part of the contractual requirements of the universal ECCE Scheme since 2010.

The *Childcare (Early Years Services) Regulations, 2016* represented a major sectoral reform, requiring that 'each employee working directly with children in an ECEC setting must hold at least a Major award in (ECEC) at Level 5 on the NFQ or a qualification deemed by the Minister to be equivalent' (Government of Ireland 2016: 12). Mirroring somewhat the Core Knowledge Areas identified in the Model Framework (DJELR 2002), the DCYA (the Department of Children, Equality, Disability, Integration and Youth [DCEDIY] since 2020) require that Major awards in ECEC must include significant content on child development birth to 6 years, early childhood curriculum and child health and welfare. Further reform of the ECEC sector in Ireland followed in 2019 with the publication of guidance on ECEC awards criteria (DES 2019).

Reforming early childhood education and care (ECEC) awards

Twenty years after Micheál Martin, TD, referenced the need to develop a strategy to raise and maintain standards relating to professional competencies (DES 1999: 5), the DES (2019) published *Professional Award Criteria and Guidelines* (PACG) *for Initial Professional Education (Level 7 and Level 8) Degree Programmes for the ECEC Sector in Ireland.* In the foreword, the then Minister for Children and Youth Affairs, Dr Katherine Zappone, T.D., stressed the need 'to future-proof and professionalize the qualifications on offer to the current and future workforce so that we can be assured that they are prepared for the responsibility to deliver high-quality learning and care experiences for their young charges' (*Ibid*.: 4). As such, the PACG seeks to support the development and review of Level 7 and 8 professional awards that lead to the formation of ECEC graduates who are fully prepared to take on the complex challenges of practice in the field. The DES further indicate that these graduates will form part of the graduate-led workforce proposed within *First 5, A Whole of Government Strategy for Babies, Young Children and their Families* (Government of Ireland 2018).

The DES (2019: 12) proposes that an ECEC professional graduate requires a combination of attributes developed through a range of experiences. Specifically these include:

- Academic attributes (e.g., establishing sound academic principles)
- Professional practice attributes (e.g., planning and developing a curriculum for children)
- Professional personal attributes (e.g., an ethical practice framework to inform practitioner practice; a capacity for reflection and critical thinking).

Premised upon *Síolta* (CECDE 2006), *Aistear* (NCCA 2009) and a competent systems approach (Urban et al. 2012), the PACG sets out the values, knowledge and practices essential for all professionals working in ECEC and specifies the integral nature of professional practice placement. A Qualifications Advisory Board (QAB) established by the DES/DCYA manages the review of new programmes for their coherence with the PACG prior to submission for validation by their authorized body (i.e., QQI or Higher Education Institutions).

QQI has also developed new awards standards for ECEC at Levels 5 and 6 (details available at: <https://www.qqi.ie/Articles/Pages/Current-consultations.aspx>). Known as Professional Award-type Descriptors (PATDs), these new award standards, for use when designing programmes leading to ECEC awards, create two new Major Awards: a Level 5 Certificate in Early Learning and Care and an Advanced Level 6 Certificate in Early Learning and Care. ECEC training providers of programmes leading to QQI awards based on the new standards must have their programmes validated by QQI before offering them to learners. Mirroring issues identified within the WDP (DES 2010), both the QQI PATD and the DES PACG make specific requirements in relation to teaching staff, and those who supervise and monitor students engaging in professional practice placement during their training.

Commenting upon the PACG, the Minister for Education and Skills, Mr. Joe McHugh, T.D., suggested that they build upon the long commitment of the DES to support the evolution of the ECEC sector in Ireland and, in particular, the professionalization of the workforce (DES 2019). He notes that:

> For the first time in the history of the sector, the workforce will have access to a suite of professional awards from entry level qualifications at Level 5 to honours degree level, that recognize the value of professionals at all these levels working in [ECEC] settings across the country. (*Ibid.*: 3)

However, as discussed in the following section, which explores the establishment of a graduate-led workforce, simply reforming awards criteria alone will not recognize the value of professionals working with young children outside the school gates.

Achieving a graduate-led workforce

First 5 proposes a 50 per cent graduate-led workforce by 2028 (Government of Ireland 2018). In spite of third level institutions offering degree level programmes in ECEC since the late 1990s (e.g., University College Cork, since 1995, Dublin Institute of Technology, since 1999 and Mary Immaculate College, since 2003), graduates currently account for 22 per cent of the workforce and qualification levels remain generally low (*Ibid.*). Without a doubt, staff turnover which stands at 23 per cent presents a considerable challenge to the establishment of a graduate-led workforce, especially as almost one third of those leaving the sector are graduates (Pobal 2019).

Staff salaries are of particular concern, with six out of ten staff earning below the living wage of €12.30 per hour (*Ibid.*). In addition, there is no correlation between qualification levels, experience and salaries for those working in, or intending to work in, the sector (Moloney 2015). It is noteworthy, therefore, that while ECEC capitation is paid directly to settings, it is not mandated that this should go to staff. There is also a tension between practical experience and graduate qualifications, as reflected in criteria associated with the higher capitation. Furthermore, as mentioned earlier, there is no mechanism to incentivize graduates to work with children aged birth to 3 years.

In order to achieve the target of establishing a graduate-led workforce, *First 5* commits to developing a Workforce Development Plan (WDP), involving collaboration between the DCEDIY and the DES. Work on developing the WDP is ongoing with the intention to ensure the appropriate number of ECEC staff at all levels in the sector, as well as setting out plans to raise the profile of careers in the sector, establish a career framework and leadership development opportunities. The WDP, which builds on the previous plan of 2010 (DES 2010), will develop a high-level vision for the sector, complete a skills forecast setting out the projected demand and supply of professionals at different qualification levels over 2020–2028 and decide on occupational roles, associated titles and qualification requirements. To date, the term 'practitioner' prevails regardless of whether somebody holds a Level 5 or a Level 8 qualification and career progression is limited. We are, however, hopeful that this matter will be addressed through the WDP and that a term more consistent with the educative nature of the role will emerge.

In a parallel process, also initiated through *First 5*, the development of a new Funding Model for the ECEC sector is underway. The international benchmark for investment in the sector is 1 per cent of GDP. Yet in spite of a 117 per cent increase in investment between 2016 and 2020 (Zappone 2019), Ireland still invests only 0.2 per cent of GDP (Early Childhood Ireland 2020). Accordingly, *First 5* commits to doubling investment to make progress towards average OECD levels of investment. We look forward to the day when Ireland will reach the 1 per cent GDP target investment, as well as the sectoral transformation such as professional remuneration and stable and consistent staff retention, that will inevitably follow.

Conclusion

This chapter establishes the slow development of the requirement for qualifications for professionals working with our youngest citizens in Ireland and the equally slow progress towards establishing a graduate-led workforce. This is in part due to a deeply entrenched split system of care and education that prevails to the present day. Led by labour market activation, the thrust of government policy has focused predominantly upon *childcare*, rather than prioritizing the rights of children to quality ECEC experiences as evinced through the UNCRC. While the State has repeatedly acknowledged the inextricable link between care and education and the relationship between staff qualifications and quality ECEC, persistent chronic under investment underscores the policy rhetoric. The sector is now in crisis with unsustainable staff turnover, which diminishes children's experiences of ECEC. The State is now embarking upon the development of a new and welcome WPD and a new Funding Model for ECEC. Issues of social justice for both children and those who care for and educate them in the early childhood period is a political imperative.

As we conclude this chapter, we are hopeful that the WDP will deliver a vision for the sector predicated on the needs and rights of children and the rights of professionals to a salary commensurate with qualifications and experience in line with professionals across the education sector (primary and post-primary). We urge the government not to view the 50 per cent graduate workforce as an end-point, but rather to view it as an interim target. The next strategy should aim for an ambitious 100 per cent graduate workforce. Nowhere else in the education sector in Ireland are we happy to have only 50 per cent of professionals trained to degree level; we must not settle for anything less for our youngest children.

Bibliography

Centre for Early Childhood Development and Education. (2006). *Síolta The National Framework for Quality in Early Childhood Care and Education.* Dublin: CECDE.

Coolahan, J. (1998). *Report on the National Forum for Early Childhood Education.* Dublin: Department of Education and Science.

Department of Children and Youth Affairs. (n.d). *Rules for ECCE Programme.* Available at: <https://assets.gov.ie/26553/8a6844640f3b422da3cff8ca18593 199.pdf>.

Department of Children and Youth Affairs. (2019). *Workforce Development Plan for the Early Learning and Care (ELC), School-Age Childcare (SAC) and Childminding Sector. Background Note and Draft Terms of Reference for the Steering Group.* Available at: <https://assets.gov.ie/26650/a384c28887494 88d8e93badc501507b3.pdf>.

Department of Education and Science. (1999). *Ready to Learn; White Paper on Early Childhood Education.* Available at: <https://www.education.ie/en/ Publications/Policy-Reports/Ready-to-Learn-White-Paper-on-Early-Childh ood-Education.pdf>.

Department of Education and Skills. (2010). *A Workforce Development Plan for the Early Childhood Care and Education Sector in Ireland.* Available at: <https:// www.education.ie/en/schools-colleges/information/early-years/eye_workfor ce_dev_plan.pdf>.

Department of Education and Skills. (2019). *Professional Award Criteria and Guidelines for Initial Professional Education (Level 7 and Level 8) Degree Programmes for the Early Learning and Care (ELC) Sector in Ireland.* Available at: <https://www.education.ie/en/The-Education-System/Early-Childhood/ professional-award-criteria-and-guidelines-for-initial-professional-education- l7-8-degree-programmes-elc-ireland.pdf>.

Department of Justice, Equality and Law Reform. (2002). *Quality Childcare and Lifelong Learning: Model Framework for Education, Training and Professional Development in the Early Childhood Education and Care Sector.* Dublin: DJELR.

Early Childhood Ireland. (2020). *Rising to the Challenge Investing in Our Future Budget 2021 Submission.* Dublin: ECI. Available at:<https://www.earlychild hoodireland.ie/wp-content/uploads/2020/09/Budget-2021-Submission- WEB.pdf>.

European Commission. (2014). *Proposal for Key Principles of a Quality Framework for Early Childhood Education and Care. Report of the Working Group on Early*

Childhood Education and Care under the auspices of the European Commission. Brussels: European Commission.

European Commission. (2019). *Council Recommendation on High-Quality Early Childhood Education and Care Systems.* C/189/4. Official Journal of the European Union. Available at: <https://eur-lex.europa.eu/legalcontent/EN/TXT/PDF/?uri=CELEX:32019H0605(01)&from=EN>.

French, G. (2007). *Children's Early Learning and Development.* Dublin: NCCA.

French, G. (2018a). *The Time of their Lives: Nurturing Babies Learning and Development in Early Childhood Settings.* Dublin: Barnardos.

French, G. (2018b). 'Tuning in to Babies: Nurturing Relationships in Early Childhood Settings'. In B. Mooney (ed.), *Ireland's Yearbook of Education 2018–2019*, pp. 105–109. Dublin: Education Matters.

Government of Ireland. (1937). *Bunreacht na hÉireann/ Constitution of Ireland.* Dublin: The Stationery Office.

Government of Ireland. (1999a). *Ready to Learn: White Paper on Early Childhood Education.* Dublin: The Stationery Office. Available at: <https://www.education.ie/en/Publications/Policy-Reports/Ready-to-Learn-White-Paper-on-Early-Childhood-Education.pdf>.

Government of Ireland. (1999b). *National Childcare Strategy: Report of the Partnership 2000 Expert Working Group on Childcare.* Dublin: The Stationery Office.

Government of Ireland. (1999c). *Qualifications (Education and Training) Act.* Dublin: The Stationery Office.

Government of Ireland. (2006a). *Towards 2016: Ten Year Framework – Social Partnership Agreement 2006–2015.* Dublin: The Stationery Office.

Government of Ireland. (2006b). S.I. No 604/2006. *Child Care (Pre-school Services) (No 2) Regulations 2006.* Available at: <http://www.irishstatutebook.ie/eli/2006/si/604/made/en/print>.

Government of Ireland. (2012). *S.I. No 28/2012. Qualifications and Quality Assurance (Education and Training) Act 2012.* Available at: <http://www.irishstatutebook.ie/eli/2012/act/28/enacted/en/html>.

Government of Ireland. (2016). *S.I. No 221/2016. Child Care Act 1991 (Early Years Services) Regulations 2016.* Available at: <http://www.irishstatutebook.ie/eli/2016/si/221/made/en/print>.

Government of Ireland. (2018). *First 5: A Whole-of-Government Strategy for Babies, Young Children and their Families.* Dublin: The Stationery Office. Available at: <https://assets.gov.ie/31184/62acc54f4bdf4405b74e53a4afb8e71b.pdf>.

Hayes, N. (2005). 'Welfare and Wellbeing: Impact of Social Policy on Early Educational Practice in Ireland'. In M. Horgan and F. Douglas (eds.), *Children of the Global Village*, Proceedings of the OMEP Ireland Conference 2004, pp. 22–31.

Hayes, N. (2010). *Early Childhood: An Introductory Text*. Dublin: Gill and Macmillan.

International Labour Organization. (2014). *Policy Guidelines on the Promotion of Decent Work for Early Childhood Education Personnel*. Available at: <http://www.ilo.org/wcmsp5/groups/public/---ed_dialogue/--sector/documents/normativeinstrument/wcms_236528.pdf>.

Melhuish, E., Ereky-Stevens, K., Petrogiannis, K., Ariescu, A., Penderi, E., Rentzou, K., Tawell, A., Leseman, P. and Broekhuisen, M. (2015). *A Review of Research on the Effects of Early Childhood Education and Care on Child Development*. Oxford: CARE with European Commission. Available at: <http://ecec-care.org/>.

Mhic Mhathuna, M. and Taylor, M. (2012). 'The Montessori Approach to Early Childhood Education'. In M. Mhic Mhathuna and M. Taylor (eds.), *Early Childhood Education and Care: An Introduction for Students in Ireland*, pp. 113–126. Dublin: Gill and MacMillan.

Moloney, M. (2021). 'Ireland's Reform Agenda: Transforming the Early Childhood Education and Care Sector into One of the Best in the World'. In W. Boyd and S. Garvis (eds.), *International Perspectives on Early Childhood Teacher Education in the 21ˢᵗ Century*. Singapore: Springer.

Moloney, M. (2014). 'Breach of Trust: Getting it Right for Children in Early Childhood Education and Care in Ireland', *NZ Journal of Research in Early Childhood Education*. Special Issue, Early Childhood Policy, 17, 71–88.

Moloney, M. (2015). *Untangling the Knots, K[not] Easy: Professional Identity in the Early Childhood Education and Care Sector*. A paper prepared for the symposium, Early Educational Alignment: Reflecting on Context, Curriculum and Pedagogy. Available at: <http://ecalignment.ie/Untangling%20the%20knots%206%2010%2015.pdf>.

Moloney, M. and O'Carroll, G. (2018). *The Proposed Apprenticeship Model*. Dublin: Education Matters. Available at: <https://educationmatters.ie/downloads/YB20172018-Early%20Childhood.pdf>.

Moloney, M. and McKenna, I. (2018). *Is It Time to Establish an Early Years Council?* Dublin: Education Matters. Available at: <https://educationmatters.ie/downloads/YB20172018-Early%20Childhood.pdf>.

National Council for Curriculum and Assessment. (2009). *Aistear: The Early Childhood Curriculum Framework*. Dublin: NCCA.

National Development Plan/Structural Cohesion Fund Evaluation Unit. (2003). *Evaluation of the Equal Opportunities Childcare Programme 2000–2006*. Dublin: NDP/CSF Evaluation Unit.

National Qualifications Authority of Ireland. (2003). *Policies and Criteria for the Establishment of the National Framework of Qualifications.* Dublin: NQAI.

Nolan, C. (2012). 'Friedrich Froebel and Early Childhood Education'. In M. Mhic Mhathúna and M. Taylor (eds.), *Early Childhood Education and Care: An Introduction for Students in Ireland*, pp. 141–46. Dublin: Gill and MacMillan.

OMNA (2000). *Final Report of OMNA – DIT/NOW Early Childhood Project 1995–2000. Life is a Learning Curve.* Dublin: Centre for Social and Educational Research, Dublin Institute of Technology.

Organisation for Economic Cooperation and Development. (2004). *OECD Thematic Review of Early Childhood Education and Care Policy in Ireland.* Paris: OECD. Available at: <https://assets.gov.ie/24598/5e8d30bb02b948ccb5fdb4bd413ab67d.pdf>.

Organisation for Economic Cooperation and Development. (2019). *Good Practice for Good Jobs in Early Childhood Education and Care.* Paris: OECD. Available at: <https://read.oecd-ilibrary.org/social-issues-migration-health/good-practice-for-good-jobs-in-early-childhood-education-and-care_64562be6-en#page1>.

Pobal. (2019). *Annual Early Years Sector Profile Report 2018–19.* Dublin: Pobal. Available at: <https://www.pobal.ie/app/uploads/2019/12/Annual-Early-Years-Sector-Profile-Report-AEYSPR-2018-19.pdf>.

Scannell, Y. (1988). 'The Constitution and the Role of Women'. In B. Farrell (ed.), *De Valera's Constitution*, pp. 124–5. Dublin: Gill and MacMillian.

United Nations. (1989). *Convention on the Rights of the Child.* New York: United Nations.

Urban, M., Vandenbroeck, M., Lazzari, A., Van Laere, K. and Peeters, J. (2012). *Competence Requirements in Early Childhood Education and Care.* Final Report. Brussels: European Commission. Directorate General for Education and Culture. Available at: <http://ec.europa.eu/education/more-information/doc/2011/core_en.pdf>.

Zappone, K. (2019). *Press Release.* Available at: <https://merrionstreet.ie/en/News-Room/Releases/Minister_Zappone_will_strengthen_child_protection_and_quality_requirements_for_early_years_services.html>.

ELIZABETH DUNPHY AND MÁIRE MHIC MHATHÚNA

7 The history and work of the Centre for Early Childhood Development and Education (CECDE) (2001–2008)

Introduction

The Centre for Early Childhood Development and Education (CECDE) was established in a context where, in Ireland, distinct traditions of 'care' and 'education' existed. State involvement in early childhood provision was uneven across the care and education divide. Apart from provision for children designated 'at risk' and in need of protection, the preschool sector had developed in a relatively ad hoc way with little State engagement with services at any level (Organisation for Economic Co-operation and Development [OECD] 2004). Meanwhile, early childhood education in infant classes (children aged 4 to 6 years) was an integral part of primary schooling from the beginning of the national system of education in Ireland from its inception in 1831 (O'Connor 2010). This gave rise to a split system of ECEC. When, at the turn of the millennium ECEC in Ireland moved to the foreground of government policy, the Department of Health was responsible for children under four and the Department of Education and Science (DES) was responsible for children aged 4 to 6. Recognition of the need to address this split was one of the overarching factors that shaped the rationale for the CECDE, the way the Agency was structured and managed, and how it progressed the task of developing and coordinating early childhood education.

This chapter offers an account of the history and work of the CECDE. It begins by describing the import, for subsequent developments in Ireland, of international and national debate regarding the development of provision for quality early childhood education and care (ECEC) in the final decade of the twentieth century. Against this background, the establishment of the CECDE is described. In chronological order, the chapter charts the work of the CECDE from its inception in 2001 until its closure in 2008. It documents the outputs of the Centre including major publications, funded PhD studies and international conferences. The significance of key outputs of the CECDE for the subsequent development of the ECEC sector are discussed. In particular, the process of the development of *Síolta, The National Quality Framework for Early Childhood Education* (CECDE 2006a), is foregrounded. The continuing influence of the framework on subsequent sectoral developments is a key theme of the chapter. Tensions and struggles culminating in the eventual closure of the CECDE in 2008 are documented. Throughout, the authors offer an insider view on the history, work and management of the CECDE, while at the same time drawing on key publications of the time to include objective commentary.

Background and context

In the decade 1990–2000, there was considerable international debate on ways of expanding the provision for ECEC, whilst ensuring an emphasis on quality (Moss and Pence 1995, Woodhead 1996). In Ireland, the 1997 programme for government, *An Action Plan for the Millennium* (Government of Ireland 1997), referenced early childhood education as an area for policy and for expenditure over the coming years. While the infant classes in primary schools provided ECEC for children aged 4 and 5 years, participation rates for children under 4 years were low compared to other European countries. A further 1,500 children availed of the DES Early Start Programme, established in 1994 in forty primary schools in designated areas of urban disadvantage. Early Start was a one-year preschool intervention designed to meet the needs of 3-to-5-year-old children deemed to be at risk of not reaching their potential within the school system.

There was also a limited but less visible number of personnel working in the preschool and childcare sector. This consisted mainly of part-time workers in small scale voluntary services with varying levels of formal qualifications, but many with rich experience of working with young children, often in disadvantaged circumstances (Department of Justice, Equality and Law Reform [DJELR] 2002). Terms and conditions of employment were often low given that there was little understanding at that time of the significance and complexity of early childhood education issues and even less state support (Coolahan et al. 2017). However, due in part to the provision of the Equal Opportunities Childcare Programme funding for capital projects, and increased staffing from 2000 onwards, a sense of vibrancy then began to grow in the sector.

Arising from the *Report on The National Forum for Early Childhood Education* (Coolahan 1998), the *White Paper on Early Childhood Education: Ready to Learn* (Government of Ireland 1999) was published. This provided for the development of an independent Early Childhood Education Agency (ECEA), charged with implementing the provisions of the *White Paper*. It also provided for an Early Years Development Unit (EYDU) within the DES to promote coordination of provision and policy formulation and to 'kickstart' developments. It was envisaged that the DES would devolve executive functions and focus on broad policy issues and high-level coordination.

There was an evident reluctance by the DES to establish the Agency in 1999. An explanation may be discerned in the statement that 'early childhood education is a relatively new area for the Department and is underdeveloped nationally' (Government of Ireland 1999: 107). An integrated perspective on care and education was certainly not yet evident in key initiatives of government. However, the *White Paper* heralded opportunities for changes in orientation of the relationship between care and education. Childcare and early childhood education had long been considered separate endeavours, both in policy development but also on the ground, and that ambivalence within the DES to the idea of an integrated approach to ECEC continued into the next decade. This dichotomy was also addressed in later reports of both the OECD (2004) and the National Economic and Social Forum (NESF) (2005).

By 2001 there was increasing interest and consequent pressure in many countries to address issues related to ECEC. *Starting Strong*, an OECD thematic study on provision and policy in twelve European countries was launched. It offered perspectives and recommendations to guide member states in developing their integrated systems (OECD 2001). This, along with expectations within the ECEC community arising from *The National Forum* (Coolahan 1998) and the *White Paper* (Government of Ireland 1999), and developments in other aligned countries, no doubt exerted some pressure on the Irish government to make a tentative move in the direction of provision of State support for children below school-going age.

Establishment of the Centre for Early Childhood Development and Care (CECDE)

In November 2001, the CECDE was announced and heralded as the forerunner of the proposed ECEA Agency. It was formally launched by the Minister for Education and Science in October 2002. A *Memorandum of Agreement* (CECDE 2001a) detailed the governance and structures of the Centre and outlined three objectives which were drawn from the 1999 *White Paper*:

- Develop a National Quality Framework (NQF) for all settings with children from birth to 6 years, including support mechanisms for staff and tools for assessment of quality
- Develop targeted interventions for children who are disadvantaged or have special needs
- Prepare the groundwork for establishment of the Early Childhood Education Agency as envisioned in the 1999 White Paper.

The Centre was jointly managed by St Patrick's College (now Dublin City University) and the Dublin Institute of Technology (now Technological University Dublin). This was a highly significant partnership which indicated willingness on the part of the two institutions, coming from two different traditions, to come together to promote the integration of care and education within the sector. The two institutions brought their own perspectives on early childhood education and this melding of perspectives led to many robust and productive debates on how ECEC should be conceptualized, and the above objectives progressed.

An annual budget (c.€1 million p.a. including salaries) was granted for each of the years the Centre was in existence. However, tensions regarding the annual approval of this budget existed from the outset and was a source of constant frustration at all levels of governance of the Centre. Each year, timely reports and requests were submitted to the DES for budget approval and each year there were long delays in securing a response. Throughout the lifetime of the Centre, this had consequential impacts on employment contracts, funded projects and the day-to-day running of the Centre.

Governance was determined by the *Memorandum of Agreement* (CECDE 2001a). The Steering Committee was chaired by a succession of DES officials. Members included an international expert on ECEC, a DES inspector and two members of each of the two institutions engaged with the project. The Steering Committee met an average of four times a year. The Management Board consisted of three members drawn from each of the two institutions. It met about ten times each year from 2001 to 2008. It established subcommittees to support the CECDE team in relation to areas such as research, budget, recruitment and communication. Membership of these boards is detailed in Note 1 at the end of the chapter.

Staffing of the Centre consisted of a Director, an Assistant Director, three Development Officers, an Information Officer/Librarian, an Administrator and several fixed-term Research Assistants (see Note 2 at the end of this chapter), though it was 2003 before the full team was in place. Three priorities were identified in the *Programme of Work: Appendix to the Memorandum of Agreement* (CECDE 2001b). These were quality of provision, coordination of provision and research into issues of curriculum, teaching methodologies and parent involvement. In 2002, the European Council agreed the Barcelona objectives for childcare facilities (European Commission 2013) and targets were set whereby Member States were to provide childcare by 2010 to at least 90 per cent of children between 3 years and the mandatory school age (6 years), and to at least 33 per cent of children under 3 years of age. This introduced a sense of urgency into developing a framework for the development of provision and policy in Ireland, and the CECDE set about putting in place the structures and processes required. The DES/Steering Committee worked closely with the Board and Director in determining how best to proceed and by mid-2002 the Centre was poised to play a central role in developments over the coming years.

The core objective of the CECDE was to develop a National Quality Framework (NQF) and initially preparing the groundwork for this was the major focus. The remit for the NQF was that it should have three elements:

- Standards that define what is understood by quality in the Irish context
- Assessment of quality
- Supporting quality in practice.

To do this the foundation of an agreed conceptual framework had to be laid, a collaborative process which proved to be challenging and lengthy, but which ultimately was very successful.

CECDE research strategy

As indicated above, the themes of quality, access, inclusion and coordination determined the scope of the work of the CECDE and these reflected the themes government was most keen to address in the decade from 1999 onwards. The CECDE Work Programme (CECDE 2003), Implementation Strategies and outputs ensured that these themes were kept to the fore in the interactions between the CECDE and the DES in the years 2001–2008.

The Research Strategy published in early 2003 was ambitious, wide-ranging and comprehensive (CECDE 2003). It sought to implement the initial CECDE Programme of Work, but also incorporated work related to the gaps and deficits that were identified in the audit of research (Walsh 2003). Its work was progressed from 2002 by the Director and staff of the Centre and by the Research Sub-Committee of the Management Board, established in early 2003. The Strategy comprised of several strands which included overarching research on how young children develop and learn in the Irish context; a national and international overview of good practices, policies and research in ECEC; quality-related research interrogating the meaning of quality in the Irish context; the key characteristics of a quality curriculum for the early years and the values underpinning the existing primary school curriculum. It also sought to investigate good practices across a range of issues central to ECEC and to examine research on aspects of educational disadvantage, particularly the need for targeted responses for children in the birth to 3 age group and research on ways of engaging parents of children often marginalized in consultative processes. Special needs education was also a focus of the Strategy, as were issues such as the transition of children from preschool to formal schooling, children's ex-periences of second language acquisition, and practitioners' perspectives about play and learning in the Irish context.

The Work Programme Implementation Strategy drawn up by the Centre for the period October 2006–December 2007 (CECDE 2006b) gives some sense of the considerable progress made in relation to its remit. It detailed the range of areas that the Centre was targeting at that point. Areas of work included, for instance, the updating of the research audit; commissioning of targeted projects; further recruitment of PhD students; procedures and mechanisms for inspection and evaluation; assessment materials and processes; testing and evaluation of *Síolta*; resource mater-ials; support issues; professional development and Delivering Equality of Opportunity in Schools (DEIS)[1] survey and support.

1　Delivering Equality of Opportunity in Schools (DEIS) was the Department of Education's action plan for educational inclusion (DES 2005).

NQF research and publications

A significant step in the development of the NQF (subsequently known as *Síolta*) was the commissioning of a literature review of the domains of learning by the CECDE. It focused on five developmental domains (physical, socio-emotional, cognitive, moral and spiritual). The review was unpublished but was reported in detail in Fallon (2005). She reported that two further sections were added to the literature review to site the domains in their historical and contemporary context. The first focused on the historical and cultural context of ECEC in Ireland from the end of the nineteenth century to 1990, and the second addressed perspectives on ECEC in Ireland from 1990.

This review was seminal to the development of the NQF. It provided the evidence base for the publication *Early Childhood in Ireland: Evidence and Perspectives* (Fallon 2005). There it was noted that issues regarding usage of diverse terminology for adults working in the sector were not resolved at that time, and indeed remain unresolved today.

The evidence from the review was presented thematically:

- Child-centred learning and development
- Holistic learning and development
- Environments for learning and development
- Relationships in learning and development
- Diversity in learning and development
- Communication in learning and development
- Play in learning and development.

These themes formed the nucleus of the NQF, augmented by insights from several key pieces of research conducted by the CECDE.

Two reviews of national and international policy, practice and research relating to quality in ECEC were undertaken: *Insights on Quality. A National Review of Policy, Practice and Research relating to Quality in ECEC in Ireland 1990–2004* (Duignan and Walsh 2004) was closely followed by *Making Connections. A Review of International Policy, Practice and Research* (Schonfeld et al. 2004.) These reports and other research reports were published in both Irish and English. The reports are available on the *Síolta* website, <www.siolta.ie>.

Insights on Quality recommended that the NQF take multiple perspectives on quality into account and should be flexible enough to take account of the changing needs of children, families and Irish society. In addition, it asserted that the framework should be child-centred and have a children's rights focus. The standards should cover indoor and outdoor environments, promote parental involvement, ensure appropriate levels of professional qualifications and ensure that an appropriate curriculum and suitable resources were in place. The importance of acknowledging existing expertise and quality assurance procedures was also recognized. *Insights on Quality* proposed that provision be made for the establishment of a national registration system for ECEC providers. It stressed that the implementation of the NQF should be the responsibility of a centralized agency for ECEC, fully supported by a coordinated infrastructure at national, regional and local level. Adequate and sustained funding was recommended as an overarching principle, as was a national data strategy on ECEC provision.

Making Connections reviewed policy, practices and research on ECEC in six countries and made recommendations relevant to the Irish context. The key recommendation was the importance of a coordinated and integrated policy framework for ECEC, either based within a single government department or through other coordinating structures (Schonfeld et al.2004). A broad-based definition of quality was required to cater for multiple perspectives and an advisory and empowering support system was deemed necessary as well as an evaluative approach to assessment. The report concluded with a plea for a wide-ranging framework of initiatives to support quality in ECEC in Ireland.

The rights of children living in disadvantage and children with special needs were the focus of *On Target* (Duignan and Fallon 2004), an audit of services for children in these circumstances. The report recommended that a national protocol for targeted interventions be developed by the relevant government departments and that a national data strategy for the ECEC sector should also be designed. In addition, it advised that flexible and integrated structures across government departments and agencies should be initiated.

The research reports discussed above supported the development of the NQF. Indeed, the NESF report of 2005 referenced the publication of reports *Insights on Quality. A National Review of Policy, Practice and Research relating to Quality in ECEC in Ireland 1990–2004* (Duignan and Walsh 2004) and *Making Connections. A Review of International Policy, Practice and Research* (Schonfeld et al. 2004) as some of the 'landmark initiatives' of the preceding fifteen years (NESF 2005: 10). It perceived the CECDE as pivotal to ongoing quality development in policy, infrastructure and service provision. Likewise, the OECD Report of 2004 commented favourably on the progress made by Ireland in relation to ECEC policy in the years from 1999 to 2004. That report gave special mention to the establishment and work of the CECDE while at the same time it identified a range of issues that provided a blueprint for policy. Many of those issues were contained in the initial *Programme of Work* of the Centre (CECDE 2001b) and were subsequently identified by the OECD (2004) as central to the realization of government policy in the years that followed.

The functions of the CECDE related to quality, coordination and the identification of best practice in curriculum, teaching methodologies and parental involvement, with a particular emphasis on the experience of children from disadvantaged backgrounds and children with special needs. The enormous volume of work generated by these functions was further augmented by several doctoral studentships, which were funded by the Dublin Institute of Technology, St Patrick's College and the CECDE (see Note 3 at the end of this chapter). The commissioning of these studies was significant in the field of ECEC at the time when academic scholarship at this level was only just beginning to flourish.

Consultation and networking

Consultation was the expectation of stakeholders who sought involvement in the development of ECEC initiatives. The CECDE was guided in its work by its Consultative Committee which comprised of over forty representatives of organizations active in the ECEC sector (see Note 4 at the end of this chapter). This group represented the views and aspirations of the range of educators and policy advocates in the ECEC sector. The detailed consultation process that took place during the development of the NQF was particularly significant in that it promoted agreement by the ECEC sector on the future direction of quality provision. Consultation meetings with practitioners and other stakeholders were held nationally, including one in the Irish language in An Cheathrú Rua, Co. Galway.

The findings from the consultative process, published as *Talking about Quality* (Duignan and Walsh 2004), indicated a huge diversity of perspectives and philosophies regarding quality and the need for quality standards to be flexible enough to accommodate this diversity. Minimum standards were to be set down for environments in all types of ECEC settings and the best interests of the child should inform all policies and practice in ECEC. Children's voices should be heard on all aspects of the development, delivery and assessment of quality in ECEC. The NQF should support national developments regarding standard setting for qualifications, mechanisms for access, transfer and progression and quality assurance procedures on education and training programmes. The NQF should facilitate the development of infrastructure to facilitate the representation of parents' perspectives in the development of policy and practice in ECEC and on parental involvement in services. *Aistear: The Early Childhood Curriculum Framework* (NCCA 2009a) was in the process of development at this time (NCCA 2004) and the stakeholders believed that the NQF should support the development and dissemination of this initiative. On a broader note, clear guidelines in relation to the development of policies, procedures and practice in a wide variety of ECEC settings was also to be included in the NQF. Government policy and initiatives should be aligned with the NQF and embedded in coordinated policy and provision of financial support.

Throughout its existence, there was a great deal of national and international interest in the work of the CECDE. The Centre staff were frequently invited to address national bodies and organizations. International recognition for the work of the Centre followed and team members regularly collaborated with colleagues and agencies at home and abroad, sharing expertise and disseminating the work of the CECDE. The Centre's website and the publication of the quarterly newsletter *Alana* ensured a very visible presence for its work.

Two very successful international conferences were organized by the CECDE in Dublin Castle. The first, on *Questions of Quality*, was held in September 2004 and the conference proceedings were published in 2005 (Schonfeld et al. 2005). The CECDE continued to pursue issues of quality provision, and in February 2007 the Centre hosted its second international conference *Vision into Practice: Making Quality a Reality in the Lives of Young Children*, aimed at stimulating exchange of ideas in relation to ensuring quality provision of ECEC. These conference proceedings were published in 2008 (O'Brien et al. 2008).

Síolta. The National Quality Framework for Early Childhood Education

Early Childhood in Ireland. Evidence and Perspectives (Fallon 2005) synthesized the implications for the NQF under the key headings of Defining Quality, Assessing Quality and Supporting Quality (Fallon 2005). Key areas included recognizing the agentic child, reciprocal relationships, assessment, diversity, staff qualifications and parental involvement. The NQF, now entitled *Síolta* (from the Irish for seeds) to signify potential for growth, was published in 2006 (CECDE 2006a), with twelve principles of quality, sixteen standards and seventy-five components of quality. This was based on a national consensus on quality indicators in all settings that cater for children from birth to 6 years (Early Years Policy Unit 2014). It was published in four manuals, one for full and part-time care, sessional care, childminders and infant classes in primary schools.

The NQF applied to a wide range of early years settings, including childminders, preschools, playgroups, crèches and infant classes in primary school. They could be state-funded, community-based or private enterprises. It was envisioned that the NQF would:

- support individual professional practice and development
- act as a focus for teamwork and team development

- act as a tool for management, strategic planning and policy development
- provide a common base for the interactions of a varied team of professionals.

It would also support formal and informal assessment processes and common understandings amongst the broad range of adults who influence the early experiences of young children (CECDE 2006a). This assessment would be primarily internal to the setting and parents.

The principles cover twelve broad areas, all integrated and interdependent (Duignan et al. 2007). These were:

- The value of early childhood
- Children first
- Parents as partners
- Relationships
- Equality
- Diversity
- Environments
- Welfare
- Role of the adult
- Teamwork
- Pedagogy
- Play.

Working out from these principles, a framework of sixteen standards in practice was developed as follows:

1. Rights of the child
2. Environments
3. Parents and families
4. Consultation
5. Interactions
6. Play
7. Curriculum
8. Planning and evaluation
9. Health and welfare

10. Organization
11. Professional practice
12. Communication
13. Transitions
14. Identity and belonging
15. Legislation and regulation
16. Community involvement.

Explanatory notes accompanied each principle and standard and the standards were further delineated by components and signposts for reflection to facilitate self-study. Guidance was also given on how the standards were interlinked with each other.

With the publication of *Síolta*, the first objective of the Centre was met.

Targeted interventions

The second objective, the implementation of targeted interventions on a pilot basis for educationally disadvantaged children and those with special needs was fast tracked in 2002 with the preparation of proposals for the provision of early childhood education targeted at children experiencing disadvantage. *On Target? An Audit of Provision of Services Targeting Disadvantage and Special Needs among Children aged Birth to Six in Ireland* was published (Duignan and Fallon 2004). This gave rise to several CECDE-commissioned large-scale research projects which focused on a range of related areas including effective ways to identify children at risk of disadvantage, parental involvement and representation among parents experiencing disadvantage, and structures to ensure their participation in decisions about ECEC. These were published as executive summaries (see Note 5 at the end of this chapter). In 2006, the CECDE-commissioned research on the nature of the ECEC provision available in Ireland. Provision available to children with special needs and effective early interventions for these children was a particular focus of the study and an executive summary was published as *Early Years Provision for*

Children from Birth to Six Years with Special Needs in Two Geographical Areas in Ireland (Kelleher et al. 2006).

Structures

The third objective of the Centre, that of preparing the way for the ECEA, was to all intents achieved by 2006. The NQF was in place, the Implementation Strategy was ready and there was a wealth of research now available on which to base policy and practice in developing the sector in an effective, integrated and coordinated way.

In retrospect, however, warning signs about the future of the CECDE were becoming evident. DES ambivalence towards the establishment of the ECEA was apparent as early as May 2004. There was some procrastination in the offering of contracts, but a new three-year contract was signed by the Director and Assistant Director in the summer of 2005. However only one-year contracts were offered to other employees from that point onwards, including those seconded to the CECDE. Also, no new Memorandum of Agreement with the DES was forthcoming despite the best efforts of the Management Board and Steering Committee. All of this left the CECDE in somewhat of a precarious position. Nevertheless, the work continued, and a new Implementation Strategy was agreed (CECDE 2006b).

At this point, pressure was building to address the issue of integration of policy and services. This pressure was exerted by, for example, the observations in the OECD Report of 2004 and those of the NESF Report of 2005. Both reports were adamant in their insistence that what was required at this point was a National Plan, leading to a coordinated system of policy implementation and the development of an effective and coordinated system of ECEC. The Early Years Education Policy Unit (EYEPU), first mooted in the White Paper (Government of Ireland 1999), was finally established in 2006. Its remit was to oversee the development of an integrated, coordinated system of early childhood education. It assumed responsibly for the preparation of plans for a phased implementation of the early childhood education dimension of DEIS, the Department's action plan for educational inclusion (DES 2005). Several of the early education initiatives supported by the DES, such as Early Start and Traveller Preschools, came within the remit of the new unit. Significantly, the EYEPU assumed responsibility for oversight of the CECDE, previously under the remit of the Central Policy Unit of the DES. It was assigned several functions related to policy development issues. The establishment of the EYEPU was the first real effort at government level to integrate the early childhood sector into the broader educational sphere. By 2007, it appeared that continuance of the Centre in this new order within the DES was again under review. This was despite earlier indications that the future of the CECDE was secure.

Closure of the CECDE

Throughout 2007/2008, members of the Management Board of the CECDE were increasingly concerned about issues that had been simmering for a considerable time. First, there were tensions between the Management Board, the Steering Committee and the DES in relation to the pension position of staff for which the Board was seeking a resolution from the DES. Second, there was the lack of employment certainty past September 2008 for staff who were on rolling contracts. Third, there were ongoing difficulties in planning the work programme arising from continued delays in confirming a budget for the Centre. The programme included providing on site mentoring services to 300 preschools, most of which were in disadvantaged areas.

In June 2007, the Board Members representing St Patrick's College and the Dublin Institute of Technology, the two Institutions managing the CECDE met with the DES Chairperson of the CECDE Steering Committee to discuss these matters. They were reassured somewhat when it was stated that the DES was in favour of putting pilot projects such as CECDE onto a statutory basis. However, it was also stated that the CECDE should move to a more operational role, particularly in relation to the early years component of DEIS. In essence, this signalled plans for a change in the role and remit of the Centre.

The closure of the Centre was announced in October 2008, effective from the end of November 2008. It was an enormous shock to all involved, including the officials of the DES who had supported and advocated for the work of the Centre within the DES. The reason given by the then Minister for Education and Science was the economic crisis that had just struck the country. It is quite likely that the issues outlined above also contributed to the decision to bring this ECEC satellite home to within government offices. Six members of staff immediately became unemployed. Two were redeployed within the DES. The ECEC community that had invested such faith in the promise of a developing and consolidating force for the sector was dismayed. There were many protests and appeals. The significant value offered by the Centre was a point frequently made by those who publicly objected, as was the loss of expertise and momentum in advancing care and education services in the early years. The government's commitment to ECEC was once again questioned publicly, as was its appreciation of the critical nature of the work that the Centre was doing.

Conclusion

The work output of the Centre was impressive by any standards, and its quality in terms of coherence, cohesiveness and relevance was to prove itself in the years that followed. The large body of rigorous research it carried out in the period 2001–2008 (see Note 5 at the end of this chapter) gives an insight into provision, policy and practice as it was during those years. Strengths as well as concerns were identified. Areas for development were highlighted, as were aspects that required further investment. CECDE research and development provided the evidence base on which recommendations for the future of the sector were made.

The *Síolta* framework, designed to assist the process of defining, assessing and supporting quality improvements in ECEC contexts, provided the basis for a major quality assurance initiative. The CECDE developed the *Síolta Quality Assurance Programme* (QAP) at the end of 2008, just as the Centre was being closed. This was a combined project between the

Department of Children and Youth Affairs (DCYA), the DES and the NCCA, and was subsequently managed by the DES from 2010.

In order to address an initial lack of clarity about the interface between *Aistear* and *Síolta*, the two frameworks were aligned. This led to the publication of the comparative document on similarities between the two frameworks (NCCA 2009b). A decade after the launch of *Síolta*, the National *Síolta/Aistear* Initiative (NSAI) was established in 2016. Its purpose was to support the implementation of both frameworks with trained mentors and other resources. *Síolta* itself is now published as one consolidated manual (DES 2017). *Síolta*, along with *Aistear*, is now a crucial component of the criteria for the Early Childhood Care and Education (ECCE) Scheme, the Better Start Mentoring Programmes and the Early Years Education Inspections. It continues to provide a key platform from which quality provision in the early years is viewed and enjoys widespread recognition both nationally and internationally.

Despite developments since the closure of the CECDE, including the establishment of a full ministerial position for Children and Youth Affairs in 2011, the fragmentation of policy development and service delivery in the sector continues. Walsh (2016) outlines the complex web of entanglement of government departments and agencies which continue to be responsible for the development and implementation of early childhood education policy. There is still no one department or agency with overall responsibility for the development of early childhood education policy and for driving a comprehensive vision. As a result, there exists an ongoing lack of coherence in terms of polices. In some instances, manageability difficulties have arisen for those seeking to implement disparate policies, with policies in health, safety and early childhood education sometimes contravening each other. For instance, it is regrettable that the Department of Health did not align with the NQF (*Síolta*) in the work that led to the publication of the Tusla *Quality and Regulatory Framework* (QRF) in 2018 (Tusla 2018).

Nevertheless, the CECDE made a major contribution to the ongoing project of developing quality in ECEC in its short lifespan and its work continues to influence policy and practice today.

Note 1: Membership of CECDE Committees

Steering Committee Members

Lesley Abbot. Manchester Metropolitan University (chair)
Richard Byrne, Department of Education and Science
John Donovan, Dublin Institute of Technology
John Fanning, Department of Education and Science
Deirdre Liddy, Department of Education and Science
Nóirín Hayes, Dublin Institute of Technology
Liam Mac Mathúna, St Patrick's College
Anne McGough, St Patrick's College
Breda Naughton, Department of Education and Science
John Quinlan, Department of Education and Science
Alan Wall, Department of Education and Science
Margaret Whelan, Dublin Institute of Technology

Board of Management Members

Siobhán Bradley, Dublin Institute of Technology
Elizabeth Dunphy, St Patrick's College
Nóirín Hayes, Dublin Institute of Technology
Marie Kennedy, Dublin Institute of Technology
Anne McGough, St Patrick's College
Máire Mhic Mhathúna, Dublin Institute of Technology
Lorna Ryan, Dublin Institute of Technology
Martin Ward, St Patrick's College

Expert Working Group on CECDE's Irish Output

Máire Mhic Mhathúna, Dublin Institute of Technology
Anne Nolan, Department of Education and Science
CECDE staff.

Note 2: CECDE Staff

Director

Heino Schonfeld

Assistant Directors

Maresa Duignan
Gemma Kiernan

Education Officers

Maresa Duignan
Ms Jacqueline Fallon
Karen Mahony
Mia O'Dwyer
Thomas Walsh

Information Officer

Peadar Cassidy

Administrators

Claire Kelly
Sharon O'Brien

Note 3: PhD Scholarships

Author and completion date	*Title of thesis*
O'Kane, Mary, 2007	The Transition from Preschool to Primary School for Children in Ireland
Brennan, Carmel, 2008	Partners in Play: How Children Organize their Participation in Sociodramatic Play
Dillon, Anna, 2011	The Acquisition of Additional Languages in the Early Years
Boyle, Anne, 2014	A Study of the Involvement of Traveller Parents in Traveller Preschools in Ireland
O'Driscoll, Sharon, 2015	The Early Years in Irish Multi-grade classes

Note 4: Membership Organizations of the CECDE Consultative Committee

Ballymun Partnership
Barnardos
Border Counties Childcare Network
Childminding Ireland
Children's Research Centre

Children's Rights Alliance/Children in Hospital Ireland

Combat Poverty Agency

Department of Education and Science

Department of Health and Children

Department of Justice, Equality and Law Reform

Department of Social and Family Affairs

Disability Federation of Ireland

Dublin Institute of Technology

Foras Áiseanna Saothair (FÁS)

Further Education and Training Awards Council (FETAC)

Forbairt Naíonraí Teo

Forum of People with Disabilities

Higher Education & Training Awards (HETAC)

High/Scope Ireland

Irish Association of Teachers in Special Education (IATSE)

Irish Farmers' Association (IFA)

Irish Montessori Education Board (IMEB)

IMPACT: Sheila Carroll

Irish National Teachers Organisation (INTO)

Iris Preschool Playgroups Association (IPPA)

Irish Steiner Waldorf Early Childhood Association

Mary Immaculate College

National Association for the Mentally Handicapped of Ireland (NAMHI)

National Children's Office

National College of Ireland

National Consultative Committee on Racism & Interculturalism

National Disability Authority

National Federation of Voluntary Bodies

National Forum of Preschool Inspectors

National Parents and Siblings Alliance (NPSA):

National Parents Council – Primary

National Council for Curriculum and Assessment (NCCA)

National Children's Nursery Association (NCNA)

Organisation Mondial d'Education Préscolaire (OMEP)

Pavee Point

RAPID

Seirbhísí Naíonraí Teo

Southern & Eastern Regional Assembly

St Nicholas Montessori Society

St Patrick's College

Traveller Preschool Teachers Association

Treoir

University College Cork (UCC)

Vision in Childcare

WITH/Cúram

Note 5: CECDE Publications (available at: <www.siolta.ie>)

Research reports

Barnardos and INTO Professional Development Unit (2006). *In-Career Development Programme for Staff and Management of Traveller Pre-schools.* Dublin: CECDE.

Cederman, K. (2006). *Synergy – An Exploration of High Quality Early Intervention for Children with Special Needs in Diverse Early Childhood Care and Education Settings.* Dublin: CECDE.

Duignan, M. and Fallon, J. (2004). *On Target? An Audit of Provision of Services Targeting Disadvantage and Special Needs among Children from birth to six years in Ireland / De Réir Sprice? Iniúchadh ar Sholáthar Seirbhísí a Dhíríonn ar Mhíbhuntáistí agus Riachtanais Speisialta i measc leanaí ó Bhreith go Sé Bliana d'Aois in Éirinn*. Dublin: CECDE.

Duignan, M. and Walsh, T. (2004a). *Insights on Quality. A National Review of Policy, Practice and Research Relating to Quality in Early Childhood Care and Education in Ireland 1990–2004 / Spléachadh ar an Ardchaighdeán. Athbhreithniú ar Bheartas, Cleachtas agus Taighde Náisiúnta a bhaineann leis an Ardchaighdeán i gCúram agus Oideachas Luathóige in Éirinn 1990–2004*. Dublin: CECDE.

Duignan, M. and Walsh, T. (2004b). *Talking About Quality Report of a Consultation Process on Quality in Early Childhood Care and Education*. Dublin: CECDE.

Fallon, J. (2005). *Early Childhood in Ireland. Evidence and Perspectives / Luath-Óige in Éirinn. Fianaise agus Peirspictíochtaí*. Dublin: CECDE.

Hanlon, L. and Hayes, N. (2006). *Early Assessment and Intervention in Educational Disadvantage*. Dublin: CECDE.

Kelleher, E., McGough, A., Ware, J., Julian, G. and Dissou, G. (2006). *Early Years Provision for Children from Birth to Six Years with Special Needs in Two Geographical Areas in Ireland*. Dublin: CECDE.

Mahony, K. and Hayes, N. (2006). *In Search of Quality: Multiple Perspectives. Executive Summary*. Dublin: CECDE.

Schonfeld, H., Kiernan, G. and Walsh, T. (eds) (2004). *Making Connections. A Review of International Policies, Practices and Research Relating to Quality in Early Childhood Care and Education*. Dublin: CECDE.

Walsh, T. (2003). *An Audit of Research on Early Childhood Care and Education in Ireland 1990–2003*. Dublin: CECDE.

Walsh, T. and Cassidy, P. (2006). *An Audit of Research on Early Care and Education in Ireland 1990–2006*, 2nd ed. Dublin: CECDE.

Conference proceedings

O'Brien, S., Cassidy, P. and Schonfeld, H. (eds) (2008). *Vision into Practice. Making Quality a Reality. in the Lives of Young Children. Conference Proceedings. International Conference 2007*. Dublin Castle 8–10 February 2007. Dublin: CECDE.

Schonfeld, H., O'Brien, S. and Walsh, T. (eds) (2005). *Questions of Quality. International Conference 2004. Conference Proceedings*. Dublin Castle, 23–25 September 2004. Dublin: CECDE.

Síolta manuals

Centre for Early Childhood Development and Education (2006a). *Síolta. The National Quality Framework for Early Childhood Education. Handbook / Síolta. An Chreatlach Náisiúnta Cáilíochta d'Oideachas na Luath-Óige. Lámhleabhar.* Dublin: CECDE.

Centre for Early Childhood Development and Education (2006b). *Síolta. The National Quality Framework for Early Childhood Education. Full and Part-time Daycare User Manual / Síolta. An Chreatlach Náisiúnta Cáilíochta d'Oideachas na Luath-Óige. Cúram Lae Lánaimseartha agus Páirtaimseartha. Lámhleabhar.* Dublin: CECDE.

Centre for Early Childhood Development and Education (2006c). *Síolta. The National Quality Framework for Early Childhood Education. Sessional Services User Manual / Síolta. An Chreatlach Náisiúnta Cáilíochta d'Oideachas na Luath-Óige. Seirbhísí Seisiúnacha. Lámhleabhar* Dublin: CECDE.

Centre for Early Childhood Development and Education (2006d). *Síolta. The National Quality Framework for Early Childhood Education.* Infant Classes User Manual. / *Síolta. An Chreatlach Náisiúnta Cáilíochta d'Oideachas na Luath-Óige. Ranganna na Naíonán. Lámhleabhar.* Dublin: CECDE.

Centre for Early Childhood Development and Education (2006e). *Síolta. The National Quality Framework for Early Childhood Education. Childminding User Manual. Síolta. An Chreatlach Náisiúnta Cáilíochta d'Oideachas na Luath-Óige. Feighlíocht Linbh. Lámhleabhar.* Dublin: CECDE.

Centre for Early Childhood Development and Education (2006f). *Síolta. The National Quality Framework for Early Childhood Education. A Guide for Parents. / Síolta. An Chreatlach Náisiúnta Cáilíochta d'Oideachas na Luath-Óige. Treoir do Thuismitheoirí.* Dublin: CECDE.

Centre for Early Childhood Development and Education & Foras Áiseanna Saothair (2007). *Síolta Research Digests / Achoimrí Taighde.* Dublin: CECDE.

Department of Education and Skills (2017). *Síolta. The National Quality Framework for Early Childhood Education.* Dublin: DES.

Training manuals

Centre for Early Childhood Development and Education (2007). *Síolta Workshop Materials / Ábhair do Cheardlanna Síolta.* Dublin: CECDE.

Centre for Early Childhood Development and Education (2008). *Síolta Implementation Toolkit.* Dublin: CECDE.

Bibliography

Centre for Early Childhood Development and Education (2001a). *Memorandum of Agreement between The Department of Education and Science, Dublin Institute of Technology and St. Patrick's College, Drumcondra.* Dublin: CECDE.

Centre for Early Childhood Development and Education (2001b). *Programme of Work: Appendix to the Memorandum of Agreement.* Dublin: CECDE.

Centre for Early Childhood Development and Education (2003). *Research Strategy: A Work in Progress.* Dublin: CECDE.

Centre for Early Childhood Development and Education (2006a). *Síolta. The National Quality Framework for Early Childhood Education. Handbook.* Dublin: CECDE.

Centre for Early Childhood Development and Education (2006b). *Work Programme Implementation Strategy: October 2006-December 2007.* Dublin: CECDE.

Coolahan, J. (1998). *Report of the National Forum on Early Childhood Education.* Dublin: The Stationery Office.

Coolahan, J., Drudy, S., Hogan, P., Hyland, A. and McGuinness, S. (2017). *Towards a Better Future: A Review of the Irish School System.* Cork: Irish Primary Principals' Network and the National Association of Principals and Deputy Principals. Available at: <https://issuu.com/ippn/docs/towards_a_better_future>.

Department of Education and Science (2005). *Delivering Equality of Opportunity in Schools (DEIS): An Action Plan for Educational Inclusion.* Dublin: DES.

Department of Education and Skills (2017). *Síolta. The National Quality Framework for Early Childhood Education.* Dublin: DES.

Department of Justice, Equality and Law Reform (2002). *Quality Childcare and Lifelong Learning: Model Framework for Education, Training and Professional Development in the Early Childhood Care and Education Sector.* Dublin: DJELR.

Duignan, M. and Fallon, J. (2004). *On Target? An Audit of Provision of Services Targeting Disadvantage and Special Needs among Children from Birth to Six Years in Ireland / De Réir Sprice? Iniúchadh ar Sholáthar Seirbhísí a Dhíríonn ar Mhíbhuntáistí agus Riachtanais Speisialta i measc leanaí ó Bhreith go Sé Bliana d'Aois in Éirinn.* Dublin: CECDE.

Duignan, M., Fallon, J., O'Dwyer, M., Schonfeld, H. and Walsh, T. (2007). 'Síolta. The National Quality Framework for Early Childhood Education', *An Leanbh Óg*, 1 (1), 40–56.

Early Years Policy Unit (2014). *Final Report on Síolta Quality Assurance Programme.* Dublin: DES. Available at: <https://www.gov.ie/en/publication/69096b-siolta-final-report-on-the-development-and-implementation-of-the-sio/>.

European Commission (2013). *Barcelona Objectives. The Development of Childcare Facilities for Young Children in Europe with a View to Sustainable and Inclusive Growth.* Luxembourg: Publications Office of the European Union.

Fallon, J. (2005). *Early Childhood in Ireland. Evidence and Perspectives / Luath-Óige in Éirinn. Fianaise agus Peirspictíochtaí.* Dublin: CECDE.

Government of Ireland (1997). *An Action Plan for the Millennium.* Dublin: The Stationery Office.

Government of Ireland (1999). *Ready to Learn: White Paper on Early Childhood Education.* Dublin: DES. Available at: <https://www.education.ie/en/Publi cations/Policy-Reports/Ready-to-Learn-White-Paper-on-Early-Childhood-Education.pdf>.

Moss, P. and Pence, A. (eds) (1995). *Valuing Quality in Early Childhood Services.* London: Paul Chapman.

National Council for Curriculum and Assessment (2004). *Towards A Framework for Early Learning: A Consultative Document.* Dublin: NCCA. Available at: <https://ncca.ie/media/1473/towards_a_framework_for_early_learning_ a_consultative_document.pdf>.

National Council for Curriculum and Assessment (2009a). *Aistear. The Early Childhood Curriculum Framework.* Dublin: NCCA. Available at: <https:// ncca.ie/media/4151/aistear_theearlychildhoodcurriculumframework.pdf>.

National Council for Curriculum and Assessment (2009b). *Aistear: The Early Childhood Curriculum Framework and Síolta, The National Quality Framework for Early Childhood Education Audit: Similarities and Differences.* Dublin: NCCA. Available at: <https://ncca.ie/media/4152/aistear__similar-ities_differences_.pdf>.

National Economic and Social Forum (2005). *Early Childhood Care and Education NESF Report 31.* Dublin: The Stationery Office.

O'Brien, S., Cassidy, P. and Schonfeld, H. (eds) (2008). *Vision into Practice. Making Quality a Reality in the Lives of Young Children. Conference Proceedings. International Conference 2007.* Dublin Castle, 8–10 February 2007. Dublin: CECDE.

O'Connor, M. (2010). *The Development of Infant Education in Ireland, 1838–1948: Epochs and Eras.* Bern: Peter Lang.

Organisation for Economic Co-operation and Development (2001). *Starting Strong.* Paris: OECD.

Organisation for Economic Co-operation and Development (2004). *OECD Thematic Review of Early Childhood Education and Care in Ireland.* Prepared by Carmel Corrigan for The Department of Education & Science. Paris: OECD. Available at: <https://www.education.ie/en/Publications/Policy-Reports/OECD-Thema tic-Review-of-Early-Childhood-Education-and-Care-Policy-in-Ireland.pdf>.

Schonfeld, H., Kiernan, G. and Walsh, T. (eds) (2004). *Making Connections. A Review of International Policies, Practices and Research Relating to Quality in Early Childhood Care and Education*. Dublin: CECDE.

Schonfeld, H., O'Brien, S. and Walsh, T. (eds) (2005). *Questions of Quality. International Conference 2004. Conference Proceedings*. Dublin Castle, 23–25 September 2004. Dublin: CECDE.

Tusla (2018). *Quality and Regulatory Framework* (QRF). Available at: <https://www.tusla.ie/services/preschool-services/early-years-quality-and-regulatory-framework/>.

Walsh, T. (2003). *Audit of Research in Early Childhood Education*. Dublin: CECDE.

Walsh, T. (2016). 'Recent Policy Developments in Early Childhood Education (ECE): A Jigsaw with too Many Pieces?', *An Leanbh Óg*, 16, 69–94.

Woodhead, M. (1996). *In Search of the Rainbow: Pathways to Quality in Large Scale Programmes for Young, Disadvantaged Children*. The Hague: Bernard van Leer Foundation.

ANNE EGAN AND SHEILA GARRITY

8 The legislative and regulatory landscape for early childhood education and care in Ireland

Introduction

The development of the early childhood education and care (ECEC) sector, within any State, will be reflective of that State's unique social and cultural history as it changes over time, as is true in the case of the Republic of Ireland. This chapter focuses on Ireland's constitutional, legislative and regulatory history, examining the impact of this on children, their education and, in particular, their early education. Over time, these changes have created a safer environment for children from a statutory perspective and have impacted on how society views and values children and childhood.

It could be argued that for most of the twentieth century, legislation in Ireland deferred to the private family realm in regard to children, only intervening where families of lesser means were seen to fail in their duties. As this chapter will outline, legislation slowly began to recognize the place of mothers, separate and distinct from the family unit, and eventually, to acknowledge that the safeguarding, welfare and rights of children were not always best protected within that traditional familial structure. However, it was not until enactment of Article 42A of the Constitution in 2015 that children's rights as equal citizens within the Republic were enshrined in law.

Whereas this volume offers as its starting point the year 1921, creating a centenary of reflection from 1921 to 2021, in order to establish context, this chapter commences its account in 1908, a time in which the present Irish State was still part of the United Kingdom of Great Britain and Ireland. From early in the twentieth century, the education and welfare of children were promoted under the *Children Act 1908*.[1] This legislation remained in place until 2001 when it was repealed by the Children Act of that year. In order to properly understand Irish legislative and regulatory history as it relates not only to education, but also to children, families, women and ECEC, one must begin with the 1908 Act.

This chapter is presented in two distinct parts. The opening part reflects the broader legislative historical context over the past century, with particular focus on legislative and constitutional changes in the early decades of the 1900s. While in theory these changes had an educational slant, in practice, they led to thousands of children remitted to reformatory and industrial schools. Progressive legislative developments affecting the lives of women, and then, children, are also outlined. By the mid-twentieth century, legislative changes in Ireland created automatic guardianship rights for all mothers, irrespective of their marital status together with increased financial independence for women. This in turn led to an increased need for childcare of preschool children.

Although this will present some overlap, the *Child Care Act 1991* offers a clear starting point for the second part of the chapter, being the mechanism by which ECEC services in Ireland received statutory recognition. Parallel to regulatory and legislative developments, emerging policy discourse in the Irish, European and international contexts increasingly promoted a rights-based perspective in matters affecting young children, with this chapter offering a historic account of advances in the Irish context. The contribution presented in the pages that follow outlines the historical, constitutional, legislative and regulatory contexts within which other chapters in this volume may be better understood.

Historical context (1908–1991)

The *Children Act 1908* was the first piece of legislation that sought to protect children, albeit protection of those in conflict with the law (Kilkelly

---

1   All sources of law, both legislative and constitutional pre-1922, is authored by His Majesty's Government (HMG). Constitutional and legislative provisions post-1922 are authored by the Government of Ireland. Full citations are found in the reference list.

2008). At the time of its introduction, it was viewed in a positive light as '[t]his Act consolidated the mass of legislation which had regulated the treatment and provision of services for children since the middle of the nineteenth century' (Buckley et al. 1997: 5). However, viewed from today's standards, it can be perceived as more parent-centred than child-centred (Ferriter 2005).

While the primary focus of amending legislation to the 1908 Act was on deviant children, other influential legislation relating to children was also in existence. The *Public Health (Medical Treatment of Children) Act 1919* governed health provision within schools, while the *School Attendance Act 1926* made it an offence for a parent to fail to send a child under the age of 14 to school.[2] As Buckley (2013: 28) suggests, children were the 'victims of the State's inability to tackle the poverty that separated families', as many parents needed their children to work in order to survive. The 1908 Act was amended a number of times, particularly by the *Children Act 1929*, allowing for the committal of children to industrial schools when parents were deemed unable to provide the necessary support. The *School Attendance Act 1926*, together with the *Children Act 1929*, led to thousands of parents being prosecuted for the non-attendance of their children at school and the transfer of these children to industrial schools (Buckley and McGregor 2018). The 1908 Act was also amended by the *Children Act 1941* which expanded the grounds under which children could be committed to reformatory and industrial schools to include begging and homelessness.

A further amendment in the *Children (Amendment) Act 1957* provided that the Minister for Education release children who had been committed, particularly if the child was unlikely to offend again and that the parents/guardians were in a position to support the child. This Act also regularized 'nursing and maintenance' of a child for 'reward', now commonly known as fostering in Ireland (Ferriter 2005).

---

2   Section 2 of the *School Attendance Act 1926* stated that a child within the context of this Act was between the ages of 6 and 14 years.

Constitutional consideration to education

The Irish Constitution is in effect the cornerstone of legislative, executive and judicial powers in the State. From a constitutional perspective, the Anglo-Irish Treaty of 1921 dissolved the legislative union between Ireland and England resulting in the formation of the Irish Free State (Thornton et al. 2016). It is notable that the Constitution adopted in 1922 was structured in the form of a set of restrictions. There were two positive principles enunciated in this document, one of which was a right to free primary education (Chubb 1978). In particular, Article 10 stated that '[a]ll citizens of the Irish Free State (Saorstát Eireann) have the right to free elementary education'. This marked a tentative break from the British tradition as Ireland now had a rights-based education system. This was the catalyst towards the enactment of the present Constitution in 1937. While Article 10 did not specify primary education, by the use of the word 'elementary', it alluded to it and by default, as the concept of ECEC did not exist in legislation at this point, excluded any reference to preschool children having the same constitutional rights as those within the school system.

Bunreacht na hÉireann, the Constitution of Ireland (Government of Ireland 1937) reflected the political climate of Ireland at that time, developed against a background of strongly conservative social and moral conditions and a weak and stagnant economy (Doyle 2004). The 1937 document specifically referenced 'education' in Article 42 by providing that the primary educators of a child is the family (Article 42.1). Article 42.4 specified that '[t]the State shall provide for free primary education …', albeit it has been argued that this Article was used to 'copperfasten' the connection between Church and State, its educational providers (primarily religious denominations) and parents, rather than a child-centred approach (Quinn 2000). However, it was not mandatory to send a child to a State school (Article 42.3). To comprehend the origins and significance of the provisions of Article 42, the legal, political, economic, social and religious context from which they evolved must be considered, notably:

> The importance of these articles lies not only in their legal protection of the family and the promotion of education, but also in the national culture they reflect. This

involves the overriding importance of the family in Ireland and the rights of families to privacy and independence in the conduct of their family responsbilities. (DES 2002: 7)

Progressive legislative development: Women

Legislative change over the last eighty years significantly impacted women's lived experiences, hence, influencing the contexts in which children were reared. The liberalization of women gradually occurred with the acceptance of women working outside the home and the provision of children's allowance in 1944. While legislative changes, such as the *Married Women's Status Act 1957* provided that courts could decide on property disputes between spouses, the main changes occurred from the 1970s onwards, as loosening of sexual conventions and social morality came to influence legislators (Lee 1989). Reflecting this liberalizing social context, a constitutional referendum in 1972 witnessed the removal of the special position of the Catholic Church in Article 44 of the Constitution (Keogh and McCarthy 2005) with legislation gradually adapting to this evolution. The backdrop to these changes was the European Economic Community (EEC) (now European Union) Directive Treaty of Rome 1957 (Council Directive 75/117/EEC) which required equal pay and treatment under Articles 119 and 189 of the Treaty of Rome and was the paving stone for equality legislation.

Financial independence

By the removal of the marriage bar for women in the civil service under the *Civil Service (Employment of Married Women) Act 1973* and the introduction of the *Employment Equality Act 1977*, mothers were increasingly working outside the home. Financial independence for women was also important. Legislation was introduced which strengthened the rights of women, and by default, protected children in their care. One such statute was the *Family Law (Maintenance of Spouses and Children) Act 1976*, which provided for maintenance to women upon separation from their husbands. A second notable example was the *Family Home Protection Act 1976* that ensured the wife's consent must be obtained prior to the family home being sold or re-mortgaged. These changes resulted in married mothers having access to assets, which were not previously available to them.

Such progressive legislation emerged against the backdrop of Article 41.2 of the Constitution, which privileged the role of women in the home. Scannell (1988 cited in Hogan 2005) suggests that this article could be viewed from two oppositional perspectives: as a 'tribute' to women's work as mothers or a recognition that mothers should not be forced to seek employment outside the home; alternatively, as an 'offensive' article that implied mother's work should be focused solely on the family. Irrespective of the position, the Constitution's drafters promoted the benefit of the woman's role for both family and society, though financial or State support has never flown from this privileging (Crowley 2013).

In addition to these legislative changes, the unmarried mothers' payments (*Social Welfare Act 1973*); the introduction of divorce (*Family Law (Divorce) Act 1996*) and the commencement of the *Equal Status Act 2000* (now *Equal Status Acts 2000–2018*) paved the way for greater opportunities for women. The latter legislation prohibited discrimination in employment under nine grounds, including gender, marital status and family status. Whereas this shifting, liberalized context facilitated women's independence, including employment outside the home, the lack of any formalized regulated or affordable childcare system created barriers.

Childcare as an economic imperative

As has been well documented through this volume, and within the literature, the Irish State historically had minimal involvement in the area of ECEC (Gallagher 2013, Hanafin 2016, Share and Kerrins 2013). The provision of childcare from the outset was primarily provided through 'market mechanisms, with limited State subsidy' (Canavan 2012: 23).

As chronicled by Kennedy (2001), the traditional nature of family life in Ireland with its reliance on a male-breadwinner model of family economic organization, the low incidence of female labour market engagement, larger family size and extended family networks, meant demand for wide-scale formalized childcare remained low through to the end of the twentieth century. However, changing economic conditions from the early 1990s coupled with a labour shortage led to Irish women, including Irish mothers, joining the workforce in record numbers (Canavan 2012, Garrity and Canavan 2017, O'Sullivan 2012).

Described as the feminization of the Irish workforce (O'Sullivan 2012) through the 1990s, females, and particularly maternal employment, increased despite the State's slow response to the childcare gap (Millar et al. 2012). This inaction was in the face of increasing calls for greater State support for ECEC from providers' organizations (DES 2002), women's groups and the trade union movement (Kennedy 2001). Through this period 'children remained largely invisible as a policy consideration' (Hayes and Bradley 2009: 25) as the emerging focus was firmly on childcare as a labour support and economic stimulus. Women and families through this time made the best of informal arrangements, including extended family care, informal childminding services (DES 2002, Gallagher 2013) and formal, though still unregulated, centre-based services (Hayes 1995). This loose amalgam of childcare provision has been described as the 'organic nature of development' of the ECEC sector through this time (Department of Justice, Equality and Law Reform [DJELR] 2002: 6).

Progressive legislative developments: Children (1964–2018)

As witnessed, legislation liberalized the place of women in Irish society over the latter part of the 1900s, influencing children and family life. Social and cultural changes have also offered enhanced legal protection for children, as their claims to rights and citizenship were strengthened, as this section will outline.

Guardianship

For much of the twentieth century, the status of the non-marital child, at common law, was illegitimate. He/she was a *filius nullius*, that is, a child of no one, with no parents or no relations, in law. As a result, natural parents of 'illegitimate' children did not possess rights to guardianship or custody of that child. Illegitimacy existed irrespective of whether a parental marriage took place subsequently, however; the enactment of the *Legitimacy Act 1931* allowed for the recognition of non-marital children following the subsequent marriage of their parents (Shatter 1997).

The right of a parent to make decisions in relation to their children, such as educational choices or consent to medical treatment, is reflected in guardianship privileges (Bracken 2018). In the early 1960s, the *Guardianship of Infants Act 1964* reinforced the view that only married parents and unmarried mothers had this right. This Act repealed all of the previous nineteenth-century legislation in relation to guardianship, which was more paternally focused (Shatter 1997). More than a decade earlier, the first legislative response to adoption was introduced through the *Adoption Act 1952*.

The reluctance by legislators to provide automatic guardianship for unmarried fathers was summed up by Duncan (cited in Walshe 2003), who suggested that many natural fathers might not have an interest in their children. Although the enactment of the *Status of Children Act 1987* did not provide for automatic guardianship for unmarried fathers, it did grant the right to apply for guardianship (Egan 2011) and equalized the rights of all children, irrespective of their circumstances at birth. A decade later, *the Children Act 1997* provided that an unmarried father could assume guardianship, with the mother's consent, if they jointly signed a statutory declaration without the necessity of court involvement. This was further updated by the *Children and Family Relationships Act 2015* granting unmarried fathers' automatic guardianship, though in limited circumstances; for example, where parents were cohabiting for one year, three months of which must occur after the child's birth.

The effect of guardianship legislation on parents, the child and ultimately, on a family's interaction with services, including educational facilities, cannot be understated. As a guardian's role is to take decisions in relation to a child's health, education and in other major areas of the child's life, in the context where an unmarried father is not a guardian, then he cannot legally guide how services interact with and provide for his child.

Child protection and safeguarding

From the 1970s onwards, there was a shift in focus particularly because of a number of reports that were highly critical of the State for failure to protect children in institutions. One of these, the *Tuairim Report* (Tuairim 1966), recommended repealing the 1908 Act and suggested that all residential child care services be administered by the Department of Health. Furthermore, the *Kennedy Report* recognized that '[a]ll children need love, care and security if they are to develop into full and mature adults' (Kennedy 1970: v). The decentralization of child care services from the Department of Education to the Department of Health by the introduction of the *Health Act 1970* was a positive move in the provision of child care services (Buckley et al. 1997). This evidenced a gradual paradigm shift towards a more child-centred approach to child protection and education. The outcome of these reports was the introduction of the *Child Care Act 1991* with the primary focus of this legislation on child protection. From an ECEC perspective, the inclusion of Part VII was ground-breaking as, for the first time preschool services were recognized in legislation. Part VII commenced in 1996, placing duties on the then Health Boards to provide special care and protection for vulnerable children. The 1991 Act, among other areas of responsibility, outlined the role of the State in the 'promotion of the welfare of children and the provision of family support services' (DJELR 2002: 9) and provided for the convening of Family Welfare Conferences as a supportive mechanism.

National guidelines in relation to the protection and welfare of children were first published in 1999 (Department of Health and Children [DHC] 1999) although they were not put on a statutory footing until the commencement of the *Children First Act 2015*. For all organizations/persons working with children, including the education and ECEC sectors, this statutorily obliges 'mandated persons' to report any child protection concerns to Tusla, The Child and Family Agency.[3] In addition, the 2015 Act obligates all services, statutory and voluntary, to have a Child Safeguarding Statement which clearly outlines the setting's reporting procedures. The Designated Liaison Person (DLP) in each service, who is statutorily obliged to report any welfare concerns to Tusla and/or act as a support for staff members who may have child protection concerns, must be clearly identified under this Act.

This duty to report runs parallel with earlier legislation, namely the *Protections for Persons Reporting Child Abuse Act 1998*, which protects any member of the public or employee of Tusla, from legal reprisals, who *bona fide* reports suspected child abuse if the allegations turn out to be false. Further, all new employees in educational settings, including ECEC settings specified under the *Child Care Act 1991*, are statutorily obliged under the *National Vetting Bureau (Children and Vulnerable Persons) Act 2012* to be vetted prior to taking up a position of employment. This legislation, which commenced in 2016, provides that An Garda Síochána disclose information in relation to previous convictions to a prospective employer following a request to do so (Bracken 2018).

Children's rights

The 1992 ratification by the Irish State of the *United Nations Convention on the Rights of the Child* (UNCRC) (UN 1989) set the scene for a new way of framing services for young children, and a shift over time in how children would come to be portrayed within the Irish context. The process of reporting State actions, under the framework of the Convention, has been credited with informing State activity from a children's rights perspective (Kiersey and Hayes 2010). A children's rights discourse can be seen framing significant policy and legislative developments in Ireland, since 1992, including: the *National Children's Strategy* (Government of Ireland 2000); the establishment of the National Children's Office in

---

3   Tusla, The Child and Family Agency was established by the *Child and Family Agency Act 2013*.

2001[4] and following the publication of the *Ombudsman for Children Act 2002*, the formation of the Ombudsman for Children's Office in 2004 (Kiersey and Hayes 2010).

However, it has been in the last decade that the most relevant legislation relating to the children of Ireland, and by default the ECEC sector, has been implemented. The call for discrete children's constitutional rights first arose as a result of a recommendation of the *Kilkenny Incest Investigation* (McGuinness 1993). Further, the United Nations Committee on the Rights of the Child recommended constitutional reform in its response to Ireland's submissions in 1998 and 2006 (Burns and McGregor 2019). Following the successful holding of a referendum on children in 2012, the *Thirty-First Amendment of the Constitution (Children) Act 2012* was passed and Article 42A was inserted into the Constitution as a stand-alone article in 2015, recognizing and protecting children as rights holders. This includes a right to express their views and the inclusion of the *best interests* principle as the paramount consideration, albeit in limited circumstances relating to adoption, guardianship, custody and access.

Regulation of early childhood education and care (ECEC) services (1991–2016)

Up to the end of the twentieth century, State attention to the area of ECEC was minimal in scope and variable in nature. What attention existed tended to be driven by locally based initiatives with their roots in voluntary, community and/or religious organizations, lacking overarching

---

4   In 2008, with the establishment of a 'super junior' Minister for Children, the department was expanded and renamed the Office of the Minister for Children and Youth Affairs (OMCYA). The Department of Children and Youth Affairs (DCYA) emerged in 2011, with the merging of responsibilities from other State departments. Following the 2020 Dáil election, further restructuring of departments concerned with ECEC resulted in the establishment of the Department for Children, Equality, Disability, Integration and Youth (DCEDIY).

national structures (Hayes and Bradley 2006). Duignan and Fallon (2004) remark that such pioneering services tended to fall along one of three prevailing imperatives: as a child protection/intervention, a family support measure, or promoting equality of opportunity for parents to upskill or seek employment. Although the lack of a national picture pre-dating the 1990s presents challenges to recording an extensive history of the State's early involvement, both the Eastern Health Board and the Southern Health Board were noted as supporting preschool services as early as the 1970s (Hayes 1983, cited in Duignan and Fallon 2004).

Whereas State funding, along with some pilot or short-lived European investment schemes and charitable supports were evident through this time (DES 2002, Hayes and Bradley, 2006), the establishment of the *Child Care Act 1991*, within the remit of the Department of Health and Children (DHC), certainly formalized and clarified the State's responsibility to support young children and their families. Making use of the regional Health Boards structure to meet the DHC's obligation under the 1991 Act to promote the wellbeing of children, the early 1990s witnessed an increase in State funding for local community preschool services, with attention focused on supporting children and families identified as being at risk or disadvantaged. Despite national overarching legislation, the development of such services remained 'ad hoc', unregulated (DJELR 2002, Hayes and Bradley 2006, Wolfe et al. 2013), 'uncoordinated, variable in quality' (Government of Ireland 1999b: 6), with regional gaps in provision through this time.

Commencement of Part VII of the Act

The Commencement of Part VII of the *Child Care Act 1991* allowed for the *Child Care (Pre-School Services) Regulations*, passed in 1996 and the follow on *Child Care (Pre-School Services) (Amendment) 1997*, setting out the responsibility for the inspection and regulation of childcare services by the DHC. Placing a statutory duty on local area-based Health Boards and involving health-oriented professionals in the inspection role, the initial lens through which ECEC services in Ireland were regulated was clearly from a health and safety perspective (DES 2002, Wolfe et al. 2013).

While generally seen as a positive first step in terms of monitoring ECEC provision (Langford 2006), and described as 'unanimously welcomed by the ECCE sector' (DJELR 2002: 6), the initial regulations offered a national context in which ECEC provision could be situated. Challenges remained, however, such as the 'non-uniform application' of the regulations and the inspection experiences across the State, and the lack or variable nature of training for members of the inspection team (DES 2002, O'Kane 2005).

Established during a time when increasing maternal employment was an economic objective of the State (DJELR 2002), the impact of the 1996 Regulations resulted in the closure of services which could not (i.e. lacked adequate physical environments) or would not (i.e. perceived as an unwelcomed administrative burden) meet the regulatory criteria and a loss of 1,846 children places (Kelly 1999, cited in O'Kane 2005). As with primary education, in this area, the State opted to provide *'for'* ECEC, rather than become the direct provider of services. As pointed out by Hayes and Bradley (2009: 25), it became the 'private responsibility of parents to make alternative care arrangements for their children while they worked', with the State maintaining an arms-length role.

Evolving Regulations

The revised *Pre-School Services (No. 2) Regulations 2006* better reflected the significant developments and emerging discourses regarding ECEC in Ireland over the preceding decade, including the underpinning *Whole Child Perspective* (Government of Ireland 2000) and the increasing rights-based understandings, though concerns remained. Domestic influences included an abundance of white papers and policy documents (Coolahan 1998, DHC 1999, DJELR 2002, Government of Ireland 1999a, 1999b), as well as the pioneering work emanating from the Centre for Early Childhood Development and Education (CECDE), established in 2001. State commitments under the Barcelona Objectives (EC 2002), the underpinning imperatives of the joint EU/Exchequer funded Equal Opportunities Childcare Programme 2000–2006 and the Organisation for Economic Cooperation and Development (OECD) *Country Note for Ireland* (OECD 2004) publication, are but a few external influences that shaped the context in which revisions of the Regulations took place, one decade on from their commencement.

Impacted by the changed organizational structure relating to health and social services in the Irish State, the regulatory responsibility for ECEC shifted from the Health Board model, to the newly established Health Service Executive (HSE) structure in 2005, prior to the publication of the revised regulations in 2006 (Government of Ireland 2006). Later, with the establishment of Tusla in 2014, the remit for the notification and inspection of preschool services was again relocated, this time to the new State agency.

Building on the existing health and safety priorities, this child protection imperative included new staffing requirements as the Garda Vetting process became necessary for all adults associated with a service. The 2006 Regulations prepared for the forthcoming National Garda Vetting Service by including reference to this impending requirement at the time of publication. The enactment of the *Child Care Act 1991 (Early Years Services) Regulations 2016* revoked the previous 2006 Regulations, establishing a 'registration' system, in law, for new services, replacing the notification system, in place since 1996. Existing services were offered a transition period to comply with the registration criteria.

Whereas the 2006 Regulations provided greater clarity on the recruitment of staff from a child protection position, it failed to make progress on the area of staff qualifications, training and quality improvement, consolidating a protectionist, health and safety focused approach to regulation of ECEC through that period. A further decade elapsed before legislation addressed staff qualifications. The 2016 Regulations set out the first statutory qualification requirement that being a one year vocational award in ECEC, a Level 5 on the National Framework of Qualifications as a minimum for all staff employed in centre-based, registered, early years services.

Towards universal provision

Early Childhood Care and Education (ECCE) Scheme

Reflecting Ireland's commitments under the Barcelona Objectives[5] (EU 2002) for universal provision of preschool education, and responding to domestic calls (Hayes 2008, NESF 2005, National Women's Council of Ireland 2005) and international benchmarking (UNICEF 2008), in April 2009, the Minister with special responsibility for Children and Young People announced a forthcoming, State-funded, Early Childhood Care and Education (ECCE) Scheme. Though reliant on the existing cohort of independent sessional service providers, the State committed to funding a three-hour, five-day per week scheme, running parallel to the thirty-eight-week primary school calendar (DHC 2010). Under contract to the State, participatory criteria for services included regulatory compliance and commitment to the spirit of the two national practice frameworks, related to quality (*Síolta*) and curriculum (*Aistear*) in ECEC settings (CECDE 2006, NCCA 2009). Funding criteria stipulated participating educators were to hold a one-year vocational award in ECEC, as a minimal qualification, as this scheme pre-dated the 2016 statutory requirement for same. Allowing for an adjustment period, by 2012 all staff working in the funded ECCE Scheme were to hold such an award. The entitlement for a child to attend this scheme was extended in 2016 to allow for two years of provision.

Inherent in the design of the ECCE Scheme, the funding criteria of a higher per diem capitation was linked to the presence of graduate-practitioners working directly in this programme. This provided a mechanism by which qualification levels across the State were positively impacted, in the absence of regulatory specificity. Whereas most graduate-practitioners were recruited to work with preschool children, this effectively created inequitable experiences in ECEC settings, from a quality perspective, for

5   EU member States committed to provide childcare places for at least 90 per cent of
     3-year-olds and 33 per cent of children under 3 years of age by 2010 (EU 2002).

children under 3 years of age. In 2010, 12 per cent of staff in registered ECEC services held a qualification equal to or above an ordinary bachelor degree (Pobal 2013), increasing to 25 per cent in 2019 (Pobal 2019). While this represents a slow but steady increase in the proportion of graduate-practitioners, progress is exacerbated by high staff turnover (SIPTU 2019) and is some way off achieving the goal of a graduate-led workforce of 50 per cent by 2030, as called for in domestic policy (DCYA 2013, Government of Ireland 2018), or the 60 per cent referred to in international reports (Urban et al. 2011).

National Childcare Scheme

Whereas the ECCE scheme addressed the affordability and universality issues in regards to 'preschool' provision, the high cost to families of full daycare services has been a perennial issue in the Irish State. This is due in large part to the reliance on the market as the primary provider of ECEC services, coupled with limited State investment (Hayes and Bradley 2006, Russell et al. 2018). Over the preceding two decades, various short-lived, non-statutory schemes attempted to address particular scenarios, be they family or service-specific, to reduce childcare fees.

The enactment of the *Childcare Support Act 2018* established the first statutory system of fee-subsidy for families in Ireland. The resultant *Affordable Childcare Scheme* (DCYA 2016), later renamed the *National Childcare Scheme* (NCS), offered both a universal and means-tested element of financial support to reduce the cost of ECEC for families. However, only families using an early years services *registered* with Tusla under the 2016 regulations, were eligible.

This restrictive criterion created the imperative to bring services historically on the margins of the early years sector into a regulatory context. Although the *Child Care Act 1991* included provision for the regulation of school-age service, the 1996, 2006 and 2016 regulations failed to address this lacuna. Unchanged since the initial 1996 regulations, the limited conditions under which home-based childcare providers (commonly known as childminders) were required to notify resulted a significant cohort, estimated to be in the area of 35,000 (DCYA 2019) remaining outside the regulatory system. This is despite childminding being considered the traditional form of childcare and the most used type of non-parental care in Ireland (*Ibid.*).

Regulatory action to extend access to the NCS to a wider cohort of families occurred with the enactment of the *Registration of School Age Services Regulations 2018*, amending the *Child Care Act 1991 (Early Years Services) Regulations 2016*. Certainly not as broad in scope as the 2016 Regulations, the amendments ensured centre-based and home-based childminding settings afforded greater oversight and protection to school-aged children than heretofore, including evidence of Garda Vetting of adults involved in the service, in line with the 2012 Act. The launch of the *National Quality Guidelines for School Age Childcare Services* (DCYA 2020) offered clarity to improve provision for this older age cohort, beyond areas addressed by the regulations, although lacking statutory enforcement mechanisms.

Whereas the 2018 amendments addressed the issue of childminding services, with respect of school-aged children, the exclusion of many families with preschool-aged children from accessing the NCS through currently unregistered childminding services remains. At present, consultations with childminding representatives have commenced with the aim of developing suitable regulations for this ECEC sub-sector, allowing for the extension of the NCS to client-families. The need to balance the unique home-based context, the providers' perspectives and experiences, with the rights of children for protection, appropriate care and quality early learning experiences is to the fore in these current deliberations (DCYA 2019, O'Regan et al. 2020).

Conclusion

The *Children Act 1908*, served as the starting point for this chapter. This Act offered a legislative foundation for most of the twentieth century, leaving a negative legacy concerning the protection and education of children in Ireland. Children who lived in poverty or were involved in petty crime were viewed as a social risk who needed protection from themselves. Education was thus provided by industrial and reformatory schools to address the perceived misconduct in these instances. These schools slowly began to shut down following recommendations from the Kennedy Report (1970).

A liberalizing societal shift from the 1960s onwards, particularly with the advancement of greater autonomy for women, impacted on children's lived experiences. That decade also saw a move from the social risk model of child care towards an increasingly developmental model (Buckley et al. 1997). These progressive changes were advanced by the ratification of the UNCRC in the 1990s, gradually influencing Irish policy related to children over the later decades; however, a protectionist viewpoint remained, ensuring a paternalistic stance on children's rights held sway for some time. The enactment in 2015 of the *Thirty-First Amendment of the Constitution (Children) Act 2012*, following a successful referendum, provided greater recognition of children as citizens, having participation rights including the right to have their voice heard in matters that affect them, depending on their age and maturity. In the area of family law, rights and responsibilities, one legislative lacuna that continues concerns unmarried fathers who remain unrecognized as guardians of their children, unless particular criteria have been met and applications undertaken. These circumstances create challenges for some fathers regarding their involvement in their children's education, particularly their early education, in terms of decision-making and partnership practices with ECEC settings.

Eighty years on from the *Children Act 1908*, the *Child Care Act 1991* set in place the legislative and regulatory framework that has since governed ECEC, as well as family support and child welfare services. Initial attention to ECEC was primarily from a labour support perspective through an economic lens. Later iterations of relevant regulations, and the accompanying policy context in which these developed, increasingly recognized the potential of early years settings as spaces through which children's rights to safe, high-quality early educational experiences could be realized.

Legislation over the past thirty years concerning mandatory reporting and vetting legislation, alongside Pre-School (1996, 2006) and Early Years Regulations (2016), has promoted a more secure and accountable environment in which children's first stage of formal education occurs. Recent State activity has extended regulatory oversight, primarily in the area of safeguarding and funding supports for school-aged children, yet meanwhile, a large cohort of home-based childminding services remain as outliers. This is despite constitutional recognition that all children, including those attending locally based childminding settings, are citizens. As such, they have as equal a claim as their peers to high-quality ECEC experiences, in regulated environments, even from a very young age.

This chapter has summarized constitutional, legislative and regulatory developments in the Republic of Ireland over the past century or so, aligning these to the evolving social and cultural context to which legislation ultimately responds. Ireland has shifted from conservative and controlling to liberalized and progressive; the societal values that have been reflected through this period have been examined through the lens of education and children's rights, and are particularly illustrated in the preceding audit of the ECEC sector. Although not without critics, it is clear that ECEC has come to be central in the lives of Irish families and that the place of the child as a rights holder has become a focus of policy, regulatory, legislative and, ultimately, constitutional change.

Bibliography

Bracken, L. (2018). *Child Law in Ireland.* Dublin: Clarus Press.

Buckley, H., Skehill, C. and O'Sullivan, E. (eds) (1997). *Child Protection Practices in Ireland: A Case Study.* Dublin: Oak Tree Press.

Buckley, S. A. (2013). *The Cruelty Man.* Manchester: Manchester University Press.

Buckley, S. A. and McGregor, C. (eds) (2018). 'Interrogating Institutionalism and Child Welfare: The Irish Case, 1939–1941', *European Journal of Social Work*, 22 (6), 1062–1072.

Burns, K. and McGregor, C. (2019). Child Protection and Welfare Systems in Ireland: Continuities and Discontinuities of the Present. In L. Merkel-Kolguin, J. D. Fluke and D. Krugman (eds), *National Systems of Child Protection*, pp. 115–138. Bern: Springer Publications.

Canavan, J. (2012). 'Family and Family Change in Ireland: An Overview', *Journal of Family Issues*, 33 (1), 10–28.

Centre for Early Childhood Development and Education (2006). *Síolta: The National Quality Framework for Early Childhood Education*. Dublin: CECDE.

Chubb, B. (1978). *The Constitution and Constitutional Change in Ireland*. Dublin: Institute of Public Administration.

Coolahan, J. (1998). *Report on the National Forum for Early Childhood Education*. Dublin: The Stationery Office.

Crowley, L. (2013). *Family Law*. Dublin: Thomson Roundhall.

Department of Children and Youth Affairs (2013). *Right from the Start: Report on the Expert Advisory Group on the Early Years Strategy*. Dublin: Government Publications Office.

Department of Children and Youth Affairs (2016). *Affordable Childcare Scheme*. Dublin: DCYA. Available at: <https://www.dcya.gov.ie/viewdoc.asp?fn=/documents/earlyyears/20161011SingleAffordableChildcareSchemeMainPage.htm>.

Department of Children and Youth Affairs (2019). *Draft Childminding Action Plan*. Dublin: DCYA. Available at: <https://www.gov.ie/en/publication/42314a-draft-childminding-action-plan/>.

Department of Children and Youth Affairs (2020). *National Quality Guidelines for School Age Childcare Services*. Dublin: DCYA. Available at: <https://www.gov.ie/en/publication/b66c5-national-quality-guidelines-for-school-age-childcare-services-guidelines-components-and-elements-september-2020/>.

Department of Education and Science (2002). *OECD Thematic Review of Early Childhood Education and Care Policy in Ireland: Background Report*. Dublin: DES.

Department of Health and Children (1999). *Children First, National Guidance for the Protection and Welfare of Children*. Dublin: The Stationery Office.

Department of Health and Children (2006). *Child Care (Pre-School Services) Regulations (No. 2) 2006*. Dublin: The Stationery Office.

Department of Health and Children (2010). *Office of the Minister for Children. Free Pre-school Year in Early Childhood Care and Education (ECCE) Scheme*. Dublin: DHC. Available at: <http://www.omc.gov.ie/viewdoc/asp?fn=%2Fdocuments%2FECCE-Scheme%2Fintro.htm&mn=chia&nlD=13>

Department of Justice, Equality and Law Reform (2002). *Quality Childcare and Life-long Learning: Model Framework for Education, Training and Professional Development in the Early Childhood Care and Education Sector*. Dublin: The Stationery Office. Available at: <https://www.education.ie/en/Schools-Colleges/Information/Early-Years/Model-Framework-for-Education-Training-and-Professional-Development-in-the-Early-Childhood-Care-and-Education-Sector.pdf>.

Doyle, O. (2004). *Constitutional Equality Law*. Dublin: Thomson Round Hall Ltd.

Duignan, M. and Fallon, J. (2004). *On Target? An Audit of Provision of Services Targeting Disadvantage and Special Needs among Children Aged Birth to Six in Ireland*. Dublin: CECDE.

Egan, A. (2011). 'Are Fathers Discriminated Against in Irish Family Law? An Empirical Study', *Irish Journal of Family Law*, 14 (2), 38–49.

European Council (2002). *Report from the Commission to the European Parliament, the Council, the European Economic and Social Committee and the Committee of the Regions*. Brussels: EC. Available at: <http://aei.pitt.edu/43345/1/Barcelona_2002_1.pdf>

Ferriter, D. (2005). *The Transformation of Ireland*. New York: Overlook Press.

Gallagher, A. (2013). 'At Home in Preschool Care? Childcare Policy and the Negotiated Spaces of Educational Care', *Children's Geographies*, 11 (2), 202–214, <http://dx.doi.org/10.1080/14733285.2013.779447>

Garrity, S. and Canavan, J. (2017). 'Trust, Responsiveness and Communities of Care: An Ethnographic Study of the Significance and Development of Parent-Caregiver Relationships in Irish Early Years Settings', *European Early Childhood Education Research Journal*. <http://dx.doi.org/10.1080/1350293X.2017.1356546>

Government of Ireland (1922). *Constitution of Ireland*. Dublin: Government Publications Office.

Government of Ireland (1926). *School Attendance Act 1926*. Dublin: Government Publications Office.

Government of Ireland (1929). *Children Act 1929*. Dublin: Government Publications Office.

Government of Ireland (1931). *Legitimacy Act 1931*. Dublin: Government Publications Office.

Government of Ireland (1937). *Bunreacht na hÉireann / Constitution of Ireland*. Dublin: Government Publications Office.

Government of Ireland (1941). *Children Act 1941*. Dublin: Government Publications Office.

Government of Ireland (1952). *Adoption Act 1952*. Dublin: Government Publications Office.

Government of Ireland (1957a). *Children (Amendment) Act 1957*. Dublin: Government Publications Office.

Government of Ireland (1957b). *Married Women's Status Act 1957*. Dublin: Government Publications Office.

Government of Ireland (1964). *Guardianship of Infants Act 1964*. Dublin: Government Publications Office.

Government of Ireland (1970). *Health Act 1970*. Dublin: Government Publications Office.

Government of Ireland (1973a). *Employment of Married Women Act 1973*. Dublin: Government Publications Office.

Government of Ireland (1973b). *Social Welfare Act 1973*. Dublin: Government Publications Office.

Government of Ireland (1976a). *Family Home Protection Act 1976*. Dublin: Government Publications Office.

Government of Ireland (1976b). *Family Law (Maintenance of Spouses and Children) Act 1976*. Dublin: Government Publications Office.

Government of Ireland (1977). *Employment Equality Act 1977*. Dublin: Government Publications Office.

Government of Ireland (1987). *Status of Children Act 1987*. Dublin: Government Publications Office.

Government of Ireland (1991). *Child Care Act 1991*. Dublin. Government Publications Office.

Government of Ireland (1996a). *Child Care (Pre-School Services) Regulations 1996*. Dublin: Government Publications Office.

Government of Ireland (1996b). *Family Law (Divorce) Act 1996*. Dublin: Government Publications Office.

Government of Ireland (1997a). *Child Care (Pre-School Services) (Amendment) 1997*. Dublin: Government Publications Office.

Government of Ireland (1997b). *Children Act 1997*. Dublin: Government Publications Office.

Government of Ireland (1998). *Protections for Persons Reporting Child Abuse Act 1998*. Dublin: Government Publications Office.

Government of Ireland (1999a). *Ready to Learn: White Paper on Early Childhood Education*. Dublin: The Stationery Office.

Government of Ireland (1999b). *National Childcare Strategy – Report of the Partnership 2000 Expert Working Group on Childcare*. Dublin: The Stationery Office.

Government of Ireland (2000). *National Children's Strategy: Our Children, Their Lives*. Dublin: The Stationery Office.

Government of Ireland (2000–2018). *Equal Status Act 2000–2018*. Dublin: Government Publications Office.

Government of Ireland (2001). *Children Act 2001*. Dublin: Government Publications Office.

Government of Ireland (2002). *Ombudsman for Children Act 2002*. Dublin: Government Publications Office.

Government of Ireland (2006). *Pre-School Services (No. 2) Regulations 2006.* Dublin: Government Publications Office.

Government of Ireland (2012). *Thirty-First Amendment to the Constitution (Children) Act 2012.* Dublin: Government Publications Office.

Government of Ireland (2012). *National Vetting Bureau (Children and Vulnerable Persons) Act 2012.* Dublin: Government Publications Office.

Government of Ireland (2013). *Child and Family Agency Act 2013.* Dublin: Government Publications Office.

Government of Ireland (2015a). *Children and Family Relationships Act 2015.* Dublin: Government Publications Office.

Government of Ireland (2015b). *Children First Act 2015.* Dublin: Government Publications Office.

Government of Ireland (2016). *Child Care Act 1991 (Early Years Services) Regulations 2016.* Dublin: Government Publications Office.

Government of Ireland (2018a). *Childcare Support Act 2018.* Dublin: Government Publications Office.

Government of Ireland (2018b). *Registration of School Age Services Regulations 2018.* Dublin: Government Publications Office.

Government of Ireland (2018c). *First 5 – A Whole of Government Strategy for Babies, Young Children and Their Families.* Dublin: Government Publications Office. Available at: <https://www.gov.ie/en/publication/f7ca04-first-5-a-whole-of-government-strategy-for-babies-young-children-and/>.

Hanafin, S. (2016). 'Regulators' Views of Quality in Early Childhood Care and Education Settings in Ireland', *Child Care in Practice*, 22 (2), 183–196. Available at: <http://dx.doi.org/10.1080/13575279.2015.1064359>

Hayes, N. (1995). *The Case for a National Policy on Early Education: Poverty and Policy, Discussion Paper No. 2.* Dublin: Combat Poverty Agency.

Hayes, N. (2008). *The Role of Early Childhood Care and Education – An Anti-Poverty Perspective.* Dublin: Combat Poverty Agency. Available at: <https://arrow.tudublin.ie/cgi/viewcontent.cgi?article=1045&context=cserrep>

Hayes, N. and Bradley, S. (2006). 'The Childcare Question'. In B. Fanning and M. Rush (eds), *Care and Social Change in the Irish Welfare Economy*, pp. 163–178. Dublin: University College Dublin Press.

Hayes, N. and Bradley, S. (2009). *Right by Children: Children's Rights and Rights Based Approaches to Policy Making in Early Childhood Education and Care: The Case of Ireland.* Dublin: Irish Research Council Humanities and the Social Sciences. Available at: <https://arrow.tudublin.ie/cserrep/36/>.

His Majesty's Government (1908). *Children Act 1908.* London: The Stationery Office.

His Majesty's Government (1919). *Public Health (Medical Treatment of Children) Act 1919*. London: The Stationery Office.

Hogan, G. (2005). 'DeValera, the Constitution and Historians', *Irish Jurist*, 40 (1), 293–320.

Kennedy, E. (1970). *Report on Industrial Schools and Reformatories*. Dublin: The Stationery Office.

Kennedy, F. (2001). *Cottage to Crèche: Family Change in Ireland*. Dublin: Institute of Public Administration.

Keogh, D. and McCarthy, A. (eds) (2005). *Twentieth-Century Ireland: Revolution and State Building*. Dublin: Gill and Macmillan.

Kiersey, R. A. and Hayes, N. (2010). 'Reporting the Rhetoric, Implementation of the United Nations Convention on the Rights of the Child as Represented in Ireland's Second Report to the UN Committee on the Rights of the Child: A Critical Discourse Analysis', *Child Care in Practice*, 16 (4), 327–346.

Kilkelly, U. (2008). *Children's Rights in Ireland: Law, Policy and Practice*. Dublin: Tottel Publishing.

Langford, S. (2006). 'The Development of Childcare Policy in Ireland During 1996–2002.' In N. Hayes and S. Bradley (eds), *A Decade of Reflection: Early Childhood Care and Education in Ireland 1996–2006. Proceedings of Centre for Social and Educational Research Early Childhood Care and Education Seminar Series 1*, November, 3, 2006. Available at: <http://www.cser.ie>

Lee, J. J. (1989). *Ireland 1912–1985*. New York: Cambridge University Press.

McGuinness, C. (1993). *Report of the Kilkenny Incest Investigation*. Dublin: Government Publications Office.

Millar, M., Coen, L., Bradley, C. and Rau, H. (2012). 'Doing the Job as a Parent: Parenting Alone, Work, and Family Policy in Ireland', *Journal of Family Issues*, 33 (1), 29–51.

National Council for Curriculum and Assessment (2009). *Aistear: The Early Childhood Curriculum Framework*. Dublin: NCCA.

National Economic and Social Forum (2005). *Early Childhood Care and Education Report*. Dublin: NESF. Available at: <http://files.nesc.ie/nesf_archive/nesf_reports/NESF_31.pdf>.

National Women's Council of Ireland (2005). *An Accessible Childcare Model*. Dublin: NWCI. Available at: <https://www.nwci.ie/learn/publication/an_accessible_childcare_model>.

Organisation for Economic Cooperation and Development (2004). *OECD Thematic Review of Early Childhood Education and Care Policy in Ireland*. Paris: OECD. Available at: <https://www.education.ie/en/Publications/Policy-Reports/OECD-Review-of-Early-Childhood-Education-and-Care-Policy-in-Ireland-Information-Note.pdf>.

O'Kane, M. (2005). 'The Effect of Regulation on the Quality of Early Childhood Services in Ireland', *Child Care in Practice*, 11 (2), 231–251. DOI: 10.1080/ 13575270500053175.

O'Regan, M., Halpenny, A. M. and Hayes, N. (2020). 'Childminders' Close Relationship Model of Praxis: An Ecocultural Study in Ireland', *European Early Childhood Education Research Journal*, 28 (5), 675–689, DOI: 10.1080/ 1350293X.2020.1817239.

O'Sullivan, S. (2012). 'All Changed, Changed Utterly'? Gender Role Attitudes and the Feminisation of the Irish Labour Force', *Women's Studies International Forum*, 35 (4), 223–232.

Pobal (2013). *Pobal Annual Survey of the Early Years Sector 2012*. Dublin: Pobal.

Pobal (2019). *Annual Early Years Sector Profile*. Dublin: Pobal. Available at: <https:// www.pobal.ie/app/uploads/2019/12/Annual-Early-Years-Sector-Profile-Rep ort-AEYSPR-2018-19.pdf>.

Quinn, G. (2000). 'Rethinking the Nature of Economic, Social and Cultural Rights in the Irish Legal Order'. In C. Costello (ed.), *Social Rights: Current European Legal Protection and the Challenge of the EU Charter on Fundamental Rights*, pp. 35–54. Dublin: Irish Centre for European Law.

Russell, H., McGinnity, F., Fahey, E. and Kenny, O. (2018). *Maternal Employment and the Cost of Childcare in Ireland*. Dublin: Economic and Social Research Institute. Available at: <https://www.esri.ie/publications/maternal-employm ent-and-the-cost-of-childcare-in-ireland>.

Share, M. and Kerrins, L. (2013). 'Supporting Parental Involvement in Children's Early Learning: Lessons from Community Childcare Centres in Dublin's Docklands', *Child Care in Practice*, 19 (4), 355–374. Available at: <http:// dx.doi.org/10.1080/13575279.2013.799457>

Shatter, A. (1997). *Family Law*. 4th ed. Dublin: Butterworths.

SIPTU (2019). *Early Years Professionals Survey*. Dublin: SIPTU.

Thornton, L., Ni Mhuirthile, T. and O'Sullivan, C. (eds) (2016). *Fundamentals of Irish Legal System*. Dublin: Roundhall.

Tuairim (1966). *Some of Our Children – A Report on the Residential Care of Deprived Children in Ireland*. London: Tuairim.

UNICEF (2008). *The Child Care Transition, Innocenti Report Card 8*. Florence: UNICEF Innocenti Research Centre. Available at: <https://www. unicef-irc.org/publications/pdf/rc8_eng.pdf>.

United Nations (1989). *Convention on the Rights of the Child*. New York: United Nations General Assembly. Available at: <https://www.ohchr.org/en/profe ssionalinterest/pages/crc.aspx>.

Urban, M., Vandenbroeck, M., Van Laere, K., Lazzari, A. and Peeters, J. (2011). *Competence Requirements in Early Childhood Education and Care. Research*

Documents. Brussels: European Commission. Directorate General for Education and Culture.

Walshe, D. (2003). 'The Legal Rights of Unmarried Biological Fathers in Ireland and England, 1997–2002: A Comparative Analysis', *Irish Journal of Family Law*, 6 (2), 2–13.

Wolfe, T., O'Donghue-Hynes, B. and Hayes, N. (2013). 'Rapid Change Without Transformation: The Dominance of a National Policy Paradigm Over International Influences on ECEC Development in Ireland 1995–2012', *International Journal of Early Childhood*, 45 (2), 191–205. DOI:10.1007/s13158-013-0090-5.

MARESA DUIGNAN AND FIONA MCDONNELL

9 An overview of the development of government regulation and inspection in the early childhood education and care sector in Ireland, 1921–2021

Introduction

This chapter addresses the evolving role of the Irish government in quality assuring the early childhood education and care (ECEC) experiences of children, under the age of 6 years,[1] in the period 1921–2021. It briefly documents developments from the inspection of infant education in national schools from the early days of the newly established Free State, through to the present day where regulation and inspection of ECEC is a complex system involving multiple actors and State agencies. The chapter examines the evolution of inspection systems across two key agencies; Tusla – the Child and Family Agency, which is the statutory regulatory body for ECEC and the Department of Education Inspectorate (DEI), which has statutory responsibility for the quality of education provision in schools and other State-funded centres of education. Particular focus is given to developments across a dynamic period of three decades, commencing with the publication of the *Child Care Act 1991* (Government of Ireland 1991). In this period, policy development relating to the quality of ECEC provision and practice advanced as did the development of inspection systems and approaches. The chapter draws upon data and research generated by the Tusla Early Years Inspectorate and the DEI during this time.

---

1   The compulsory age by which children must have enrolled in primary education.

In order to explore the key developments above, the chapter is divided into three distinct sections; firstly a brief overview of early childhood education inspection in schools by the Department of Education, secondly a review of the registration and inspection system carried out by Tusla; and finally the Early Years Education Inspections (EYEIs) in Early Learning and Care settings by the DEI.

Section one: Inspection of early childhood education in schools

In her book *The Development of Infant Education in Ireland, 1838– 1948: Epochs and Eras*, O'Connor provides an overview of the growth and development of 'infant education' in the context of primary schools. Whilst the compulsory education age range was set in 1926, encompassing children from 6 to 14 years, there is evidence of a long tradition of early enrolment in primary school by children aged 3 and 4 years (O'Connor 2010). This has continued in the intervening decades, with the majority of children enrolled in the infant classes of primary school by their fifth birthday (DES 2019, Ring et al. 2016). Inspection of the education system, including provision for 'infants', was established in parallel with the setting up of a national system of education in 1831 (later to become known as primary school education). As John Coolahan details, '… it was the accepted wisdom of the day that a State supported education system should include a formal inspectorial dimension to ensure that regulations were fulfilled and teachers were accountable for their performance' (Coolahan with O'Donovan 2009: 17).

While it is not possible to go into detail on the decades of development of the education Inspectorate here, it is worth noting that the functions of the Inspectorate have been intrinsically bound to the development of the education system generally and the curriculum in particular (Coolahan with O'Donovan 2009, O'Connor 2010, Walsh 2012). The strong connection between the focus of education and wider social, cultural and economic developments influencing Irish society is particularly evident in the provision of infant education. From the restoration of the Irish language and culture in the early years of the fledgling Irish Free State, to the early interventions that aimed to mitigate social and educational disadvantage (e.g. establishment of Rutland Street Preschool [1969] and Early Start Programme [1994]), educational provision for children under 6 years of age has a long tradition in Ireland; and an equally long tradition of oversight by the DEI. Inspection in the early years of primary school included a focus on the teaching workforce through probationary visits to newly qualified teachers[2] as well as evaluation of teaching and learning in practice using a range of inspection models, such as whole school evaluation, incidental inspection and curriculum evaluation (Department of Education and Skills [DES] 2016a). A strong emphasis has been placed upon self-evaluation in schools as a strong foundation for quality in both provision and practice of education (DES 2016b). In general, this oversight of early years education has been exercised in the context of infant classes in primary schools funded by the Department of Education. The small but notable exception to this is the Early Start units established in 1994 in forty primary schools identified as providing for the needs of children at risk of educational disadvantage (DES 2014).

The DEIs long history of evaluating early education provision and practice in schools was augmented in the early 2000s by policy initiatives to develop and publish both a national curriculum framework and a national quality framework for early childhood education. The output of these initiatives, *Síolta, the National Quality Framework for Early Childhood Education* (Centre for Early Childhood Development and Education [CECDE] 2006) and *Aistear, The Early Childhood Curriculum Framework* (NCCA 2009) have become progressively more embedded in government policy pertaining to the development of quality in ECEC over the ensuing decade. They are at the heart of formative initiatives which will impact on the future of the ECEC system in Ireland, including national standards

---

2   These visits ceased to be the responsibility of the Department of Education and Skills in 2013 with the introduction, by the Teaching Council of Ireland, of the Droichead programme of induction (Smyth et al. 2016).

and guidelines for initial professional education for the ECEC workforce (DES 2019) and are a core element of the contract with the Department of Children, Equality, Disability, Integration and Youth (DCEDIY) to provide the Early Childhood Care and Education (ECCE) scheme of free pre-school (Department of Children and Youth Affairs [DCYA] 2020: section 8.1). In 2014, they also provided the foundations for the development of the EYEI model which commenced in 2016.[3]

Section two: Inspection and regulation of ECEC undertaken by Tusla

This section addresses the inspection and regulation of ECEC provision and practice outside of that funded by the Department of Education. It first provides an overview of the work of the Tusla Early Years Inspectorate.

In contrast to the organization of infant education in the school system, and the accompanying inspection oversight, provision of publicly funded ECEC services for children under the age of 6 years in the period from 1921 to the 1990s was sparse. This can largely be attributed to the low level of participation by women in the Irish labour market which reduced the need for non-parental care for young children. The 'principle of subsidiarity'[4] also exerted strong influence over the development of social policy relating to the family with a consequent reluctance by the State to intervene

---

3   The national practice frameworks for early childhood education, *Aistear* and *Síolta*, commissioned by the DES, were developed between 2002 and 2009. *Aistear* (the curriculum framework) and *Síolta* (the quality framework) together provide a clear set of criteria and guidelines to inform capacity building in the early years sector. The frameworks also support practitioners to provide high-quality early learning experiences for children aged birth to 6 years in Ireland irrespective of where the learning experiences are provided.

4   Effectively this principle, articulated in the 1931 encyclical of Pope Pius XI, advocates a low level of State intervention in matters which should be determined by the individual. In Ireland this was influential in the development of the Irish Constitution of 1937 and ensured that the rights of the family to self-determination would not be undermined by State intervention.

in the provision of supports for non-parental childcare (Kennedy 2001, Duignan 2011). This principle goes some way to explaining the dearth of legislation, regulation and policy pertaining to the welfare and wellbeing of children in this period.

The *Children's Act 1908*[5] was a landmark piece of legislation for the care of children in Ireland at the time of its publication, introducing, as it did, compulsory education and giving children a separate legal status (Kiernan and Walsh 2004). It could also be argued that over time it evidenced the invisibility of children in social policy, as it remained the primary legislation underpinning the care of children in Ireland, until it was fully replaced by the *Child Care Act 1991*, almost a century later (Hayes 2002).

In the absence of State provision of ECEC services, a variety of actors became involved in the provision of a varied range of services for children. These included philanthropic and religious institutions providing services for children at risk as a result of poverty or disability, as well as individuals and organizations motivated by the implementation of educational philosophies and approaches (Duignan 2011). The legacy of these decades of 'laissez-faire' approach to national policy by the State was a complex picture of ECEC provision characterized by difference and diversity and little evidence of coordination or coherence (CECDE 2004, Duignan 2011, Walsh 2016). This is not to say that there was no evidence of effort to raise standards and quality of ECEC provision in this time frame; rather, that these efforts were inhibited by a persistent lack of resources and coordinated national leadership and policy frameworks (CECDE 2004, Duignan 2011).

Statutory regulation of ECEC: Legislative and regulatory context

The *Child Care Act 1991* (Government of Ireland 1991), which replaced the *Children's Act 1908*, was a ground-breaking, wide-ranging piece of

---

5   The *Children's Act 1908*. Available at: <https://www.legislation.gov.uk/ukpga/Edw7/8/67/contents/enacted>.

legislation having at its core the welfare of children who were not in receipt of adequate care and protection. Part VII of the *Child Care Act
1991* gave effect to the *Child Care (Pre-School Services) Regulations 1996*
(Government of Ireland, 1997) which made provision for the notification and inspection of preschool services. Providers of preschool services
were required to notify the Health Board that they were providing a preschool service. Inspection of notified preschool services commenced in
1997 and these inspections were undertaken by Public Health Nurses
and Environmental Health Officers as the authorized officers employed
by the Health Board. The 1996 Regulations attracted some criticism for
focusing on the health and safety of preschool settings rather than child
development and the quality of children's experiences. O'Kane (2005)
confirms some positive improvements in the quality of care were evident
as a result of their implementation.

The regulations were revised in 2006 (Government of Ireland
2006) and addressed some of the previous criticism with the inclusion of
Regulation 5 which placed a greater emphasis on the health, welfare and
development of the child. Regulation 5 introduced the assessment of both
structural and process quality based on the whole child perspective, as outlined in the National Children's Strategy (Government of Ireland 2000),
and underpinned by the United Nations Convention on the Rights of the
Child (UNCRC) (UN 1989). In 2011, the preschool Inspectorate implemented an evidenced based assessment to support preschool providers to
meet the requirements of Regulation 5 (Government of Ireland 2006) as
recommended by Hanafin et al. (2009).

The *Child Care Act 1991* was amended in 2013 by the insertion of PART
VIIA into the *Child and Family Agency Act 2013* (Government of Ireland
2013). This amendment to the legislation was far reaching and transforma-
tive and included key changes for the regulation of early years services giving
effect to revised regulations in 2016 (Government of Ireland 2016a, 2016b).
The definition of early years services was expanded in the 2016 regulations
to include a school-age service or a preschool service, and the requirement
to be registered and approved to open before commencing operation was
defined. Tusla was also prescribed enhanced enforcement powers which
included the authority to propose the attachment of conditions to the

registration of early years services, refuse the registration of a service and make a proposal to remove a service from the early years register. Within the 2016 regulations (which are the current regulations), there is provision for a right of reply by individuals directly to Tusla in relation to the registration processes. The minimum qualification requirements to work directly with children in an early years service are also established. The legislation and regulations set out the requirements to operate a quality early years service and the role of the Inspectorate in this regard is to assess, monitor and promote the safety and quality of care in accordance with the regulations.

Throughout 2016, the Tusla Early Years Inspectorate facilitated a national roll out of fourteen regional briefing meetings to support the early years sector to implement the required regulatory changes. In excess of 3,800 early years providers attended the regional briefings. In 2016 a national survey of early years providers was carried out for the purpose of improving the inspection process (Tusla 2016). The findings of the survey identified that the vast majority of respondents (70 to 85 per cent) agreed or strongly agreed that the inspection process was rigorous and robust, focused on the correct areas and was fair and appropriate. The findings also identified that service providers understood what was required of them and that the Inspectorate was responsive to queries arising (Tusla 2016). It is, however, ultimately the responsibility of the early years service provider to ensure that the service complies with legislative and regulatory requirements.

Governance structures

Early years services which include preschools, playgroups, day nurseries, crèches, daycare (childminders catering for more than three preschool children) or other similar services which cater for preschool children not attending a recognized school have been regulated by an independent statutory regulator since 1997 (Government of Ireland 1997). The Area Health Boards, which became the Health Service Executive (HSE) in 2005 (Government of Ireland 2004) had responsibility for the inspection of all notified preschool services to ensure the safety, health and welfare of children from 1997 to January 2014. In January 2014, this responsibility was transferred to the new Child and Family Agency, Tusla, established under the *Child and Family Agency Act 2013* (Government of Ireland 2013). The inspection of early years services came under a national governance structure within Tusla`s Quality Assurance Directorate in 2015 with the appointment of a national manager for the Early Years Inspectorate. The governance of the Early Years Inspectorate was further strengthened in July 2018 with the integration of all children's regulatory functions into Children's Services Regulation (CSR) and the appointment of a National Service Director for CSR (Tusla 2019, 2020a). Since the introduction of early years regulation, the Early Years Inspectorate has evolved both innovatively and proactively to meet the legislative and regulatory responsibilities across the three pillars of registration, inspection and enforcement.

Registration

The introduction of the revised regulations in 2016 resulted in a number of structural, process and system changes being implemented by the Tusla Early Years Inspectorate. This included the establishment of a centralized department for the registration and inspection of approximately 4,600 early years services (Tusla 2016). The Inspectorate's registration functions include the initial registration of new services, processing the continued registration of existing services and the receipt and management of representations on behalf of registered providers in relation to proposed decisions made by the registration panel. In addition, the registration office receives, processes and manages incidents which are deemed to be notifiable (i.e. any notification of proposed changes in circumstances of service provision, parents feedback or concerns about an early years service) (Tusla 2021a). Information relating to registered early years services which are operating outside of their registration status is managed by the registration office as are renewals of registration of early years services on a three yearly basis. All early years service providers applying for or having a Tusla registered early years service are subject to the processes of inspection.

Tusla Early Years Inspections

The purpose of inspection is to

> promote and monitor the safety and quality of care and support of the child in early years provision in accordance with the regulations. The Inspectorate implements its role by assessing applications for registration and by inspecting registered services. (Tusla 2020a: 16)

The regulatory inspection processes are underpinned by the principles of proportionality, accountability, effectiveness, fairness, reasonability and transparency (Department of the Taoiseach 2004; Walshe and Shorthall 2004). Equally all inspections of early years services are undertaken in a structured and consistent manner where children's wellbeing is at the heart of the inspection process. There are a number of different types of inspections, such as 'Fit For Purpose' (FFP) inspections; this inspection type applies where the service provider has made an application to Tusla to have its service registered. Inspections may also be conducted when a service provider notifies the Tusla Early Years Inspectorate of a change in circumstances in their service provision. However, the vast majority of inspections are undertaken in relation to existing registered services, with some inspections being undertaken in response to concerns received about an early years service by Tusla (Tusla 2020a).

Evidence of compliance with the regulations is assessed during the inspection process using a triangulation methodology which includes observation of practice, discussion with the provider and staff and a review of the documentation available. Four thematic areas were identified from an analysis of findings of inspection reports in 2014 (Hanafin 2014). These themes provided an overarching framework for the assessment of regulatory compliance on inspection. Regulatory inspection to assess compliance with the 2016 Regulations seeks to determine the extent to which:

- The service is well governed
- The health, welfare and development of each child is supported in the early years service
- Children are safe in the early years service and
- The premises being used for the early years service is safe, suitable and appropriate for the care and education of children (Hanafin 2014).

The inspection methodology of early years services is underpinned by a strong evidence base which includes the annual analysis of inspection reports (Hanafin 2014, Tusla 2015, 2016, 2018a, 2021b) and the *Quality and Regulatory Framework* (Tusla 2018b). The Framework presents how the Inspectorate assesses early years services' compliance with the 2016 Regulations (Government of Ireland 2016b). The methodology of inspection by the Tusla Early Years Inspectorate has transitioned through many iterations since 1997 in response to legislative, regulatory, policy and contextual developments, resulting in the current standardized, coordinated and proportionate approach. Following inspection, the service provider is issued with a draft inspection report. The service provider is afforded a right of reply which includes an opportunity to correct any factual inaccuracies and to detail corrective and preventive actions (CAPAs)[6] which will be undertaken to address any practice identified as non-compliant. In addition, the early years service provider has a right to make a representation to the Tusla Early Years Inspectorate. The final inspection report on completion of the inspection and editorial process is published and available on the Tusla website.[7]

6   Corrective and Preventive Action (CAPA) is an opportunity for the registered provider to respond to each non-compliance identified in the early years inspection report. A Corrective Action is the action taken to rectify or eliminate the non-compliance identified. A Preventive Action is the ongoing action (if any) which is required to ensure that the non-compliance does not reoccur.
7   Inspection Reports: <https://www.tusla.ie/services/preschool-services/creche-inspection-reports/>.

Enforcement

The majority of early years services are found on inspection to be compliant with the majority of regulations inspected (Tusla 2021b). As the statutory regulator, the Tusla Early Years Inspectorate encourages compliance through promoting improvement, monitoring and assessing compliance and responding to non-compliance. In determining appropriate and proportionate regulatory enforcement action, consideration is given to the nature of the risk, the provider's response and engagement through the CAPA process, and the provider's previous history of compliance. The escalation of an early years service through the enforcement process involves a number of steps, including some or all of the following; compliance meeting(s) with the registered provider, regulatory enforcement meeting(s) and / or escalation of the service to the National Registration and Enforcement Panel. Enforcement can include the application of conditions of registration, a proposal to remove the service from the register and prosecution.[8]

It is acknowledged that it is difficult for a regulator to measure the outcomes for children following the inspection process. As an initial step, the Tusla Early Years Inspectorate has commenced measuring the impact of inspection on regulatory compliance. From 2016 to 2020, following analysis of 500 randomly selected non-compliant regulations, the Tusla Early Years Inspectorate can demonstrate an improved rate of compliance of over 80 per cent from inspection to publication (Rouine et al. 2020, Tulsa 2021b). All of the work of the Tusla Early Years Inspectorate is underpinned by agreed standard operating procedures and processes which support statutory registration, inspection and enforcement (Tusla 2016).

As an Inspectorate, Tusla recognizes and values the importance of quality early years provision in supporting children's development, learning and wellbeing. Tusla is committed to supporting early years service providers in meeting regulatory requirements. However the primary role of

---

8   A Guide to Regulatory Enforcement in Early Years Settings <https://www.tusla. ie/services/preschool-services/a-guide-to-regulatory-enforcement-in-early-years-settings/>.

Tusla Early Years Inspectorate is to ensure that children are safe and have quality early years experiences. In this regard, with the best interest of the child at the centre of the inspection process, the Early Years Inspectorate will apply proportionate enforcement where necessary.

Collaboration

The Early Years Inspectorate, while retaining its regulatory independence, continuously strives to be transparent in its practices and to work collaboratively with all stakeholders in the early years sector nationally and internationally. It is in this context of service improvement and collaborative engagement that Tusla established a number of stakeholder groups, including The Early Years Consultative Forum (2015),[9] The Early Years Regulatory Support Forum (2017)[10] and The Education Establishments Forum (Tusla 2020a). Tusla's collaborative work also includes ongoing engagement with statutory and voluntary organizations to support continuous quality improvement.

In 2019, the Early Years Inspectorate sought parents' views on reflecting the voice of parents in the inspection process through a nationwide consultation with parents of children who attend early years services (Tusla 2021a). Tusla recognizes the involvement of parents in their child's care and education and acknowledges that this involvement is widely considered as crucial to the development and wellbeing of the child (Domina 2005, Jeynes 2012). Within this context, the Tusla Early Years Inspectorate is developing mechanisms to ensure that the voice of parents and guardians are heard and inform the inspection process (Tusla 2021a).

9   Early Years Consultative Forum: <https://www.tusla.ie/services/preschool-services/early-years-inspectorate-update/>.
10   Early Years Regulatory Support Forum: <https://www.tusla.ie/services/preschool-services/early-years-inspectorate-update/>.

New and future developments

The Tusla Early Years Inspectorate is committed to continuous improvement of its regulatory systems. Priority developments focus on the design and implementation of systems that are effective and conform to international best practice. Regulation strategy is designed to foster an ethos of advancing children's safety, development and wellbeing by strengthening partnership and communication with stakeholders. As an Inspectorate, Tusla recognizes and values the importance of quality early years provision in supporting children's development and wellbeing. The inclusion of the voice of the child in the inspection process as described by Molloy (2018) is recognized by the Tusla Early Years Inspectorate as an important element in measuring the quality of early years provision. The inspection of childminders has also been committed to in *First 5: A Whole of Government Strategy for Babies, Young Children and their Families 2019–2028* (Government of Ireland 2018). The Tusla Early Years Inspectorate is committed to this policy agenda and has conducted a review of the registration, regulation, inspection and enforcement processes in six jurisdictions to support this policy direction and future implementation (Tusla 2020b).

Section three: Education inspection of ECEC in the Early Learning and Care[11] (ELC) sector

The genesis of the current programme of EYEIs in the ELC sector was the commission, received by the DEI from the DCYA in 2014, to develop an

---

11   Early Learning and Care (ELC) is a term used in *First Five: A Whole of Government Strategy for Babies, Young Children and their Families 2019–2028* to refer to a service for children that is a regulated arrangement to provide education and care for children from birth to compulsory primary school age. It includes centre-based provision and home-based regulated provision but excludes grandparental care and the early years of primary school (Government of Ireland 2018: 26).

evaluation initiative to examine the scope and nature of children's early educational experiences in the ECCE scheme of free preschool education that had been established by the DCYA in 2010. The DEI responded purposefully and extended its established inspection remit to encompass universal State-funded early education provision in diverse settings. These included private, commercial early education services with a multiplicity of governance, staffing and curricular approaches. Despite the challenges that this commission presented, the DEI's long experience of conducting inspections that respond to changing cultural, theoretical and educational perspectives provided a strong foundation upon which to develop a new quality-focused inspection regime.

From the beginning, enrolment figures for the ECCE scheme demonstrated that it had been overwhelmingly successful in terms of children's participation and parents' approval. However, concerns raised by an investigative media report *'Breach of Trust'* (RTE, 28th May 2013)[12] about the quality of practice in a small number of early years settings served to reinforce national and international research findings that participation in ECEC can impact negatively on children if the quality of their experiences is poor (European Commission 2013, Eurydice and EACEA 2009, Oireachtas Library and Research Service 2020).

The government response to this investigative media report was the announcement in Budget 2014 of a National Quality Agenda for the Early Years.[13] This initiative provided resources for a range of measures including a review of the statutory inspection system operated by Tusla, the establishment of a national quality support service for early years services (now known as Better Start) and the establishment of a Learner Fund to support staff in early years services to improve their qualification profile, in advance of the introduction of minimum qualification levels for practitioners in 2016. The agenda also made provision for the establishment of EYEIs as an essential element. In particular, it recognized that the focus on process quality, self-evaluation and inspection for improvement, embedded in the DEI's approach to inspection in the wider school system, had the potential

12   <https://www.rte.ie/news/2013/0529/453276-childcare-frances-fitzgerald/>.
13   <https://www.dcya.gov.ie/viewdoc.asp?DocID=3019>.

to encourage and enhance the capacity of the ELC sector to embed the use of the *Aistear* and *Síolta* frameworks in practice. In turn, this would leverage the pedagogical potential and substantial State investment in quality in ECEC that these two frameworks represented. As the Minister for Children and Youth Affairs stated in the Oireachtas on 30th May 2013:

> We are working to develop a more comprehensive and broader-based inspection regime for pre-schools; moving away from a narrow focus on compliance only, to a greater focus on children's outcomes, including educational development and child wellbeing.[14]

Development of the Early Years Education Inspections (EYEI) model

Between 2013 and 2015, the DEI conducted extensive research on best practice in ECEC which influenced the development of the EYEI model. A draft quality framework was developed and an inspection process designed. An important element of this development work was the piloting of the new inspection model in Early Start units in primary schools. This benefited from cross-fertilization of approaches and ideas within both the DEI and the Tusla Early Years Inspectorate and included the participation in pilot inspections of inspectors from both organizations. These processes were largely based upon the inspection for improvement approach to inspection in primary and post-primary schools (Hislop 2017). The EYEI model is underpinned by a number of principles including:

- Early childhood is a significant and distinct time which must be nurtured, respected, valued and supported in its own right
- The role of the practitioner within early education settings is central
- Children should be active agents in their learning and development, and enabled to achieve their potential as competent, confident

14   <http://merrionstreet.ie/en/Category-Index/Society/Child-Protection/work-underway-on-pre-school-quality-agenda-fitzgerald.html>.

learners, through high-quality interactions with their environment and early childhood practitioners
- Play is central to the learning and development of young children
- The role of parents as children's primary educators is recognized and supported
- The ongoing development of quality through co-professional dialogue between practitioners in early years settings and DES early years inspectors is promoted (DES 2018a).

The quality framework that guides evaluation of practice in the EYEI model addresses the following four areas of practice:

- Area 1 – Quality of context to support children's learning and development
- Area 2 – Quality of processes to support children's learning and development
- Area 3 – Quality of children's learning experiences and achievements
- Area 4 – Quality of management and leadership for learning.

Each of these four areas is further elaborated to encompass a total of twenty learning outcomes and a series of 'signposts for practice' to assist both inspectors and practitioners to come to a common understanding of how these outcomes might be identified and evaluated. The application of the inspection framework in practice is detailed in a *Guide to Early Years Education Inspection* (DES 2018a).

Throughout the latter half of 2015 and early 2016, a structured consultation process was facilitated to afford an opportunity to all stakeholders in the ELC sector across Ireland to provide constructive comment and feedback on the draft EYEI model. This consultation included a field trial in diverse ELC settings and a programme of public seminars to hear feedback from these settings on their experience of inspection using the draft EYEI model. The approach to inspection that emerged from the consultation process involved processes that recognize and encourage sharing of the diverse professional wisdom that exists across the ELC sector. Pre-evaluation meetings, engaging with staff and children during the course of the inspection, and opening the post-inspection feedback meetings to all staff are some of the key characteristics that were endorsed by the ELC sector.

Provision of the opportunity to review and contribute to the inspection report through factual verification and setting response processes were also widely welcomed (DES 2018b).

A major change to the inspection model arising from consultation was the move from an unannounced to an announced inspection (DES 2016e). This reflected understanding and agreement by the DEI of the need for preparation of young children for the arrival of new adults into the ELC setting. The new inspection model was approved and authorized by the Ministers for Education and Skills and Children and Youth Affairs in April 2016. To reinforce the introduction of EYEIs, the grant agreement for ELC settings in receipt of funding to deliver the ECCE Programme of free preschool was amended to include the following text in section 8.1:

> The Grantee shall permit representatives and agents of the Grantor to attend at the premises of the Grantee and shall permit access to the Grantee's premises and personnel for the purposes of inspection and audits. These shall include, but not be limited to, inspections and audits carried out by the early years (pre-school) inspectorate, the inspectorate of the Department of Education and Skills .... (DCYA 2020)

Full national roll out of EYEIs commenced on 14th April 2016.

Implementation of the EYEI model

Since the appointment of the first nine early years inspectors to the DEI in November 2015, resource allocation from the DCYA (and more recently the DCEDIY) has allowed for the expansion of the service to nineteen early years inspectors in 2020. Each inspector has achieved a minimum required qualification of an honours bachelor degree in ECEC and at least five years experience of leadership in early childhood provision and practice (Public Appointments Service 2015). Additional resources provided though the DEI allow for the allocation of two (whole-time equivalent) posts filled by primary inspectors with experience and expertise in early childhood education. This team is managed by an Assistant Chief Inspector who also contributes to the DES early years policy brief.

Since commencement, over 2,600 inspections have been completed in a diverse range of ELC settings on contract to deliver the ECCE programme. Each inspection to date has been selected randomly from the total list of eligible ELC settings. The DEI coordinates with the Tusla Early Years Inspectorate to ensure that there is no coincidence of inspection visits. The Tusla inspections are given priority over DEI inspections. Each visit is negotiated with the individual ELC setting to take account of the size and location of the setting. Observation of all learning areas, both indoors and outdoors, is carried out and time is provided to ensure professional conversations with staff are facilitated. The number of contracted settings varies slightly from year to year due to the predominantly private, commercial nature of provision in the ELC sector. However, based upon an average of 4,200 settings on contract per annum, the DEIs coverage of the sector stands at approximately 65 per cent in March 2020.[15] Inspection reports arising from this programme of inspection are published on the Department of Education website.[16]

In 2017, a review of inspection findings from the first tranche of inspection was completed. A composite report was published to share the early insight arising from EYEIs in early 2018 (DES 2018b). In the main, the settings inspected in the first year of EYEIs were small in scale with one preschool session targeted as the focus of inspection. Analysis of inspection reports identified that the majority of ECEC settings were highly committed to providing safe, inviting and positive experiences to support children's early learning. However, there were particular challenges evident in relation to practices that are essential to the provision of high-quality early learning. These were categorized as relating to:

15   The advent of the Covid-19 Global pandemic resulted in the closure of all schools and ELC settings on 12th March 2020 with a concomitant suspension of inspection activity. Inspection resumed in April 2021 with Follow-Through Inspection Circular 0020/2021. <https://www.gov.ie/en/circular/f84fa-arrangements-for-inspection-of-early-learning-and-care-elc-settings-april-june-2021/>.

16   <https://www.education.ie/en/publications/inspection-reports-publications/Early-Years-Education-Reports/>.

- Curriculum development and implementation
- Leadership for learning
- Partnership with parents
- Inclusive practice and managing diversity
- Supporting transitions.

In addition to analysis of inspection reports, a survey of staff in the settings inspected was also conducted to inform the review. The survey findings provided perspectives from practitioners about the practical challenges they were facing in providing high-quality early learning. They highlighted the challenging context for professional practice within the ELC sector. Respondents noted that the capacity of the workforce varied across settings due to the diverse qualification profile of staff and the limited availability of continuing professional development. It was further reported that retention of qualified staff was impeded by the low status and poor terms and conditions of employment of the workforce and that high turnover of staff was a key factor in limiting the capacity of the sector to deliver high-quality educational programmes.

In September 2017, a Follow-through Inspection Model was developed and introduced. This inspection model is carried out in settings that have had a published report for at least one year. It allows for progress against the 'Actions Advised' from the previous EYEI to be reviewed and evaluated. The report of the Follow-through Inspection is processed through the same editorial stages as the full EYEI report and is also published on the Department of Education website.

In early 2018, the scope of EYEIs was expanded to include larger scale ELC settings which were operating multiple ECCE sessions. These inspections require a team of inspectors to support the inspection process and are carried out over a longer time period than inspections in small settings which are typically completed in one working day. In keeping with the consultative nature of inspection model development in the DEI, a trial phase for these larger scale, multi-room EYEIs was completed. Participants in the trial were invited to offer critical feedback on this experience and make suggestions for amendments to the inspection model. At this time, opportunity to review the quality framework for EYEI was also offered to all stakeholder and partners in the ELC sector. The cumulative effect of this work was the publication in June 2018 of a revised *Guide to Early Years Education Inspection* (DES 2018a). While the review process did not result in any change to the four areas or the twenty outcome statements that elaborate the focus of the EYEI quality framework, a broad range of additional 'signposts for practice' were suggested to improve the clarity of the framework in areas such as inclusion and leadership for learning. Inspections informed by this revised guide commenced in September 2018.

Quality assuring education inspection

The DEI is committed to ensuring that its inspection processes in all educational settings – early years, primary, post-primary and centres for education – are of very good quality. The ultimate goal in this regard is to embed the use of quality assurance mechanisms in inspection work to ensure that evaluations meet the high standards articulated in the *Code of Practice for the Inspectorate* (DES 2015). The procedures are in place to ensure this includes the:

- Requirement for inspectors to work according to a code of practice: The Code sets out four key principles that provide the standards that inform, guide and govern the Inspectorate's work:
    o A focus on learners
    o Development and improvement
    o Respectful engagement
    o Responsibility and accountability
- Development of quality frameworks (DES 2016a, 2016b, 2016c, 2016d, 2018a) around which inspectors gather evidence and reflect before drawing conclusions and making their evaluative judgements. While inspectors use the frameworks flexibly to inform their work as they monitor and report on quality in schools and early years settings, the frameworks nonetheless support consistency in evaluations
- Detailed published procedural guidance for every model of inspection
- An initial professional development programme for inspectors
- Continuing professional development (CPD) of inspectors in relation to inspection matters

- Ongoing evaluation by the Inspectorate of its procedures and protocols with a view to improvement and regular updating of inspection practice
- Asking stakeholders (e.g. practitioners, owner/managers, management committees, etc.) for their views about inspections
- An editing and clearance procedure for all published inspection reports
- An inspection review procedure which provides a fair and transparent process to examine concerns raised about inspections (DES 2015).

The development and implementation of EYEIs has followed these procedures with the exception of post-evaluation questionnaires in each early years service. Procedures to support this activity, and consultation with parents and children during early years education inspection, are currently being developed.

A common agenda

Despite the separate responsibilities of the DEI and the Tusla Early Years Inspectorate, it is evident that both systems have a common agenda and objectives towards provision and practice of high-quality ECEC. Despite the constraints of their respective statutory and regulatory remits, very good co-professional working and positive relationships have been established between the two Inspectorates to ensure that their activity is coordinated to avoid overlap of inspection in ECEC services. A memorandum of understanding is in place to support the sharing of data and to facilitate this coordination. The two Inspectorates are also members of the Operations Systems Alignment Group (OSAG), chaired by the DCEDIY. This structure is designed to foster communication and a coordinated approach across all of the agencies with oversight functions in relation to the operation of the ECEC sector. Under the auspices of this group, the staff of the two Inspectorates have participated in joint professional development conferences in 2018 and 2019.

Future policy directions

It is evident from recent national policy development in Ireland that the value and importance of high-quality services for children in their earliest years, and their families, has been accepted and endorsed by the State (Government of Ireland 2018). It has also been accepted that children do not experience their learning and care as separate actions but as intrinsically connected aspects of a continuum of learning, development and growth that is lifelong. The implications of this policy perspective for the provision of publicly funded services in the ECEC sector is that such services must be enabled to deliver coherent, consistent and continuous quality in provision and practice, irrespective of the settings in which they take place.

Given the history of the evolution of the ECEC sector, realizing the goal of providing high-quality ECEC provision for all children will require investment and change at many levels of the system. Evaluation for improvement and accountability will play a central role in supporting these processes. The implementation and enforcement of statutory regulation and the provision of clearly communicated standards and guidance to support effective practice together with the publication of comprehensive quality assurance reports to all stakeholders provide the strong foundations upon which to build a truly world-class ELC system in Ireland. The DEI and the Tusla Early Years Inspectorates will act in the best interests of all children to oversee, encourage and enhance the provision of high-quality ECEC, in all its diversity, and at every stage in the continuum of early childhood.

Bibliography

Centre for Early Childhood Development Education (2004). *Insights on Quality: A National Review of Policy, Practice and Research Relating to Quality in Early Childhood Care and Education in Ireland 1990–2004*. Dublin: CECDE. Available at: <http://siolta.ie/media/pdfs/01_insights_on_quality.pdf>.

Centre for Early Childhood Development Education (2006). *Síolta, The National Quality Framework for Early Childhood Education*. Dublin: CECDE.

Coolahan, J. with O'Donovan, P. (2009). *A History of Ireland's School Inspectorate 1831 to 2008*. Dublin. Four Courts Press.

Department of Children and Youth Affairs (2020). *Grant Agreement for ECCE Scheme 2020/21*. Dublin: DCYA. Available at: <https://earlyyearshive.ncs.gov. ie/ECCE-contract-2020.pdf>.

Department of Education and Skills (2014). *Focussed Policy Assessment Early Start Programme*. Early Years Education Policy Unit. Dublin: DES. Available at: <https://www.education.ie/en/Publications/Education-Reports/Focus sed-Policy-Assessment-Early-Start-Programme-Early-Years-Education-Policy-Unit.pdf>.

Department of Education and Skills (2015). *Code of Practice for the Inspectorate*. Dublin: DES.

Department of Education and Skills (2016a). *A Guide to Inspection in Primary Schools*. Dublin: DES. Available at: <https://www.education.ie/en/Publicati ons/Inspection-Reports-Publications/Evaluation-Reports-Guidelines/A-Guide-to-Inspection-in-Primary-Schools.pdf>.

Department of Education and Skills (2016b). *School Self-Evaluation Guidelines 2016–2020. Primary*. Dublin: DES. Available at: <https://www.education.ie/ en/Publications/Inspection-Reports-Publications/Evaluation-Reports-Gui delines/School-Self-Evaluation-Guidelines-2016-2020-Primary.pdf>.

Department of Education and Skills (2016c). *Looking at Our School 2016: A Quality Framework for Primary Schools*. Dublin: DES.

Department of Education and Skills (2016d). *Looking at our School 2016: A Quality Framework for Post-primary Schools*. Dublin: DES.

Department of Education and Skills (2016e). *A Guide to Early-Years Education-Focused Inspections in Early-Years Settings Participating in the Early Childhood Care and Education (ECCE) Programme*. Dublin: DES.

Department of Education and Skills (2018a). *A Guide to Early Years Education Inspection*. Dublin: DES. Available at: <https://www.education.ie/en/Publi cations/Inspection-Reports-Publications/Evaluation-Reports-Guidelines/ guide-to-early-years-education-inspections.pdf>.

Department of Education and Skills (2018b). *Insights and Future Developments. A Review of Early-Years Education-focused Inspection: April 2016–June 2017*. Dublin: DES. Available at: <https://assets.gov.ie/25246/9d33fa1d458644c98 dde7069477a1351.pdf>.

Department of Education and Skills (2019). *Professional Award Criteria and Guidelines for Initial Professional Education (Level 7 and Level 8) Degree Programmes for the Early Learning and Care (ELC) Sector in Ireland*. Dublin: DES. Available at: <https://assets.gov.ie/30316/784a2158d8094bb7bab40f2064358221.pdf>.

Department of the Taoiseach. (2004). *Regulating Better*: Dublin: Government Publications Office.

Domina, T. (2005). 'Leveling the Home Advantage: Assessing the Effectiveness of Parental Involvement in Elementary School', *Sociology of Education*, 78 (July), 233–249.

Duignan, M. (2011). *The Growth of Professionalism in Early Childhood Education and Care in Ireland*. Unpublished PhD Thesis, University College Cork. Available at: <http://library.ucc.ie/record=b2029856>.

European Commission (2013). *Commission Recommendation of 20 February 2013 – Investing in Children: Breaking the Cycle of Disadvantage*. EUR-LEX. Available at: <http://eur-lex.europa.eu/legal-content/EN/ALL/?uri=CELEX%3A320 13H0112>.

Eurydice and EACEA (2009). *Tackling Social and Cultural Inequalities through Early Childhood Education and Care in Europe*. EACEA. Available at: <http://eacea.ec.europa.eu/about/eurydice/documents/098EN.pdf>.

Government of Ireland (1991). *Child Care Act*. Dublin: The Stationery Office.

Government of Ireland (1997). *Child Care (Pre School Services) Regulations 1996 and Child Care (Pre School Services) (Amendment) Regulations 1997*. Dublin: The Stationery Office.

Government of Ireland (2000). *National Children's Strategy: Our Children, Their Lives*. Dublin: The Stationery Office.

Government of Ireland (2004). *Health Act 2004*. Dublin: Office of the Attorney General.

Government of Ireland (2006). *Child Care (Pre-School Services) (No 2) Regulations 2006 and Child Care (Pre-School Services) (No 2) (Amendment) Regulations 2006*. Dublin: The Stationery Office.

Government of Ireland (2013). *Child and Family Agency Act 2013*. Dublin: Office of the Attorney General.

Government of Ireland (2016a). *Child Care Act 1991 (Early Years Services) Regulations 2016*. Dublin: Government Publications Office.

Government of Ireland (2016b). *Child Care Act 1991 (Early Years Services) (Amendment) Regulations 2016*. Dublin: Government Publications Office.

Government of Ireland (2018). *First 5: A Whole of Government Strategy for Babies, Young Children and Their Families*. Dublin: Government Publications Office.

Hanafin, S., Brooks, A. M., McDonnell, F., Rouine, H. and Coyne, I. (2009). 'A Whole-child Perspective Assessment Guide for Early Years Settings', *Community Practitioner*, 82 (10), 22–26.

Hanafin, S. (2014). *Report on the Quality of Pre-school Services: Analysis of Pre-school Inspection Reports*. Dublin: Tusla.

Hayes, N. (2002). *Children's Rights, Whose Right? A Review of Child Policy Development in Ireland*. Studies in Public Policy 9. Dublin: The Policy Institute, Trinity College.

Hislop, H. (2017). *A Co-professional Approach to Inspection for Accountability and Improvement: Progress and Prospects in the Irish Context*. Inaugural Public Lecture to mark the incorporation of the Centre for Evaluation, Quality and Inspection within the DCU Institute of Education. Available at: <https://assets.gov.ie/25255/637a9e4e8dcb4c348ddad47fcf407702.pdf>.

Jeynes, W. (2012). 'A Meta-analysis of the Efficacy of Different Types of Parental Involvement Programs for Urban Students', *Urban Education*, 47 (4), 706–742.

Kiernan, G. and Walsh, T. (2004). 'The Changing Nature of Early Childhood Care and Education in Ireland', *Irish Educational Studies*, 23 (2), 1–18.

Kennedy, F. (2001). *Cottage to Crèche: Family Change in Ireland*. Dublin: Institute of Public Administration.

Molloy, D. (2018). *Taking Account of the Voice of the Child within the Regulatory Inspection Process of Early Years Services*. Galway: National University of Ireland Galway.

National Council for Curriculum and Assessment (2009). *Aistear: The Early Childhood Curriculum Framework*. Dublin: NCCA.

Oireachtas Library and Research Service (2020). *L&RS Note: Public Provision of Early Childhood Education: An Overview of the International Evidence*. Available at: <https://data.oireachtas.ie/ie/oireachtas/libraryResearch/2020/2020-06-16_l-rs-note-public-provision-of-early-childhood-education-an-overview-of-the-international-evidence_en.pdf>.

O'Connor, M. (2010). *The Development of Infant Education in Ireland, 1838–1948: Epochs and Eras*. Bern: Peter Lang.

O'Kane, M. (2005). 'The Effect of Regulation on the Quality of Early Childhood Services in Ireland', *Child Care in Practice*, 11, 231–251.

Public Appointments Service (2015). *Candidate Information Booklet. Early Years Inspectors at The Department of Education and Skills*. Available at: <http://www.wccc.ie/wp-content/uploads/2015/05/Information-Booklet-Early-Years-Inspectors-DES.pdf>.

Ring, E., Mhic Mhathúna, M., Moloney, M., Hayes, N., Breathnach, D., Stafford, P., Carswell, D., Keegan, S., Kelleher, C., McCafferty, D., O'Keeffe, A., Leavy, A., Madden, R. and Ozonyia, M. (2016). *An Examination of Concepts of School Readiness among Parents and Educators in Ireland*. Dublin: Department of Children and Youth Affairs.

Rouine, H., McDonnell, F. and Hanafin, S. (2020). 'Making a Difference: The Impact of Statutory Inspection on the Quality of Early Years Services', *Child Care in Practice*, 1–11. DOI: 10.1080/13575279.2019.1701410.

Smyth, E., Conway, P., Leavy, A., Darmody, M., Banks, J. and Watson, D. (2016). *Review of the Droichead Teacher Induction Pilot Programme*. Dublin: Economic and Social Research Institute. Available at: <https://www.education.ie/en/Publications/Education-Reports/Review-of-the-Droichead-Teacher-Induct ion-Pilot-Programme-Executive-Summary.pdf>, accessed 19 April 2021.

Tusla (2015). *Annual Report 2015 of Tusla Child and Family Agency's Early Years Inspectorate*. Dublin: Tusla.

Tusla (2016). *Annual Report 2016 of Tusla Child and Family Agency's Early Years Inspectorate*. Dublin: Tusla.

Tusla (2018a). *Annual Report 2017 of Tusla Child and Family Agency's Early Years Inspectorate*. Dublin: Tusla.

Tusla (2018b). *Quality and Regulatory Framework*. Dublin: Tusla.

Tusla (2019). *Children's Services Regulation Annual Report 2018*. Dublin: Tusla.

Tusla (2020a). *Child and Family Agency: Children's Services Regulations Report 2019*. Dublin: Tusla.

Tusla (2020b). *The Registration, Regulation, Inspection and Enforcement Processes of Childminders; An International Review*. Dublin: Tusla.

Tusla (2021a). *Tusla Early Years Inspections – Parents Consultation*. Dublin: Tusla.

Tusla (2021b). *Early Years Inspection Reports 2018–2019: Analysis and Trends*. Dublin: Tusla.

United Nations (1989). *United Nations Convention on the Rights of the Child*. Geneva: United Nations.

Walsh, T. (2012). *Primary Education in Ireland, 1897–1990: Curriculum and Context*. Bern: Peter Lang.

Walsh, T. (2016). 'Early Childhood Care and Education in Ireland 2016'. In B. Mooney (ed.), *Education Matters Yearbook 2016–17*, pp. 107–112. Dublin: Education Matters.

Walshe, K. and Shorthall, S. M. (2004). 'Social Regulation of Healthcare Organizations in the United States: Developing a Framework for Evaluation', *Health Services Management Research*, 17 (2), 79–99.

NOEL PURDY AND DIANE MCCLELLAND

10 Provision for early childhood education and care in Northern Ireland, 1921–2021

Introduction

This chapter aims to chart the policy and practice trajectory for early childhood education and care (ECEC)[1] in Northern Ireland from 1921 to the present day. Rather than making claims to represent an exhaustive history, the chapter will focus on four central aspects of ECEC during the period: the emergence and evolution of government legislation and policy; the evolution of and tensions around curriculum content; the enduring debate about the development of a professional ECEC workforce; and a brief overview of contemporary and future challenges facing the sector. The scope of the chapter will encompass education and care for children aged birth to 6 years, thus including provision of childcare and preschool education (both statutory and non-statutory) as well as formal schooling for children aged 4 to 6 years.

By way of contextual introduction, Northern Ireland has a population of around 1.9 million (Northern Ireland Statistics and Research Agency [NISRA] 2020) with a school population of over 344,000 children (Department of Education [DE] 2021). A distinctive feature of the education system is that children are obliged to start formal education in the September following their fourth birthday (Walsh 2007). Prior to starting primary school, around 90 per cent of 3-year-old children (n=23,112) attend

---

1   In Northern Ireland, the broader term Early Years provision is often preferred to early childhood education and care (ECEC) and commonly refers to the 0–6 age range.

funded preschool education settings: almost half are funded voluntary
and private (non-statutory) preschool centres (i.e. playgroups and day
nurseries), while the remainder are state-funded (statutory) stand-alone
nursery schools or nursery units attached to primary schools (DE 2021).

The development of policy

Northern Ireland was formally established by the *Government of Ireland
Act 1920*. The new jurisdiction comprised the northern six counties of
Ireland in which, at the time, there was a two-to-one majority of Protestant-
Unionists over Catholic-Nationalists (Farren 1986). The new Ministry of
Education, established on 7th June 1921, quickly began making arrange-
ments for the transfer of services from Dublin (Government of Northern
Ireland 1923). However, before making any reforms, the newly appointed
Minister of Education, Lord Londonderry, established a Departmental
Committee of Enquiry (known as the Lynn Committee after its chair,
R. J. Lynn MP) in September 1921 to 'enquire and report on the existing
organization and administration of the Educational Services' (Ministry
of Education for Northern Ireland 1922: 7). Thus began a decade of often
bitter wrangling as political and religious leaders vied to exert an influence over the new education system. Although referred to as a 'tawdry
and often tediously complicated tale' (Akenson 1973: 87), the period is
nonetheless highly significant as it epitomizes the nature of broader social
and political life in Northern Ireland in the 1920s, dominated by political and religious power struggles. Contact with the new Free State was
limited; official relations with the South were often hostile; and instead,
the pioneers of early years education in Northern Ireland looked east to
Great Britain for inspiration and support.

As a result, the education debate at the time focused almost entirely
on issues around government funding of schools, religious instruction
and church influence over the appointment of teachers. Where there was
a focus on curricular content, this related primarily to opportunities taken
by the (Protestant-dominated) Lynn Committee to develop a curriculum

('programme of instruction') which would instil loyalty to the British Empire and thwart any resurgence of interest in the Irish language, which was treated with some considerable suspicion by Unionists. The Final Report of the Lynn Committee (Ministry of Education for Northern Ireland 1923) was generally dismissive of infant education and recommended that the age of admission to primary school should be raised from three to four 'from motives of economy as well as on hygienic grounds' (para. 56). However, support was expressed by the Lynn Committee for the provision of nursery schools especially in 'crowded urban areas' where 'suitable women' could care for these young children rather than have them play in the streets 'under no guidance or restraint' (para. 54–55).

Although the resulting *Education Act (Northern Ireland) 1923*, often referred to as the Londonderry Act, did empower local education authorities to provide nursery education (where the children's 'health, nourishment and general welfare' (para. 11) could be attended to), economic challenges as well as political tensions dominated affairs to such an extent that there was barely a mention of nursery education in official Ministry of Education papers of the 1920s and no available State funding for nursery education for more than a decade. Nonetheless it was during this politically fraught decade that the first nursery in Ireland (North or South) opened its doors for the first time on 5th November 1928 in a church hall on the (working-class) Donegall Road, Belfast. The Arellian Nursery was founded by the Past Pupils' Association of Richmond Lodge (from which the name originates: the 'R.L.-ians') whose philanthropic intentions were to offer nursery provision to the young children of working mothers. In 1936 the second nursery school, McArthur Nursery, opened in Belfast, privately funded by the former pupils of another prestigious school, Methodist College, and the following year a third nursery school opened beside Edenderry Mill on the Crumlin Road, Belfast (McNeilly 1973).

The first significant milestone in government support for nursery education was the introduction of financial aid from the Ministry of Education under the 1937 Nursery Regulations (Ministry of Education for Northern Ireland 1937). To secure funding, the Ministry would inspect the provision and had to be satisfied that 'adequate arrangements are made for attending to the health, nourishment and physical welfare of the children' (para. 8), with no mention made of the adequacy of education or programmes of instruction.

The expansion of nursery provision in Northern Ireland was, however, significantly constrained by the onset and financial consequences of the Second World War (1939–1945) and by the UK-wide policy position which focused on nursery provision solely to meet social need in disadvantaged contexts. This was clearly illustrated at the end of the war by the wording of an (English) Ministry of Health circular which stated that 'the proper place for the child under two is at home with his mother' and that nursery places would only be allocated to children aged 2 to 5 years whose mothers 'are constrained by individual circumstances to go out to work or whose home conditions are in themselves unsatisfactory from the health point of view, or whose mothers are incapable for some reason of undertaking the full care of their children' (Ministry of Health 1945: 4). Despite the duty placed on local education authorities in the *Education Act (Northern Ireland) 1947* to secure the provision of nursery schools or nursery classes for children under five, the growth of nursery education in Northern Ireland from 1945 to 1972 was 'slow and erratic' (Cockerill 1990: 16) with commentators attributing this variously to financial constraints (McNeilly 1973), societal conservatism (Cockerill 1990) and opposition from the conservative Catholic Church hierarchy (O'Rawe 1997, McGrath 2000). While some progress was made during the 1970s with the reorganization of local government, the creation of the Education and Library Boards, and the personal commitment of Lord Melchett (a direct rule Labour Minister of State with responsibility for education and health in Northern Ireland), the implementation of the resulting 1978 White Paper, *Day Care and Education for the Under Fives in Northern Ireland: Policy and Objectives* (Department of Health and Social Services [DHSS] and DE 1978), fell victim to the electoral defeat of the Labour government at Westminster in 1979 and the ensuing decade of Thatcherite cuts to public spending.

It was not until the late 1990s, heralded by a new Labour government under Tony Blair and the devolution of power to the Northern Ireland Assembly following the Belfast/Good Friday Agreement in 1998, that significant progress was made in the form of the *Pre-School Education Expansion (PEEP)* programme (DE 1998). The aim of the programme was to create over 9,000 new high-quality funded preschool places (statutory, voluntary and private) by 2002, and in the longer term, to provide a full year of preschool education for every child whose parents wanted it. While initially targeted at children from socially disadvantaged backgrounds, by 2008–2009 provision had increased from 45 to 97 per cent of children in their immediate preschool year (Northern Ireland Audit Office [NIAO] 2009). The other highly significant element of the programme was the partnership approach to be developed for the first time between the statutory and voluntary/private sectors (there was an intention for the additional numbers to be divided in roughly equal numbers between the sectors), with providers required to adhere to common quality standards as assessed by the Education and Training Inspectorate (ETI).

The PEEP programme was a key element in the inter-departmental Northern Ireland Childcare Strategy *Children First* (DHSS, Training and Employment Agency [T&EA], DE 1999) which marked a concentrated effort to move away from fragmentation of responsibility towards a more integrated approach (Walsh 2007). *Children First* proposed a variety of measures to be taken by government to 'ensure that high quality, affordable childcare for children up to the age of fourteen is available in every community in Northern Ireland' *(Ibid.:* 5). Its long-term aim was to integrate early education and childcare and arose from the Inter-Departmental Group on Early Years (created in 1995) which included representatives from the DHSS, DE and Department of Economic Development as well as the ETI and the Social Services Inspectorate. Among its actions were the creation of four new regional Childcare Partnerships to take forward the strategy, and a commitment to implementing the Sure Start programme in Northern Ireland for the first time (with £9.9m funding until 2002). Introduced to Northern Ireland in July 2000, Sure Start is a universal programme targeted at parents and children under the age of 4 living in the 25 per cent most deprived wards in Northern Ireland. Funded by the DE since 2006, Sure Start projects deliver a wide variety of services which are designed to support children's learning skills, health and wellbeing, and social and emotional development. In 2015, a review of Sure Start services reported that thirty-nine projects had been established in Northern Ireland, enabling the provision of support to around 43,450 children aged under 4 and their families (DE 2015). The budget for Sure Start projects for 2020–2021 is £27m, an increase of £1.5m on the previous year.

The government's commitment to Early Years was further demonstrated through the consultation process on the draft *Early Years 0–6 Strategy* (DE 2010) which had four key objectives: to improve the quality of early years provision; to improve engagement with parents, families and communities; to improve equity of access to quality early years provision; and to encourage greater collaboration among key partners to promote greater integration in-service delivery. Noteworthy in the draft strategy was the 'drive for cohesion in the policies and services affecting early years' *(Ibid.:* 5) and the acknowledgement of the need for a highly skilled, well-qualified workforce across both the statutory and the private/voluntary sectors. This draft Strategy was subsequently revised by *Learning to Learn: A Framework for Early Years Education and Learning* (DE 2013) which set out more explicitly than ever before the policy aim that all children should have equal opportunities to achieve their potential through 'high quality early learning experiences' (DE 2013: ii). Among the five key policy objectives were a commitment to providing equitable access to services; supporting the holistic development of children; addressing barriers to learning and reducing the risk of social exclusion; and encouraging and supporting parents in their role as 'first and ongoing educators' (para. 4.6).

The development of curriculum

Just as the trajectory of government policy in relation to ECEC in Northern Ireland has been characterized by periods of inactivity punctuated by periods of rapid reform, the development of curricular provision for the sector has also been far from linear.

Given the philanthropic motivation of the founders of the first charitable nurseries in inner-city working-class areas, it is hardly surprising that there was a strong focus on children's health rather than formal learning in the earliest provision. The Arellian Nursery (founded in 1928), for instance, aimed to provide 'a healthy diet of good wholesome food eaten in the company of adults and friends; plenty of exercise and fresh air in the school field and garden and in the nearby park; regular medical and dental checks – the nurse attended the school daily; the doctor weekly; opportunities to wash …' (McCavera 1988: 3). Nonetheless, alongside such healthcare concerns, Arellian's first Superintendent, Miss Dorothy Moore, a Froebel-trained teacher, affirmed that every child would 'have the freedom and the possibilities for playing and developing through his play at his own rate, which is every child's right' (Moore 1930: 8).

By contrast, within the earliest Ministry of Education programmes of instruction for 'infant classes' within elementary schools, there was no explicit mention of play *per se*, though in addition to speaking, reading, drawing, number, songs and games, the children were to engage in 'educational handwork' comprising 'building, bead-threading, sorting and arranging various materials according to size, shape or colour, modelling in clay or other plastic material, lacing and buttoning, very simple paper work' (Ministry of Education for Northern Ireland 1928: 10).

Despite the introduction of government funding for nursery education in 1937, any further development of ECEC curricular provision was naturally halted by the onset of war two years later. During the Second World War, the Nursery Schools' Association was asked by the Northern Ireland Ministry of Home Affairs to form a Nursery Centres Committee to facilitate the evacuation of city children to nurseries outside Belfast. In addition, industrial nurseries were established in Belfast for children whose mothers were involved in the war effort. In each of the war-time nursery centres, the curriculum corresponded very closely to that of existing nursery schools (McCavera 1988: 13).

While the post-war development of nursery education was slow and piecemeal, the mid 1950s heralded a significant revision of the primary curriculum (including children aged from 4 to 8 years) marked by a shift in emphasis from 'a curriculum-centred system to a child-centred system' with a focus on 'activities to be fostered and interests to be broadened' (Ministry of Education for Northern Ireland 1955: 5). There is, however, little evidence to suggest that this had any significant impact on classroom practice, and it was not until a nursery expansion programme in the 1960s accompanied by a series of departmental circulars, guidance and resources in the 1970s that a more centralized focus began to emerge. These circulars led in 1977 to the DE publishing a handbook and video to support nursery practitioners known as *Well Begun, Theory into Practice in a Nursery School*. Following this in the 1980s the primary sector developed a range of curricular support materials entitled *Primary Guidelines* which in turn led to the publishing of the *Northern Ireland Nursery Guidelines* in 1989 (Carville 2019).

Meanwhile, prompted by the lack of statutory investment, the playgroup movement which had begun in England as a 'self-help response by mothers to the lack of nursery education' (Brophy and Statham, 1994: 64) likewise emerged in Northern Ireland as a series of parent-led groups during the 1960s. As the number of playgroups expanded, the Northern Ireland Pre-School and Playgroups Association (NIPPA, renamed *Early Years – the organisation for young children* in 2007) was formed on 21 September 1965. Having grown steadily since its formation, Early Years now employs over 200 staff, and works alongside a range of local, national and international partners (Smith 2015, Early Years 2020). In terms of pedagogy and curriculum, Early Years delivers a range of programmes which seek to improve practice by applying an appropriate play-based, evidence-informed curriculum (Early Years 2020).

The statutory educational landscape of the 1980s was dominated by the roll out of the highly prescriptive, assessment-led Northern Ireland Curriculum under the 1989 Education Reform Order (mirroring the landmark Education Reform Act in England and Wales the previous year). While there may have been a growing awareness of the importance of play in the early years (e.g. the Rumbold Report 1990), the reality for 4-year-olds in primary classrooms under the new Northern Ireland Curriculum was exposure to a formal curriculum with clearly defined attainment targets and level descriptors (Walsh 2007).

By contrast, as preschool provision expanded through the 1980s and 1990s (as a result of the PEEP programme), additional statutory guidance emphasizing the importance of high-quality learning experiences was published for adoption in all funded settings (statutory and voluntary) e.g., the *Northern Ireland Nursery Guidelines* (Northern

Ireland Curriculum Council 1989) and the Council for the Curriculum, Examinations and Assessment (CCEA's) *Curricular Guidance for Pre-School Education* (1997, revised in 2006 and 2018). The CCEA guidance outlines the anticipated progress of children's learning by the end of the preschool year in each of the six Areas of Learning: Personal, Social and Emotional Development; Physical Development and Movement; Language Development; Early Mathematical Experiences; The Arts; The World Around Us. Importantly, the guidance (CCEA 2018: 5) acknowledges the continuum of learning from home and/or childcare settings, parent and toddler groups and programmes for 2-year-olds (such as SureStart), through the preschool year and into The Foundation Stage (years 1 and 2 of primary education).

Unique to Northern Ireland, the Foundation Stage was built on the success of the Enriched Curriculum, a pioneering curriculum devised jointly by CCEA and the Belfast Education and Library Board to address the perceived shortcomings of the formal statutory curriculum, especially in disadvantaged areas (Hunter and Walsh 2014). The Enriched Curriculum was implemented from September 2000 with (initially) a group of six schools in the Greater Shankill area of Belfast and was specifically designed to be more play-based and activity-led than the rigidity of the Northern Ireland curriculum. Aiming to remove the early experience of persistent failure by young children exposed to formal methods at an early age, the Enriched Curriculum placed a greater emphasis on oral language development and activity-based mathematical activities. The success of the Enriched Curriculum project (McGuinness et al. 2009, Walsh et al. 2010) was reflected in the subsequent development of the Foundation Stage of the *Northern Ireland (Revised) Primary Curriculum* (CCEA 2007). The Foundation Stage Curriculum builds on children's experiences of home and/or the preschool curriculum and, echoing the play-based principles set out in the Arellian nursery almost a century earlier, affirms that children learn best when learning is 'interactive, practical and enjoyable' and when they are 'involved in play that is challenging, takes account of their developmental stage and needs and builds on their own interests and experiences' (CCEA 2007: 15).

The development of a professional Early Years workforce

In Northern Ireland, as in other jurisdictions, there has been slow recognition of the importance of adequately remunerating a highly qualified professional workforce for the ECEC sector, and there remains a stubborn disparity between qualifications and salaries in the statutory and non-statutory preschool sectors (McMillan 2008). Training options for Early Years professionals are also many and varied, including vocational, graduate and postgraduate qualifications, part-time and full-time programmes, pre-service and in-service pathways. There is only a requirement for Qualified Teacher Status within nursery schools and nursery unit classes attached to primary schools.

The origins of the continuing divergence can be traced back to the immediate post-partition years, when the *Final Report of the Lynn Committee* (Ministry of Education for Northern Ireland 1923) paid scant attention to infants and made it clear that there were economic, practical and hygienic reasons why the youngest children (aged under 4 years) should not be permitted in elementary schools, making it clear that their care need not be entrusted to fully qualified and salaried teachers. Nonetheless, while the Ministry of Education paid little regard to the qualifications of those working with young children, once again the pioneering example of the Arellian Nursery serves as an important and influential outlier: its first superintendent, Miss Dorothy Moore, was Froebel-trained and its earliest annual reports all cite Grace Owens' visionary *Aims of the Nursery School* (Moore 1930). Although still unfunded by government, such progressive work did not go entirely unnoticed. In 1934, the Right Hon. H. M. Pollock, Minister of Finance (and former chair of the 1922 Committee for the Training of Teachers for Northern Ireland), visited the Arellian Nursery school and reported that he was '… very impressed that Froebel certificated teachers were willing to work for the miserable salaries we gave them' (McNeill 1949: 9).

When funding was finally introduced by means of the Nursery School Regulations in 1937, it was stipulated that 'Superintendents and Assistant Superintendents … should have satisfactorily completed a course of training approved by the Ministry, in a recognised training college, and should either during such course or subsequently have attended a special course of training to fit them for work in nursery schools' (Ministry of Education for Northern Ireland 1937: 111). This was further supported by the appointment of nursery tutors to both Stranmillis and St Mary's Colleges in 1947, allowing infant studies students to opt to train to work in nursery schools from 1948 (McMillan 2008). A graduate route for nursery teachers was only introduced thirty years later with the nursery option of the B.Ed. degree programme (and ten years after the introduction of the B.Ed. for primary and secondary teachers). This was followed in due course by the introduction of the Early Childhood Studies degree programme at Stranmillis in 1996, the one-year Postgraduate Certificate in Education (PGCE) in Early Years in 2000 and the MA in Early Childhood Studies in 2006. It is hoped that a part-time taught doctorate in Early Years Education could be offered through Stranmillis in the next few years.

While parity of qualification and salary has now been achieved in the statutory ECEC sector in Northern Ireland, the qualification landscape remains more challenging and diverse within the voluntary and private sector (McMillan 2008). Following the establishment of NIPPA in 1965, there was a more concerted effort to offer appropriate training to childcare practitioners, often self-funded and extra-mural, but nonetheless frequently oversubscribed (Smith 2015). By 1996 NIPPA was facilitating training to over 1,200 students, providing most of the training and continuing professional development for staff in the voluntary and private sector (Walsh 2007).

Despite the short-term financial implications, it could be argued that a significant opportunity to bring parity between the statutory and non-statutory sectors was missed when *Children First – the Northern Ireland Childcare Strategy* (DHSS, T&EA and DENI 1999) required funded preschool settings in the voluntary and private sectors to employ a leader qualified to National Vocational Qualification (NVQ) Level 3 with other staff qualified to Level 2. While statutory nursery settings are required to employ a graduate teacher for every class, voluntary/private sector settings are required only to 'arrange support from a qualified teacher or other suitably qualified early years specialist' shared between a number of preschools (DENI and DHSS 1998: 15). Many nursery school teachers were opposed to this development and the British Association for Early Childhood Education (BAECE) likewise expressed great concern at the prospect of early years education being delivered by practitioners who were not qualified teachers (Sutherland 2006, Walsh 2007). This concern is evidenced by the findings of the *Effective Pre School Provision in Northern Ireland* (EPPNI) study (Melhuish et al. 2006) which found that staff training and qualifications were associated with higher quality of provision and that overall quality was higher in nursery schools and classes than in playgroups. The researchers concluded that this was 'likely to be related to higher staff qualifications' (Melhuish et al. 2006: 7). In response, NIPPA called for additional funding to develop a graduate work-force and to 'prevent the perception that there is a 'two-tier' structure of service between the voluntary/community and statutory sector provision' (NIPPA 2005: 6). The importance of a 'highly qualified workforce' with access to appropriate support was noted in the *Early Years Strategy 0–6* (DE 2010: 17) and has been followed by more recent calls for investment in a high-status professional early childhood workforce (Fitzpatrick 2020, McMillan 2017).

While there is clear evidence of continued inequity in terms of salaries and qualifications, there is nonetheless evidence of progress over recent decades. All funded preschool settings are inspected by the ETI, while voluntary and private settings are also subject to Health and Social Care Trust (HSCT) annual inspections. The most recent *Chief Inspector's Report (2016–2018)* highlighted that in recent years '… outcomes for children attending voluntary and private settings have steadily improved. The im-proved capacity of those staff who have attained a degree level qualification in early years education is evident in better professional understanding of how to improve outcomes and provision' (ETI 2018: 54).

Contemporary challenges

Despite the progress made over the course of the past century, many chal-lenges remain. In terms of government policy, ECEC now occupies a much more prominent position than ever before. The clearest articulation of this current prioritization is Outcome 12 of the *Draft Programme for Government Framework 2016–2021* of the Northern Ireland Executive (2016): 'We give our children and young people the best start in life.' It is further acknowledged that the delivery of this outcome can be supported through 'high quality early years provision, excellence in education and by building the confidence and capability of families and of communities to help children and young people to fulfil their potential' (NI Executive 2016: 44). The *Draft Programme for Government* uses a series of indicators to measure performance against outcomes, and here one of the key population indicators for Outcome 12 is Indicator 15: the percentage of children who are at the appropriate stage of development in their immediate preschool year. While there is currently no universal health check at age three (the immediate preschool year), the proposed source of such data is the 3+ Health Review, which is currently being rolled out across Northern Ireland. It is hoped that this will improve the identification of children's needs in their preschool year and allow this important population data to be recorded using the Personal Child Health Record (also known as the Red Book) documentation. In 2018–2019, this developmental review was offered to children in 60 per cent of preschool settings in four Health Trusts and 100 per cent of children in the Northern HSCT area.

More recently, the *Children's Services Co-operation Act (Northern Ireland) 2015* required the Northern Ireland Executive to adopt a cross-departmental Children and Young People's Strategy. The *Children and Young People's Strategy 2020-2030* (Northern Ireland Executive 2020) was formally adopted by the restored Executive on 10th December 2020. Led by the DE (but requiring input from all nine departments) and based around a set of eight shared outcomes for the wellbeing of children and young people, this Executive Strategy will be accompanied by a Delivery Plan supported by a new cross-departmental Monitoring and Reporting Group. In terms of government policy, therefore, there is little doubt that the argument for cross-departmental co-operation to address the needs of children has finally been won in principle. Time will tell if the aspirational high-level outcomes are met in practice.

A further priority for government over the coming months is the publication of an Executive Childcare Strategy for Northern Ireland, a commitment expressed in the *New Decade, New Approach* political agreement of January 2020 (Smith and Coveney 2020). Building on the responses to the 2015 consultation as well as developments in childcare across other jurisdictions since then, the Strategy will propose a range of actions (requiring Executive approval and considerable funding) to address the twin aims of supporting children's development and promoting parental employment.

However, many difficulties still need to be tackled. In the 1920s and 1930s, the pioneers of nursery provision in Northern Ireland recognized the greatest need in disadvantaged communities and established the first nurseries to provide care for working-class children whose mothers were working in local mills and factories. Almost a century later, there is evidence that children from disadvantaged backgrounds in Northern Ireland still do not enter school on a level playing field, despite successful targeted interventions such as the Sure Start Programme. For instance, a recent report (Save the Children 2017) found that there was a consistent attainment gap in Northern Ireland between children aged 7, 11 and 14 growing up in poverty and their peers, and that it is likely to be easier to tackle this achievement gap in the early years rather than waiting until post-primary school, a finding confirmed by larger international studies (e.g. Organisation for Economic Co-operation and Development [OECD] 2018). However, while there is a wealth of evidence to confirm the link between attainment at aged 16 (measured by the percentage of children securing five+ GCSEs at grade A*-C) and social disadvantage (measured by the proxy of Free School Meal Entitlement), there is currently a gap in our knowledge of the correlation between levels of social disadvantage and developmental/learning outcomes in young children in Northern Ireland. There is little reason to suggest the situation would be very different from a recent study conducted in England (Andrews et al. 2017) which found the attainment gap between disadvantaged and non-disadvantaged children to be equivalent to 4.3 months when children start school (aged 5). It is hoped that this data gap may be resolved at least in part by the data gathered by the 3+ Review.

The 3+ Review has the potential to greatly improve identification of special educational needs (SEN), and to provide early intervention, as well as to provide useful regional data on the extent of those needs. A recent NIAO Report (2020), echoing a study of parental experiences of the mainstream SEN system (Purdy et al. 2020), highlighted systemic shortcomings in the system operated by the (regional) Education Authority to identify, assess and meet the needs of children with SEN. It is reported that the Education Authority spent £311m on SEN in 2019–2020, that there has been a 36 per cent increase in the number of children with a statement of SEN in the past nine years, and that 85 per cent of statements were issued outside the twenty-six-week statutory limit in 2019–2020. The report concludes that there is a need for 'an urgent overhaul' of the SEN policies, processes and procedures.

Most recently of all, the impact of the Covid-19 pandemic has had an unprecedented impact on everyone in Northern Ireland, including our youngest children. From 23rd March to 30th June 2020, all schools were closed with the exception of the provision of supervision in schools for vulnerable children and the children of essential/key workers. All non-statutory childcare settings also closed. Education in the 2020–2021 school year was further disrupted by rising infection rates, enforced periods of self-isolation and a two-week 'circuit breaker' half-term holiday in October 2020 followed by a further extended period of school closures from January to March 2021 (though special schools remained open throughout this period). Research carried out across Northern Ireland (Walsh et al. 2020) during the first lockdown highlighted that levels of parental education and employment status were strong mediators of home-schooling experience, with better educated parents spending more time and feeling more confident supporting their children's learning than those with fewer or no qualifications who were also more likely to be essential/key workers. Parents/carers reported that their younger children were generally happier at home than their older siblings, but that they missed the daily interaction with their peers and teachers. Experiences ranged from, on the one hand, confident, highly educated parents relishing the opportunity to spend more time learning alongside their children, safely cocooned from the pandemic threat, to, on the other hand, highly stressed working parents struggling to access online resources with limited technology, lacking confidence in their own abilities and battling to motivate their children to engage in learning during the 'nightmare' of lockdown. Evidence from this study confirms the findings of other national studies (Institute for Fiscal Studies 2020, Sutton Trust 2020) that the experience of the pandemic has exacerbated existing inequalities in our education system with children from poorer backgrounds having less access to online resources and parental support, spending less time learning, and submitting less work than their less disadvantaged peers and those attending private schools.

Conclusion

This short history of the development of ECEC in Northern Ireland has highlighted the considerable progress made over the past century in terms of the growing recognition of the importance of high-quality early years provision by a well-qualified, appropriately supported professional workforce. However, the often hard-fought battle is not yet won and there remain enduring challenges which must be addressed by government, including the need to professionalize the entire workforce (statutory and non-statutory), to provide equitable remuneration right across the sector, to fund the sector adequately to meet the increasingly complex needs of children and to ensure that all children, irrespective of background, have equal access to the highest standards of care and education.

In some ways the contemporary challenges faced by the ECEC sector in Northern Ireland are vastly different from those of a century ago, and yet there are some striking similarities including the struggle to secure adequate funding, training and recognition; the need to address the impact of social disadvantage and families struggling to make ends meet, compounded by ill-health and the legacy of inter-community conflict; the duty to care for the holistic development of the child: physical, emotional and cognitive; the tension between conflicting curricular and pedagogical approaches; and perhaps, most strikingly, the obvious commitment of the workforce to give tirelessly of themselves day after day to offer our youngest children 'the best start in life'. In this regard, it seems that little has changed since Miss M. McNeill, Honorary Secretary of Arellian Nursery School, wrote in 1930 of the privilege she and her colleagues felt as they undertook their pioneering work:

> It has been wonderful to us who have worked in the Nursery School to see our children growing stronger and healthier, spending day after day in happiness, and developing both mentally and physically, absolutely in front of our eyes. But it is not only that, we do feel that there is a deeper influence and it is this, more than anything else which makes the Nursery School worthwhile. To feel that we can really give all this is at once a great privilege and a great responsibility. (Moore 1930: 3)

Bibliography

Akenson, D. H. (1973). *Education and Enmity: The Controlling of Schooling in Northern Ireland 1920–1950*. Belfast: Institute of Irish Studies, Queen's University Belfast.

Andrews, J., Robinson, D. and Hutchinson, J. (2017). *Closing the Gap? Trends in Educational Attainment and Disadvantage*. London: Education Policy Institute.

Brophy, J. and Statham, J. (1994). 'Measure for Measure: Values, Quality and Evaluation'. In P. Moss and A. Pence (eds), *Valuing Quality in Early Childhood Services*, pp. 61–75. London: Paul Chapman.

Carville, S. (2019). *The Pre-school Curriculum in Northern Ireland: Where Have We Come From?* Belfast: CCEA. Available at: <https://ccea.org.uk/downloads/docs/ccea-asset/Curriculum/History%20of%20Pre-School%20in%20NI.pdf>.

Children's Services Co-operation Act (Northern Ireland) 2015.

Cockerill, P. (1990). *Nursery Education in Northern Ireland: An Overview*. Unpublished MEd Dissertation, Queen's University Belfast.

Council for the Curriculum, Examinations and Assessment (2007). *The Northern Ireland Curriculum Primary*. Belfast: CCEA.

Council for the Curriculum, Examinations and Assessment (2018). *Curricular Guidance for Pre-School Education*. Belfast: CCEA.

Department of Education (1998). *Investing in Early Learning*. Bangor: DENI. Available at: <https://www.education-ni.gov.uk/sites/default/files/publications/de/investing-in-early-learning.pdf>.

Department of Education (2010). *Early Years (0–6) Strategy*. Bangor: DENI. Available at: <https://www.education-ni.gov.uk/sites/default/files/publications/de/early-years-strategy.pdf>.

Department of Education (2013). *Learning to Learn: A Framework for Early Years Education and Learning*. Bangor: DENI. Available at: <https://www.education-ni.gov.uk/sites/default/files/publications/de/a-framework-for-ey-education-and-learning-2013.pdf>.

Department of Education (2015). *Independent Review of the Sure Start Programme*. Bangor: DENI. Available at: <https://www.education-ni.gov.uk/sites/default/files/publications/de/final-report-review-of-sure-start.pdf>.

Department of Education (2021). *Annual Enrolments at Schools and in Funded Pre-school Education in Northern Ireland*. Bangor: DENI. Available at: <https://www.education-ni.gov.uk/sites/default/files/publications/education/Revised%20February%202021%20-%20Annual%20enrolments%20at%20schools%20and%20in%20funded%20presc....pdf>.

Department of Education and Department of Health and Social Services (1998). *Investing in Early Learning: Pre-School Education in Northern Ireland*. Belfast: The Stationery Office.

Department of Health and Social Services and Department of Education Northern Ireland (1978). *Day Care and Education for the Under Fives in Northern Ireland: Policy and Objectives*. Belfast: HMSO.

Department of Health and Social Services, the Training and Employment Agency and the Department of Education Northern Ireland (1999). *Children First: The Northern Ireland Childcare Strategy*. Belfast: DHSS, TandEA and DENI.

Early Years (2020). *HighScope Ireland Institute*. Belfast: Early Years. Available at: <https://www.early-years.org/highscope/>.

Education Act (Northern Ireland) 1923.

Education Act (Northern Ireland) 1947.

Education and Training Inspectorate (2018). *Chief Inspector's Report 2016–2018*. Belfast: ETI.

Farren, S. (1986). 'Nationalist-Catholic Reaction to Educational Reform in Northern Ireland, 1920–1930', *History of Education*, 15 (1), 19–30.

Fitzpatrick, S. (2020). '*A Professional Early Childhood Workforce for a Peaceful, Shared and Sustainable Northern Ireland*'. Presentation delivered at BERA Research Commission 'Competing Discourses of Early Childhood Education and Care', Stranmillis University College, Belfast (26 February).

Government of Ireland Act (1920).

Government of Northern Ireland (1923). *Report of the Ministry of Education for the Year 1922–23*. Belfast: Public Record Office of Northern Ireland.

Hunter, T. and Walsh, G. (2014). 'From Policy to Practice? The Reality of Play in Primary School Classes in Northern Ireland', *International Journal of Early Years Education*, 22 (1), 19–36.

Institute of Fiscal Studies (2020). *Learning during the Lockdown: Real-time Data on Children's Experiences during Home Learning*. London: IFS. Available at: <https://www.ifs.org.uk/publications/14848>.

McCavera, P. (1988). *Nursery Education: 60 Years On (1928–1988)*. Belfast: Northern Ireland Centre for Learning Resources.

McGrath, M. (2000). *The Catholic Church and Catholic Schools in Northern Ireland*. Dublin: Irish Academic Press.

McGuinness, C., Sproule, L., Trew, K. and Walsh, G. (2009). *The Early Years Curriculum Evaluation Project, End of phase 2, Report 1, Overview, Evaluation Strategy and Curriculum Implementation*. Belfast: CCEA. Available at: <https://ccea.org.uk/downloads/docs/ccea-asset/Curriculum/EYE CEP%20End-of-Phase%202%20Report%201%3A%20Overview%3A%20Evaluation%20Strategy%20and%20Curriculum%20Implementation.pdf>.

McMillan, D. (2008). *Education and Care: Implications for Educare Training in Northern Ireland*. Unpublished PhD thesis, Queen's University Belfast.

McMillan, D. (2017). 'Towards the Playful Professional'. In G. Walsh, D. McMillan and C. McGuinness (eds), *Playful Teaching and Learning*, pp. 198–212. London: Sage.

McNeill, M. (1949). *21 Years – A Growing, Short History of Arellian 1928–1949*. Belfast: A. T. Boyd.

McNeilly, N. (1973). *Exactly Fifty Years: The Belfast Education Authority and Its Work (1923–1973)*. Belfast: Blackstaff Press.

Melhuish, E., Quinn, L., Hanna, K., Sylva, K., Sammons, P., Siraj-Blatchford, I. and Taggart, B. (2006). *Effective Pre-school Provision in Northern Ireland (EPPNI) Summary Report*. Bangor: DENI.

Ministry of Education for Northern Ireland (1922). *Interim Report of the Departmental Committee on the Educational Services in Northern Ireland*. Belfast: HMSO.

Ministry of Education for Northern Ireland (1923). *Final Report of the Departmental Committee on the Educational Services in Northern Ireland*. Belfast: HMSO.

Ministry of Education for Northern Ireland (1928). *Programme of Instruction for Public Elementary Schools*. Belfast: HMSO.

Ministry of Education for Northern Ireland (1937). *Nursery School Regulations*. Available at: <https://www.legislation.gov.uk/nisro/1937/30/pdfs/nisro_1937 0030_en.pdf>.

Ministry of Education for Northern Ireland (1955). *Report of the Primary Schools Programme Committee*. Belfast: HMSO.

Ministry of Health (1945). *Nursery Provision for Children under Five: New Arrangements. Circular on Welfare 221/45*. London: HMSO.

Moore, D. (1930). *Annual Report of the Arellian Nursery School 1929–1930*. [Public Record Office of Northern Ireland] D3020/3/1.

Northern Ireland Audit Office (2009). *Pre-School Education Expansion Programme*. Available at: <https://www.niauditoffice.gov.uk/sites/niao/files/media-files/the_pre-school_education_expansion_programme.pdf >.

Northern Ireland Audit Office (2020). *Impact Review of Special Educational Needs*. Available at: <https://www.niauditoffice.gov.uk/sites/niao/files/media-files/242135%20NIAO%20Special%20Education%20Needs_Fnl%20Lw%20Rs%20%28complete%29.pdf>.

Northern Ireland Commons (1923). III 360, 17 April 1923.

Northern Ireland Curriculum Council (1989). *Nursery Education Guidelines: The Curriculum*. Belfast: NICC.

Northern Ireland Executive (2016). *Draft Programme for Government Framework 2016–2021*. Available at: <https://www.northernireland.gov.uk/sites/default/files/consultations/newnigov/draft-pfg-framework-2016-21.pdf>.

Northern Ireland Executive (2020). *Children and Young People's Strategy 2020-2030*. Available at: <https://www.education-ni.gov.uk/sites/default/files/publications/education/final-execuitve-children-and-young-people%27s-strategy-2020-2030.pdf>.

NIPPA (2005). *A Response to the DB Budget Statement by Peter Hain from NIPPA – The Early Years Organisation*. <http://www.nippa.org/pages/Funding/Funding1.html>, accessed 31 July 2007.

Northern Ireland Statistics and Research Agency [NISRA] (2020). *2019 Mid-year Population Estimates for Northern Ireland*. Belfast: NISRA. Available at: <https://www.nisra.gov.uk/sites/nisra.gov.uk/files/publications/MYE19-Bulletin.pdf>.

Organisation for Economic Co-operation and Development (2018). *Equity in Education – Breaking Down Barriers to Social Mobility*. Paris: OECD. Available at: <http://www.oecd.org/education/equity-in-education-9789264073234-en.htm>.

O'Rawe, A. (1997). *Nursery Education: The Changing Years 1928–1997*. Unpublished M Ed Dissertation, Queen's University Belfast.

Purdy, N., Beck, G., McClelland, D., O'Hagan, C., Totton, L. and Harris, J. (2020). *Too Little, Too Late – The Views of Parents/Carers on Their Child's Experiences of the Special Educational Needs (SEN) Process in Mainstream Schools*.

Stranmillis University College, Belfast: Centre for Research in Educational Underachievement.

Rumbold Report (1990). *The Rumbold Report: The Report of the Committee of Inquiry into the Quality of the Educational Experience Offered to 3 and 4 Year Olds.* London: HMSO.

Save the Children (2017). *Tackling the Poverty-Related Gap in Early Childhood Learning in Northern Ireland.* Belfast: Save the Children. Available at: <https://www.savethechildren.org.uk/content/dam/global/reports/education-and-child-protection/tackling-poverty-related-gap-ni.pdf>.

Smith, W. B. (2015). *Early Years, Crossing Boundaries: 50 Years of Ambition for Young Children.* Belfast: Early Years.

Smith, J. and Coveney, S. (2020). *New Decade, New Approach.* Belfast: Northern Ireland Office.

Sutherland, A. (2006). 'Including Pre-School Education'. In C. Donnelly, P. McKeown and B. Osborne (eds), *Devolution and Pluralism in Education in Northern Ireland,* pp. 64–78. Manchester: Manchester University Press.

Sutton Trust (2020). *COVID-19 and Social Mobility. Impact Brief #1; School Shutdown.* Available at: <https://www.suttontrust.com/wp-content/uploads/2020/04/COVID-19-Impact-Brief-School-Shutdown.pdf>.

Walsh, G. (2007). 'Northern Ireland'. In M. Clark and T. Waller (eds), *Early Childhood Education and Care: Policy and Practice,* pp. 51–82. London: Sage.

Walsh, G., McGuinness, C., Sproule, L. and Trew, K. (2010). 'Implementing a Play-based and Developmentally Appropriate Curriculum in NI Primary Schools: What Lessons have we Learned?', *Early Years: An International Journal of Research and Development,* 30 (1), 53–66.

Walsh, G., Purdy, N., Dunn, J., Jones, S., Harris, J. and Ballentine, M. (2020). *Homeschooling in Northern Ireland during the COVID-19 Crisis: The Experiences of Parents and Carers.* Stranmillis University College, Belfast: Centre for Research in Educational Underachievement. Available at: <https://www.stran.ac.uk/research-paper/creu-home-schooling-during-covid/>.

NÓIRÍN HAYES AND THOMAS WALSH

·Conclusion

Introduction

The ambition behind this book was to reflect on the emergence of early childhood education and care (ECEC) as a system in Ireland from 1921 to 2021. In many ways the story that unfolds is one of two parts. For almost the entire twentieth century those services that were available were provided by voluntary organizations, community groups and charitable organizations with minimal State engagement until the publication of the Preschool Regulations in 1997 (Government of Ireland 1996). While each contributor has brought a unique lens to the history of ECEC, the picture that emerges is remarkably consistent. Chapters exhibit agreement that the ECEC system developed in a largely ad hoc manner, with powerful personal commitment and common cause in relation to the role of adults, the importance of play and the needs of children. In parallel with these developments, early childhood education was provided within primary schools for children aged 4 years and older. However, there was little evidence of cross-departmental coordination at a policy level. Indeed, by the mid-1990s up to eight government departments had some level of responsibility for early childhood services, largely dictated by the funding stream available to them.

Contributors also illustrated, from a variety of perspectives, the significant changes in Irish society brought about by economic and demographic changes which have prompted a shift from a traditional conservative society towards a more outward looking and progressive one. This, in turn, has changed the dynamics of family life and brought attention to the dual role and responsibility of the family and the State in relation to the care and education of young children. Despite the variety of topics covered, there were a number of points of agreement that emerged from each chapter reflecting the evolution of ECEC at both the professional and academic level. This chapter outlines some of the key influences and changes that have brought us to our current position and reflects on learning from the past that can guide us through the opportunities and challenges of today's ECEC landscape. To achieve this, the chapter addresses the following themes:

- Diverse origins: shared understandings
- Influencing factors across time
- The care/education divide
- Departmental auspices
- Funding ECEC
- Supporting quality ECEC
- Qualifications, education and training
- A vision for ECEC.

Diverse origins: Shared understandings

In a book with such a range of contributors addressing such a variety of topics, it is encouraging to see many points of agreement and a shared hope for a future that supports and sustains a cohesive and integrated system of ECEC. There is general consensus that early childhood settings are no longer regarded as merely safe places for children to be cared for while parents work or attend to other pressing matters. Rather, they are recognized, in all their different varieties, as influential miocrosystems in which children learn and develop and where their rights and needs are met in a way that recognizes and respects them. The evidence, nationally and internationally, confirms the importance of the quality of ECEC as a key feature influencing children's early learning experiences and outcomes while also meeting the economic and political ambitions of governments. Research illustrates that quality ECEC, underpinned by principles which view children as active partners in the integrated and ongoing process of learning, facilitates children's development and learning in environments that are well planned, where staff are well trained, confident and supported in their work. The importance of early childhood educators to the quality of provision was implicit across all chapters and made explicit in some, such as Chapters 3, 6, 7 and 10.

A feature of the history of ECEC in Ireland has been the important role played by civic society, key individuals and organizations working together to ensure that children remain of central importance whatever the context of service provision. The energy and passion of those providing ECEC and advocating for cohesive State support across the period was commented on by a number of authors, with Chapters 1, 4 and 7 particularly drawing attention to the growth of an informed and rich practice base as an abundant source of knowledge informing the policy developments of the last thirty years. More importantly perhaps was the overarching belief that there remains an energy and a knowledge base to inform future directions in ECEC policy.

Influencing factors across time

From the earliest explorations, services intersecting the lives of young children have been influenced by external factors. A central macro influence identified by many of the chapters, especially Chapters 1 and 8, has been the Irish Constitution and its commitment to a traditional image of family structure and responsibility for the care of young children. The evidence provided suggests that this view continues in ECEC policies and reflects the power of a historic distancing of the State from direct involvement in family affairs. Nonetheless, with the passage of time the constitutional influence has been tested in a number of different ways, most recently – and of particular relevance to ECEC – by the Citizens' Assembly on Gender Equality (Citizens' Assembly 2021).

However, as outlined in Chapters 5 and 6, the influence of European thinking before the creation of the Free State can be seen with the emergence of an interest in the work of Froebel and Montessori. Despite some local resistance to these approaches to education, both models of practice continue to impact on curricular and pedagogical thinking.

In a more general way, and unsurprisingly, the experiences in the UK have had an influence on ECEC development despite early efforts to break that connection in infant education through the politicization of primary education in the first decades of the twentieth century, a point expanded on in Chapters 3 and 10. By mid-century, one can see the impact of new thinking evident in the development of the playgroup movement but also in the changes to the primary school curriculum. Alongside this, as outlined in Chapter 4, was a growing interest in the potential of Irish language settings, the naíonraí, to maintaining and growing the use of the Irish language in communities both within and outside the Gaeltacht areas.

European and world influences began to have a significant impact on ECEC thinking, practice and policymaking by the 1970s, with developments such as the establishment of OMEP (Ireland) and its support for enhanced training and advocacy for increased policy support for the sector. Other external influences identified include the UN Convention on the Rights of the Child, the EU Quality Framework and the Organisation for Economic Co-operation Development (OECD) report *Starting Strong I* (OECD 2001). These all provided a context for awareness raising about the importance of ECEC to all children and its additional potential for children considered at risk. In addition, the economic imperative of investing in early childhood came to the fore as both an enabler for increased female participation in the workforce as well as a key long-term educational investment. Despite the impact these influences have had on the ground, the pace of State support for ECEC has been piecemeal. However, during the 1970s Europe did begin to influence policy in the area of equality and legislation, as outlined in Chapters 2 and 8, and this led on to legal changes which in turn led to the growth in female participation in the workforce and increased demands for childcare services. However, the State was slow to respond in terms of supporting the growth and development of an ECEC system and exhibited limited and differential engagement depending on the service type, characteristics of the family and the age of children attending.

One significant influencing factor noted by some authors was the financial crisis of 2008. The economic climate that followed had an unexpected impact on ECEC leading, in part, to the closure of the Centre for Early Childhood Development and Education (CECDE) as outlined in Chapter 7, while also heralding the first direct engagement of government in the provision of universal free preschool for children of 3 years of age. It is interesting to observe, as described in Chapters 2, 6 and 9, the effects of this policy decision across areas such as workforce development, qualifications, inspection and regulation. While a welcome contribution to the costs of ECEC for parents, it has led to a situation that privileges – financially and in terms of staff qualifications – those settings providing the free preschool year.

The care/education divide

Since the turn of this century, there has been an overarching consensus among academics and policymakers that the earliest educational level for children, that prior to compulsory education, comprises the integration of care and education in a unique way. The Introduction describes how this reflects the age cohort it supports and has a focus on development and learning; the synergy of both is captured in the choice of term used to refer to this level, early childhood education and care (ECEC) (Neuman 2018, OECD 2001).

The history of ECEC reported in this book highlights the provenance, and continuation of a conceptual and structural split between education and care in Ireland. In terms of terminology, the distinction can be seen in the references at policy level to childcare as a service to parents which cares for their children and early education as a service to children which focuses on their education. In the twentieth century, childcare emerged informally in the shape of a variety of different service types including day nurseries, preschools, playgroups, naíonraí and so forth. Over time these services came under the remit of, primarily, the Department of Health (DoH). Early education, on the other hand, was provided within a school structure and, by mid-century, included the pilot compensatory preschool programme at the Rutland Street preschool. These services came under the Department of Education (DoE).

The split system of policy focus that the care/education divide perpetuates was identified as contributing to the fragile and fractured state of ECEC in Ireland today. For instance, Chapter 9 identified it as a source in the differential regulation and inspection, different systems of professional support and conditions of service across the sector. It was also a source of frustration in relation to continuity of experience for young children where 4- and 5-year old children could experience significantly different learning environments as described in Chapters 3 and 5 and where, latterly, settings for children under 3 years of age are in receipt of significantly less support – both financial and resource – than those of 3 years and over.

Despite the trends in policy which maintain a distinction between care and education, the key curricular and quality frameworks informing ECEC pedagogy, *Aistear* (National Council for Curriculum and Assessment [NCCA] 2009) and *Síolta* (Centre for Early Childhood Development and Education [CECDE] 2006), respectively, were recognized as offering rich sources of guidance for integrated, quality and inclusive practice. Significantly these documents emerged from close collaboration across the sector and captured the experiences of early educators across both curricular and pedagogical traditions of ECEC provision. Chapters 5 and 7 describe how the development of these frameworks began at a time of great activity and ambition for the ECEC system and with the support of the Department of Education and the Office of the Minister for Children (OMC) which was formed in 2005.

In a continuation of the cooperation initiated with the development of *Síolta* and *Aistear,* educators from both ECEC settings and within the junior classes of the primary school are once again collaborating with the current review of *Aistear* and the development of a new Primary Curriculum Framework. These partnerships reflect a significant move towards respecting the unique nature of ECEC as a significant and important level of education and acknowledging that professionals from both have valuable contributions to make in terms of curricular and pedagogical continuity for children, a point stressed in Chapter 5.

Departmental auspices

Chapter 10 outlines the history of ECEC development in Northern Ireland and, in so doing, it captures the value of a continuity in policy attention across the century considered. While departmental responsibility for different aspects of ECEC varied at times, there was always a clear commitment to the idea of ECEC as a system and, latterly, efforts at creating an integrated policy approach led to close cooperation between the Department of Health and Social Services (DHSS) and the Department of Education (DE). By 2010, the DE in Northern Ireland had full responsibility for early years policy.

Clarity in relation to departmental responsibility and integrated policy development has not been the experience on the rest of the island. Despite moves at practice level to develop an integrated approach to enhance continuity of learning experiences across the ECEC lifespan, a significant challenge identified in almost all chapters has been the absence of a key department with responsibility for development, regulation and support of ECEC. This weakness within the system was noted by the OECD in a review of early childhood services (OECD 2004) and efforts to address it led, over time, to the establishment of a Department of Children and Youth Affairs (DCYA) in 2011.

The first department with responsibility for the regulation and support of the ECEC system was the DoH. Chapters 2 and 9 describe how, in 1997, each of the Department's Health Boards established a team of Preschool Inspectors who were notified of operating settings and carried out inspections under a system of statutory regulations. These inspection teams remain under a broad health remit and, since 2018, settings have been required to register and to comply with standards set out in the *Early Years Quality and Regulatory Framework* (Tusla 2018). However, at the turn of the century with the publication of *National Childcare Strategy* (Government of Ireland 1999a), the Department of Justice, Equality and Law Reform (DJELR) took over responsibility for childcare. While the Preschool Inspectorate remained within the DoH, the DJELR created a series of different mechanisms to coordinate the development of the childcare system, which became consolidated with the establishment of the DCYA. Despite efforts to strengthen cross-departmental engagement, however, individual departments continued to work separately resulting in the continued separation of policy development across various departments and units within departments.

The impact of this dispersal of responsibility was identified as problematic across a number of different dimensions within the ECEC system. For instance, as noted in Chapter 6, responsibility for workforce development was originally the responsibility of the DJELR (2003) and later taken up by the DoE (DES 2010). While a number of reports were published over time, the issue of workforce development continued to be challenging and responsibility now rests with the Department of Children, Equality, Disability, Integration and Youth (DCEDIY) which has established a Steering Group to produce a Workforce Development Plan. The final report from this group is due at the end of 2021.

Another area where differing departmental policies have had an impact is in regulation and inspection as described in Chapters 8 and 9. Under the *Child Care Act 1991 (Early Years Services) Regulations 2016* (Government of Ireland 2016), all ECEC services are subject to inspection by the Tusla Early Years Inspectorate. In settings providing the free preschool years, Pobal, working on behalf of the government, carries out compliance inspections for the DCEDIY and, in addition, the Early Years Education Inspection team of the DoE visit these settings to evaluate the quality of the nature, range and appropriateness of their early educational experiences. Both Chapters 1 and 2 note that ECEC settings have identified this regulatory approach to be a significant burden.

Funding ECEC

The source of funding can have a significant influence on the direction of policy. This can certainly be seen in relation to the impact that the availability of European funding had on the development of childcare in 2000. In 1999, two influential policy documents were published, the

National Childcare Strategy (Government of Ireland 1999a) and *Ready to Learn: The White Paper on Early Childhood Education* (Government of Ireland 1999b) and their influence has been referenced in Chapters 2 and 7. At the time, European funding was available to implement the *National Childcare Strategy* and, while this was welcomed by the sector, it did constrain the freedom of development as it tied the provision of childcare primarily to an employment equality measure rather than supporting its growth as a service to children and their families. The direction the Strategy took was wide ranging and the measure of its success was the number of childcare places provided. Building on a committed but fragile, poorly funded and locally driven sector, the Strategy required the involvement of the private sector to meet targets and this was the foundation for the market model of ECEC that we now have.

The funding approach taken by the *National Childcare Strategy* also privileged the development of centre-based services over smaller, family style, home-based childminding services, as noted in Chapter 8. Despite the limited funding available to childminding, it continues to be an important service for children and their families and policy has recently moved to regularize and register childminding. The challenge will be to develop a system of monitoring and regulation that will respect the unique nature of childminding as a specific form of ECEC.

When compared to investment in ECEC during the twentieth century, investment into the system has grown substantially in the early part of this century. Nonetheless, in international terms, Ireland continues to invest relatively little in the ECEC infrastructure. Maintaining the historical distancing of State from family affairs, the direction of investment continues to be directed to parents to cover childcare costs. As noted in Chapter 8, this investment strategy resulted in multiple funding streams which became both difficult to navigate and to administer. To combat this, the DCYA introduced a more streamlined funding system, the National Childcare Scheme. However, the restrictive criteria for accessing funding has been criticized as likely to penalize families already marginalized. In a move to address difficulties with the funding model, the DCEDIY have commissioned an Expert Working Group to review the current funding model and it is due to report by the end of 2021.

Supporting quality ECEC

Over the years, there have been many different initiatives and supports developed to enhance quality ECEC in Ireland. Chapter 1 illustrates how the emergence of preschools, naíonraí and day nurseries from the 1960s led to a growth in membership organizations and how attention was directed at providing education and training opportunities for members. Chapter 7 describes how colleges responded through providing certificate courses which would later expand to the provision of degree and postgraduate programmes. Mid-century saw the beginning of a trend in conferences and seminars bringing ideas from research and international practices to Irish early childhood educators. A common theme in the chapters was the enthusiasm and passion for learning that was evident from the earliest days among early childhood professionals. Following the enactment of the preschool regulations in 1997 (Government of Ireland 1996) and the publication of the *National Childcare Strategy* (Government of Ireland 1999a), there was an increase in State attention to quality ECEC provision. Chapter 7 describes how the DES, in response to a recommendation of the *White Paper on Early Childhood Education,* supported the establishment of the Centre for Early Childhood Development and Education (CECDE) in 2002. One of the key objectives of the Centre was to develop a research and practice informed National Quality Framework and the culmination of this work was the publication and dissemination of the *Síolta* quality framework, which is still in use today as part of the *Aistear/Síolta Practice Guide* (NCCA 2015).

In addition to the DES support for the development of *Síolta,* the DCYA supported a number of quality initiatives described in Chapter 2. Under the Equal Opportunities Childcare Programme (EOCP) and its successors, voluntary organizations were supported to work with their members on quality-related activities. In addition, a number of County and City Childcare Committees developed quality guidelines. Building on the dissemination of the *Síolta* framework, the DCYA supported the National Early Years Access Initiative (NEYAI) with the intention of supporting a number of projects so that the learning from an evaluation of impacts over a four-year period would provide a legacy for enhanced practice across ECEC in general. Similarly, exchequer investment, initially supported by philanthropy, also funded a series of Prevention and Early Intervention and Area Based Childhood (ABC) programmes to identify models of practice to support quality ECEC provision. In 2016, the DCYA launched the Access and Inclusion Model (AIM) so that quality ECEC would be available to all children, regardless of their abilities. This initiative was supported by investment in a focused training module on Leadership for Inclusion (LINC) available to early childhood educators to promote inclusion in ECEC settings. In parallel with these various programmes, and in response to an exposé of poor practices in certain settings, a Quality Agenda, detailed in Chapter 9, was launched in 2013. It approached the issue of supporting quality practice through a combination of strengthened regulation and inspection and the establishment of the Better Start National Early Years Quality Development agency.

While individually many of these quality initiatives are laudable, they reflect a policy approach that is programmatic and service focused rather than systemic and integrated. This has been found to be problematic for developing a sustainable ECEC system as it centres attention on particular services or initiatives rather than considering how services relate to each other and the wider policy environment. In addition, model or demonstration programmes are often not scalable and don't reach all children, which can lead to inequalities that get perpetuated over time. Finally, a programmatic/services approach does not build capacity into the overall ECEC system, can be inefficient and may not have the sustainable supports to achieve intended goals (Kagan 2016). In a hopeful development, the current early years strategy *First Five* (Government of Ireland 2018) indicates that it will address this history of a programmatic approach observing that:

> the *First 5* Strategy sets out how to develop a system of integrated, cross-sectoral and high-quality supports and services – an effective early childhood system – that will help all babies and young children in Ireland to have positive early experiences. The Strategy explains why this system should be developed, what it should look like, and most importantly, the necessary actions. (*Ibid.*: 12)

Qualifications, education and training

Evidence suggests that a central plank in achieving quality ECEC is the qualification and quality of the early childhood educators working directly with children. For most of the period covered in the book, there was no requirement for staff to hold a particular qualification, apart from primary teachers in the junior and senior infant classes of the primary school who are required to have a graduate qualification. Notwithstanding this, the evidence provided in, for instance, Chapters 1, 4, 6 and 10, shows a continuing interest and willingness among many of those working in ECEC to train and to continue their education, often within the context of their work and at significant cost to themselves.

Mandating a minimum qualification for ECEC provision was brought in following the introduction of the free preschool year scheme in 2010. Initially this requirement was only for educators working within the scheme but, since 2016, all early childhood educators working in ECEC settings have been required to hold a minimum qualification of a one year vocational certificate. As a consequence of investment through the EOCP, there was a rapid growth of ECEC services over the first decade of the twenty-first century. In the absence of a parallel, coordinated approach to upskilling those providing those ECEC services, there was a proliferation of qualifications across the system resulting, as outlined in Chapter 6, in a list of over 500 recognized qualifications for working in the free preschool year. Since 2016, in a move to link qualification to enhanced funding, and thus enhance quality, room leaders in the free preschool scheme are required to hold a more advanced qualification with compliant settings receiving an associated increased subsidy. Recently, the DES has published criteria for awards leading to qualifications in ECEC at degree and sub-degree level and this is detailed further in Chapter 6. It is anticipated that, over time, this reform will rationalize qualifications and will have a positive impact on the wider ECEC system.

A vision for ECEC

The great strength of the island of Ireland's ECEC system that emerged from the chapters of this book is the passion and commitment of educators, academics and advocates. Many examples are provided throughout of how individuals saw the possibilities and challenges of their time and responded through leadership, organization and enhanced practice. Organizations were created and sustained throughout the 100 years surveyed and, where one organization waned, another waxed. While individual groups and organizations had their own focus, as for instance with preschool playgroups as described in Chapter 1 and the naíonraí as related in Chapter 4, there was a move towards sharing knowledge with the development of the curricular and quality frameworks.

References to the fragility of the ECEC system were implicit throughout the book with many observations of the challenges presented by a policy context which was late to come into the story, fragmented in terms of leadership and reactive rather than proactive in policy responses to developing needs and challenges. The reactive nature of policy development can be seen in the many legislative and policy documents, reports and evaluations referenced across all chapters.

By way of responding to this situation and looking to the future, five of the ten chapters specifically referenced the importance and potential of developing a vision of ECEC that could inform a future ECEC strategy in the Republic of Ireland. Although not explicitly stated, this does suggest that the current early years strategy, *First 5: A Whole of Government Strategy for Babies, Young Children and their Families* (Government of Ireland 2018) does not provide such a vision. By contrast, while committing to supporting quality ECEC provision, the Strategy goes on to state that:

> given the importance of parental care in the first year and the evidence that shows
> prolonged periods in centre-based ELC can have a negative impact on children's
> cognitive and socio-emotional outcomes, particularly for younger children, *paid*

parental leave and wider supports for parents to balance caring and work have been prioritised in this Strategy. (Ibid.: 87) [emphasis added]

To further the implementation of strategy, the DCEDIY has commissioned the publication of the Workforce Development Plan and a report from an Expert Working Group on a Funding Model. These reports will provide an opportunity for reflection and response and a space for considering how best to address the continued limitations within the ECEC system.

Conclusion

Although the idea of this book was conceived in 2018, the chapters were written and edited during the Covid-19 pandemic. In the early stages of the pandemic, it became clear how central ECEC services were to maintaining a functioning society and how reliant many parents were on their ECEC settings and staff. It also became clear just how fragile the system is and highlighted some of the weaknesses of the predominantly market model in operation in Ireland. The idea of childcare as a public service began to be discussed in the media and among some politicians and has been supported by, among others, the Citizens' Assembly on Gender Equality. This experience and the associated discussions and debate, alongside the consideration of the forthcoming departmental reports, provide an opportunity to re-imagine ECEC and to develop an ambitious and forward thinking strategy informed by a thoughtful and realistic vision. In the absence of a stated policy vision for ECEC, one can find the basis for a vision in the shared principles and values that guide the curricular and quality frameworks, *Aistear and Síolta* and underpin the *Diversity, Equality and Inclusion Charter and Guidelines* (Government of Ireland 2016). As this volume attests, these documents continue to guide day-to-day practice in ECEC and, having been developed in close collaboration with the broad ECEC community, they offer a context within which to continue the journey towards an excellent, high-quality ECEC system.

The book has brought together a diversity of authors, who, through their individual contributions have woven a rich narrative identifying the source of many of the central aspects of the current ECEC system across time. Within this narrative, a number of commonalities have emerged and these form the basis on which to look towards the next steps in the development of ECEC. We trust that the present volume will prove influential and effective in initiating discussion and debate. In addition, we hope it will lead to ambitious policy and practice developments towards transforming the ECEC system into one that enriches the lives of children, their families, early childhood educators and society at large. Finally, we offer this volume as a touchstone for future scholars working in this relatively new academic discipline.

Bibliography

Centre for Early Childhood Development and Education (2006). *Síolta – The National Quality Framework for Early Childhood Education*. Dublin: CECDE.

Citizens Assembly (2021). *Recommendations of the Citizens' Assembly on Gender Equality*. Dublin: The Stationery Office. Available at: <https://www.citizensassembly.ie/en/news-publications/press-releases/recommendations-of-the-citizens-assembly-on-gender-equality.html>.

Department of Education and Skills (2010). *A Workforce Development Plan for the Early Childhood Care and Education Sector in Ireland*. Dublin: DES. Available at: <https://www.education.ie/en/schools-colleges/information/early-years/eyc_workforce_dev_plan.pdf>.

Department of Justice, Equality and Law Reform (2003). *A Review of Progress to End 2003 on the Implementation of the Equal Opportunities Childcare Programme 2000–2006*. Dublin: DJELR.

Government of Ireland (1996). *Child Care (Pre-School Services) Regulations 1996*. Dublin: The Stationery Office.

Government of Ireland (1999a). *National Childcare Strategy: Report of the Partnership 2000 Expert Working Group on Childcare.* Dublin: The Stationery Office.

Government of Ireland (1999b). *Ready to Learn: White Paper on Early Childhood Education.* Dublin: DES. Available at: <https://www.education.ie/en/Publications/Policy-Reports/Ready-to-Learn-White-Paper-on-Early-Childhood-Education.pdf>.

Government of Ireland (2016). *Child Care Act 1991 (Early Years Services) (Amendment) Regulations 2016.* Dublin: The Stationery Office.

Government of Ireland (2018). *A Whole of Government Strategy for Babies, Young Children and Their Families 2019–2028.* Dublin: The Stationery Office.

National Council for Curriculum and Assessment (2009). *Aistear: The Early Childhood Curriculum Framework.* Dublin: NCCA.

National Council for Curriculum and Assessment (2015). *The Aistear/Síolta Practice Guide.* Dublin: NCCA. Available at: <https://www.aistearsiolta.ie/en/>.

Neuman, M. (2018). 'Improving Policies for Young Children through Comparison and Peer Review'. In N. Hayes and M. Urban (eds), *In Search of Social Justice: John Bennett's Lifetime Contribution to Early Childhood Policy and Practice*, pp. 10–22. London: Routledge.

Organisation for Economic Co-operation and Development (2001). *Starting Strong I.* Paris: OECD.

Organisation for Economic Co-operation and Development (2004). *Thematic Review of Early Childhood Education and Care Policy in Ireland.* Paris: OECD.

Tusla (2018). *Early Years Quality and Regulatory Framework.* Dublin: Tusla.

Appendix
Key milestones and events on the ECEC landscape
1900–2021

Year	Event
1900	• *Revised Programme of Instruction* in National Schools is published
1907	• Women's National Health Association is founded
1908	• *Children Act 1908* is introduced
1914	• The Civics Institute of Ireland is founded
1922	• Constitution of Ireland (1922) is published
	• First *National Programme Conference* report is published
1923	• Henrietta Street Crèche is established
1926	• Second *National Programme Conference* report is published
1934	• *Revised Programme of Instruction for Primary Schools* is published
1937	• Constitution of Ireland (Bunreacht na hÉireann) 1937 is adopted
1946	• Association Montessori International Teachers (Ireland) is established
1948	• *Revised Programme for Infants* is published
	• Organization Mondiale pour l'Education Prescolaire (OMEP) is established
1951	• *An Naí Scoil: The Infant School – Notes for Teachers* is published
1955	• St Joseph's day care nursery, Cork Street is established
1965	• *Investment in Education* report is published
	• Second Vatican Council concludes its deliberations
1966	• Organization Mondiale pour l'Education Prescolaire (OMEP) (Ireland) is established
1969	• Irish Preschool Playgroups Association (IPPA) is founded
	• Rutland Street Project is established
1970	• *Health Act 1970* establishes Health Boards
	• St Nicholas Montessori Society for Ireland is founded
	• Association for the Welfare of Children in Hospital Ireland (now Children in Hospital Ireland) is established
1971	• *Primary School Curriculum* 1971 is published
1973	• Commission on the Status of Women report is published
	• Ireland joins the European Economic Community (EEC)
	• Gaelscoileanna is established (reconstituted as Gaeloideachas in 2014)

Year	Event
1974	• Na Naíscoileanna Gaelacha is established (name changed to Na Naíonraí Gaelacha in 1979)
	• B.Ed degrees introduced for primary school teachers
1978	• An Comhchoiste Réamhscolaíochta Teo is established (name changed to Forbairt Naíonraí Teo. in 2003)
	• Bord na Gaeilge is established (known as Foras na Gaeilge since 1999)
1979	• Na Naíonraí Gaelacha is established (name changed from Na Naíscoileanna Gaelacha)
1980	• *Task Force on Child Care Services* report is published
1983	• *Working Party on Childcare Facilities for Working Parents* report is published
	• Childminding Ireland is founded
1985	• *Inter-departmental Working Party on Women's Affairs and Family Law Reform* report is published
1986	• The Civics Institute of Ireland ceases to operate
1988	• National Children's Nurseries Association (NCNA) is established
1989	• The United Nations Convention on the Rights of the Child (UNCRC) is published (Ireland ratifies the UNCRC in 1992)
	• Barnardos is established as an independent organization in Ireland
1990	• *Review Body on the Primary Curriculum* report is published
	• *Primary Education Review Body* report is published
1991	• *Child Care Act 1991* is introduced
1992	• Irish Steiner Kindergarten Association is established (now known as Bláthú Steiner Early Childhood Association)
1993	• National Education Convention is held in Dublin Castle
1994	• Early Start pilot project commences
1995	• White Paper on Education, *Charting our Education Future*, is published
1996	• *Child Care (Preschool Services) Regulations 1996* are introduced
1997	• Preschool inspections commence
	• Seirbhísí Naíonraí Teo is established (subsumed into Comhar Naíonraí na Gaeltachta in 2004)
1998	• National Forum on Early Childhood Education is held in Dublin Castle

Year	Event
1999	• White Paper on Early Childhood Education, *Ready to Learn,* is published
	• *National Childcare Strategy* is published
	• *Primary School Curriculum* 1999 is published
2000	• *National Children's Strategy, Our Children, Their Lives* is published
	• Equal Opportunities Childcare Programme (EOCP) 2000–2006 commences
2001	• Centre for Early Childhood Care and Education (CECDE) is established
	• National Council for Curriculum and Assessment (NCCA) is established on a statutory basis
	• *Child Care Act 2001* is introduced
	• National Children's Office is established
2002	• *Ombudsman for Children Act 2002* is introduced
	• Barcelona Targets are published
	• *Model Framework for Education, Training and Professional Development* is published
2003	• National Framework of Qualifications (NFQ) is established
	• Forbairt Naíonraí Teo is established (replacing An Comhchoiste Réamhscolaíochta Teo)
2004	• Organisation for Economic Cooperation and Development (OECD) Review of ECEC in Ireland is published
	• Ombudsman for Children office is established
	• Comhar Naíonraí na Gaeltachta is established (replacing Seirbhísí Naíonraí Teo)
	• *Towards a Framework for Early Learning: A Consultative Document* is published by the NCCA
2005	• National Economic and Social Forum (NESF) report on ECEC is published
	• Health Service Executive (HSE) is established, replacing earlier Health Boards
	• Office of Minister for Children is established
2006	• *Child Care (Preschool Services) Regulations 2006* are published
	• National Childcare Investment Programme (NCIP) commences
	• Early Childcare Supplement is introduced
	• *Síolta, The National Quality Framework for Early Childhood Education* is published

Year	Event
2008	• CECDE ceases to operate • Office of the Minister for Children and Youth Affairs is established (replacing the Office of Minister for Children)
2009	• *Aistear, The Early Childhood Curriculum Framework* is published
2010	• ECCE/Free Preschool Year scheme is introduced • *Aistear* Tutor Initiative established by the Association of Teacher Education Centres in Ireland (ATECI) and NCCA
2011	• Department of Children and Youth Affairs (DCYA) is established • IPPA and NCNA merge into Early Childhood Ireland (ECI)
2012	• Children's rights referendum passed amending Article 42 of the Constitution
2013	• *Right from the Start* is published
2014	• Tusla, the Child and Family Agency, is established • Better Start National Early Years Quality Development agency is established • Gaeloideachas established (replacing Gaelscoileanna)
2015	• *Children First Act 2015* is introduced • Article 42A on children's rights is included in the Constitution • *Aistear Síolta Practice Guide* is published
2016	• *Child Care Act 1991 (Early Years Services) Regulations 2016* are introduced • ECCE scheme extended to two years • ECCE scheme introduces higher capitation for room leaders with degree level qualifications • Minimum qualifications introduced for ECEC professionals • DES Early Years Education Inspections commence • National *Síolta Aistear* Initiative commences • Access and Inclusion Model (AIM) is introduced • *Primary Language Curriculum/Curaclam Teanga na Bunscoile* introduced to infant classes
2017	• New draft primary mathematics curriculum for infant classes published for consultation by the NCCA
2018	• *First 5, A Whole of Government Strategy for Babies, Young Children and their Families 2019–2028* is published • *Childcare Support Act 2018* (underpinning the National Childcare Scheme) is introduced • *Mo Scéal* transition materials published by the NCCA

Year	Event
2019	• National Childcare Scheme announced, replacing the Affordable Childcare Scheme
	• *Professional Award Criteria and Guidelines for Initial Professional Education (Level 7 and Level 8) Degree Programmes for the Early Learning and Care (ELC) Sector in Ireland* are published
	• Steering Group appointed to develop a Workforce Development Plan
	• Expert Working Group appointed to develop a new Funding Model for Early Learning and Care and School Age Childcare
2020	• Establishment of the Department of Children, Equality, Disability, Integration and Youth (DCEDIY), replacing the DCYA
	• *Draft Primary Curriculum Framework* is published for consultation
2021	• *Nurturing Skills: The Workforce Plan for Early Learning and Care and School-Age Childcare 2022–2028* is published.
	• *Partnership for the Public Good: A New Funding Model for Early Learning and Care and School-Age Childcare* is published.

Notes on contributors

CARMEL BRENNAN, PhD, has worked at all levels of education, in both the formal and informal sectors. Her interest in early childhood was fostered by her work as a playgroup leader, as Director of Quality in the Irish Preschool Playgroups Association (IPPA) and as Director of Practice with Early Childhood Ireland. Her PhD thesis locates play as children's gateway to belonging in the cultural, intellectual, and social life around them. She lectures on the subject, has authored several publications, contributed book chapters and presented at conferences internationally.

MARESA DUIGNAN, PhD, is Assistant Chief Inspector in the Department of Education. As a member of the senior management team in the Department of Education Inspectorate, she has special responsibility for the implementation of the national programme of Early Years Education Inspections in early learning and care settings and schools. She also manages research and development activities to inform and support national early years policy and promote quality improvement in early years education provision and practice.

ELIZABETH (LIZ) DUNPHY, PhD, was a primary teacher from 1978 to 1998. She is now Emeritus Associate Professor of Early Childhood Education at Dublin City University. Liz served as Chairperson/Board Member of the CECDE (2001–2008). At the invitation of the National Council for Curriculum and Assessment (NCCA), she chaired The Expert Advisory Group established to support the development of *Aistear: The Early Childhood Curriculum Framework*. She is currently Chairperson of the NCCA's Early Childhood and Primary Mathematics Development Group which supports the development of the new primary mathematics curriculum.

ANNE EGAN, PhD, lectures at undergraduate and postgraduate level at the School of Political Science and Sociology, NUI Galway. She returned to education as a mature student having worked previously as Legal Secretary. Her doctoral research related to the rights and responsibilities of fathers in the Irish legal context. Anne delivers the module 'Child and Family in Irish Law' on the BA in Early Childhood Studies and Practice at NUI Galway and supervises research students in the course.

ARLENE FORSTER is Chief Executive of the National Council for Curriculum and Assessment (NCCA). The NCCA advises the Minister for Education on curriculum and assessment in early childhood education, primary and post-primary schools. Arlene began her career teaching in the early years of primary school. On joining the NCCA, she led the development of *Aistear: the Early Childhood Curriculum Framework* and, more recently, the review and redevelopment of the curriculum for primary schools. She was also centrally involved in the *Aistear Tutor Initiative*.

GERALDINE FRENCH, PhD, is Associate Professor, Head of School of Language, Literacy and Early Childhood Education and Programme Chair of the Masters of Education in Early Childhood Education in the Institute of Education at Dublin City University. She has published in the areas of professional practice in early childhood education and care, supporting early language, literacy and numeracy and nurturing babies' and toddlers' learning and development through a 'slow' relational pedagogy.

SHEILA GARRITY, PhD, is Academic Director of Early Childhood programmes at NUI Galway and oversees undergraduate, postgraduate and CPD Awards for early childhood educators offered through the Centre for Adult Learning & Professional Development. A Senior Researcher at the UNESCO Child & Family Research Centre, NUI Galway, Sheila's research focus is on early years as a family support. Dr Garrity also contributes to scientific panels for conferences and academic publications, and on policy-focused State Working and Stakeholder groups at a national level.

NÓIRÍN HAYES, PhD, is Visiting Academic at the School of Education, Trinity College Dublin and Professor Emerita, Centre for Social and

Educational Research, Technological University Dublin. Working within a bio-ecological framework of development and through a child rights lens, she teaches and researches in early childhood education and care (ECEC) with a particular focus on early learning, curriculum and pedagogy and ECEC policy. She is the convenor of the Researching Early Childhood Education Collaborative (RECEC) at Trinity College and OMEP Champion and Advocate for Early Childhood Education and Care, Ireland (2021–2024).

MAIRÉAD MAC CON IOMAIRE was central in developing the Gaeltacht early years services as far back as 1978 when she had the opportunity of opening the first Gaeltacht Naíonra. She worked as Manager/Director of both Seirbhísí Naíonraí Teo and Comhar Naíonraí na Gaeltachta up to her retirement in 2019. Seirbhísí Naíonraí Teo and Comhar Naíonra na Gaeltachta provided full back up service for Gaeltacht early years education. She also published books on songs, rhyme and games including *Scéilín Scéilín and Dreoilín Dreoilín*. She has won debating and acting awards and loves to travel.

DIANE MCCLELLAND is an English and Literacy Lecturer at Stranmillis University College, Belfast, where she lectures on the BEd Primary, Post-Primary and PGCE Programmes. Diane taught for twenty-six years as a primary school teacher, particularly within Foundation Stage and Key Stage One, as well as fulfilling the role of Literacy Coordinator. Her main research interests include literacy for all ages, play-based learning, outdoor learning, history of education and the development of education in Uganda.

FIONA MCDONNELL, SRN; PHN; MSc, has worked in inspection services for almost twenty-five years and led the strategic reform, development and expansion of the Early Years Inspectorate. She is currently the National Service Director for Children's Services Regulation in Tusla. She is a member of several national and international regulatory forums. Central to her work is the alignment of regulation practice informed by the commitment to consultation and working in collaboration with stakeholders and keeping the child central in decision-making within regulatory policy.

MÁIRE MHIC MHATHÚNA, PhD, is a researcher in early childhood education and second language learning in the early years. She was Assistant Head of School of Languages, Law and Social Sciences, Technological University Dublin (formerly Dublin Institute of Technology) from 2009 to 2017 and previously worked as Lecturer in early childhood education, a primary teacher and an early years practitioner. She is the chair of the Quality Advisory Board for degree level programmes in Early Childhood Education and Care. Her research interests and publications include second language learning, family language policy and professionalization in the early childhood education and care sector.

MARY MOLONEY, PhD, is a lecturer, researcher and author at the Department of Reflective Pedagogy and Early Childhood Studies at Mary Immaculate College, Limerick. Her research interests include early childhood teacher education; international early childhood policy and practice, professionalization, governance and inclusion. She is currently President of OMEP Ireland, an international non-governmental and non-profit organization concerned with all aspects of early childhood education and care.

MAURA O'CONNOR, PhD, is retired Lecturer in Education at St Patrick's College, Dublin City University, where she specialized in early childhood education. She has worked as Primary School Teacher and School Principal. She has written numerous articles on early childhood education and care in Ireland and has made presentations at several national and international conferences. Her book entitled *The Development of Infant Education in Ireland, 1838–1948: Epochs and Eras* (Peter Lang 2010) was the winner of the Kevin Brehony Book Prize, awarded by the History of Education Society (UK) in 2014.

NOEL PURDY, PhD, is Director of Research and Scholarship and Head of Education Studies at Stranmillis University College, Belfast where he is also Director of the Centre for Research in Educational Underachievement. He lectures at undergraduate and postgraduate level and has a particular research interest in educational underachievement, special educational needs and tackling bullying in schools. He chaired the ministerial Expert Panel on Educational Underachievement in Northern Ireland 2020–2021.

THOMAS WALSH, PhD, is Associate Professor and Deputy Head of the Department of Education, Maynooth University. His teaching and research interests include history of education, education policy, early childhood education and curriculum studies. Prior to joining Maynooth University, he worked as Primary School Teacher, as Development Officer in the Centre for Early Childhood Development and Education, and as Primary school inspector.

Index

Printed by
CPI books GmbH, Leck